THE BUI

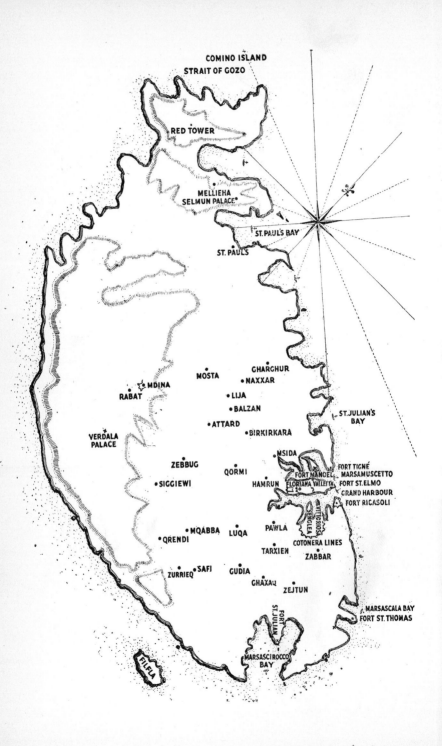

THE

BUILDING OF MALTA

during the period of
the Knights of St. John of Jerusalem
1530 – 1795

J. QUENTIN HUGHES

M.C., B.ARCH., PH.D., A.R.I.B.A.

LONDON — 1956

Alec Tiranti Ltd.

THE TIRANTI LIBRARY

Architectural Principles in the Age of Humanism
by RUDOLF WITTKOWER, demy 8vo, £1 5s.

Boullée's Treatise on Architecture
by HELEN ROSENAU, demy 8vo, £1 1s.

Italian Gardens of the Renaissance
by SHEPHERD & JELLICOE, demy 8vo, £1 5s.

Geometry in Egyptian Art
by E. CHRISTIE KIELLAND, demy 8vo, £1 10s.

Ten Books on Architecture
by L. B. ALBERTI, crown 4to, £1 15s.

The Building of Malta 1530–1795
by J. QUENTIN HUGHES, demy 8vo, £2 2s.

ALEC TIRANTI LTD., 72 CHARLOTTE STREET, LONDON, W.1

Made and printed in the United Kingdom

Foreword

I should like to express my appreciation of the kindness and courtesy I have received from so many people and, in particular, I should like to thank Mr. V. F. Denaro, the Director of the Royal University of Malta, Mr. Olaf Golcher, Mr. Pearse S. Hubbard, Professor Le Patourel, the Librarian and Staff of the Royal Library of Malta, Mr. Norbert Lynton, Dr. Edward Sammut, Sir Hannibal Scicluna, Professor Rudolf Wittkower, and Mr. Charles Zammit.

I should also like to mention my gratitude to the Honorable Minister of Works and Reconstruction in Malta for permission to reproduce the drawings in this book, to Capt. Bussetil for his untiring efforts to search out so many drawings for me, to the Director of the Valletta Museum for permission to reproduce figures 97,115,118, 125,127,135,153,155,215,279,284,287,290,312,317,320 and 325, and to the Officer in charge of the Government Tourist Bureau for permission to reproduce figures 98,176,217, and 282.

Finally, my special thanks go to Mr. Cassar Pullicino for so much valuable advice, and to my wife for her constant help and forbearance.

Contents

III. PALACES, PUBLIC BUILDINGS, AND HOUSES

IV. BUILDING MATERIALS AND METHODS OF CONSTRUCTION

List of Illustrations

Introduction

THERE has been no work dealing with the architecture of Malta which is at all comprehensive in its contents, its descriptions, and its illustrations. The other arts have fared no better. This may be partly explained by the traditional disregard for the visual arts by the British armed forces which have protected the island for more than a hundred years, and by the lack of opportunity afforded in Malta for the production of important illustrated books. The loss has been a serious one; for Malta possesses a wealth of architecture probably richer than any that may be found in other parts of the British Commonwealth—an architecture which, if only for the large number of monuments in so small an area, should have been remarked upon, and which in quality can stand comparison with the more publicised areas of southern Italy and Sicily.

The general history, the two hundred and fifty odd years during which the Knights of the Order of St. John of Jerusalem were resident in Malta, is adequately related in numerous books written in several languages. A good bibliography occurs in Boisgelin, *Ancient and Modern Malta*.

As official historian to the Order, Giacomo Bosio recorded its history from the earliest times up to the year 1552 with a second part published in 1630 by Carlo Aldobrandini. This history contains some dates, and refers to the early defences of Malta and the Turkish assault. The French history by Vertot, published in 1726, whilst giving a useful year to year account of the actions of the Order's forces and a relation of some of the important events on the island, makes very little reference to works of art, or to architects and artists. Abela, the Maltese historian to the Order, is more interested in events which happened in Malta itself, and his work, which was first published in 1647 and was later amended and considerably enlarged (1772–80) by Giovanni Antonio Ciantar, is one of the most valuable sources whereby to date and describe the island's monuments.

Achille Ferres, *Descrizione storica delle chiese,* is invaluable for its compilation of data on the works of art and artists, but it is not

1

illustrated and is not fully descriptive of either paintings or architecture. Published in 1888, it is one of the last important books of any size to deal with the subject. Hellwald and Rossi give full particulars, up to 1924, of the bibliography of the Order.

Other books which follow suffer from errors or omissions. They are either too short to be worth while or they do not cover new ground; or again, and this is a common fault, they fail to give references to the statements of the dates and designers of buildings.

I have chosen for my subject the period between 1530, when the Knights arrived on Malta, and the year 1798, when they were expelled by Napoleon and the French fleet. These years were among the most prosperous and prolific in Maltese history, and the period may be treated comprehensively because of its precise boundaries and the small area of land involved; though, with the exception of Rome, Malta's monuments are more tightly packed than anywhere in the world.

For the spelling of the names of Maltese villages and towns I have chosen to adopt the nomenclature of Braun's *Works of Art in Malta* as this contains a full list of the parishes and is the most recent statement of a problem which is continually in a state of flux. Street names are normally given in English and Maltese on the island, though a few years ago most of them had Italian names. During the sovereignty of the Knights the streets had Italian names, many quite different from what they are today. This has made it difficult at times to trace some of the smaller buildings on the islands.

It remains to assess the importance of the architecture of this period in the general history of Malta and in the wider field of Mediterranean art.

In the preceding centuries, under Angevin (1266–82), Aragonese (1283–1479), and Castilian domination (1479–1530), the Maltese islands did not prosper greatly and the quantity of building was small, with important buildings, such as palaces and the cathedral, being confined to the capital in the centre of Malta.

The Knights of the Order of St. John, which in 1113 under the leadership of Raymond du Puy, had been formed into a military brotherhood, fought a rearguard action from the shores of Palestine when in 1291 they had been forced to evacuate Acre. After a temporary sojourn in Cyprus (1291–1310) they occupied the island of Rhodes in the Aegean. The first major attack of the Turks in 1480 was successfully repulsed, but this reversal led them to bring up a

2

more powerful army against the Knights, who in 1523, after a prolonged siege, were forced to come to terms. The capitulation was an honourable one and the Convent was permitted to embark with its belongings and evacuate the island. In their withdrawal the Knights were accompanied by many of the Greek inhabitants of Rhodes.

After a great deal of tiresome negotiation, ably conducted by Grand Master de l'Isle Adam, the Convent was offered the islands of Malta and Gozo by King Charles V of Spain, but only on condition that they defended his desert outpost at Tripoli. Not without some misgivings did they accept these barren islands and the desert fortress whose insufficient defences rested insecurely upon shifting sand. But, largely through the driving force of the Grand Master, the Order of St. John accepted the terms of the gift and sailed for Malta in 1530, where they landed on 26 October.

In the first years of their occupation the Knights were engaged in fortifying the Birgu on the land which lay to the east of the ancient fort of St. Angelo, and in building for themselves a church, eight modest auberges, and a hospital.

Their architectural style is simple and Melitan 'fat' mouldings are constantly employed. These mouldings, and others which were used, are primitive, and there seems to have been no architectural influence from Italy despite the fact that several Spanish and Italian engineers visited the island at this time. What influences there were had come from Rhodes and Cyprus, and the Venetian islands which were often visited by the galleys of the Order. The period up to the great siege in 1565 is the period of the 'Melitan Style'.

After the siege, the Knights set about building a new city on the headland behind Fort St. Elmo which they called Valletta, after their Grand Master. It was in the new city, which rose up on the heights where once the Turkish batteries wrought such devastation, that the important buildings of the Order were built.

The first essential was to secure the island against further attacks, so work proceeded on the defences of Valletta from the date of its foundation in 1566; while the building of churches and palaces was not taken up in earnest until about 1571. The tremendous enthusiasm which followed the foundation of the new city saw the erection of the important Conventual church of St. John, the Magisterial palace, a new hospital, and the eight new auberges, along with numerous private houses. But this spate of building and the tremendous expenditure on the fortifications soon exhausted the treasury of the Knights.

The activity of the Order brought new prosperity to the Maltese themselves and the population grew at an unprecedented speed. From fewer than 15,000 persons when the Knights arrived in Malta, it had fallen to 10,000 during the siege of 1565, and then rose rapidly, by 1632[1], to the prodigious figure of 51,750. In spite of the years of famine which occurred from time to time (about 1536 until well after 1650), and the ravages of the plague epidemics which were particularly serious in 1592 and 1676, the population in 1798 had grown to 90,000 in Malta and 24,000 in the neighbouring island of Gozo. This steady and rapid increase in population brought with it the need for new churches and houses, which seems to have been satisfied in spite of the shortage of the funds of the Order[2] and the economies effected by the Knights in their building programme.

The first building period of the Knights, which dates from about 1571 until about 1600, shows strong traces of Mannerist influences from Italy, although some Early Baroque tendencies are discernible. Nevertheless, the architecture still reflects the stern military discipline of the Religion.

When the Knights, through lack of funds, were forced to cut down on their building programme, the Maltese themselves erected many large parish churches for their ever-expanding villages. Some of these show the belated influence of Spanish Renaissance, but their character is more restrained. In the constant use of the Latin cross plan, it is evident that the teachings of the Counter Reformation had not passed unnoticed.

Toward the end of the seventeenth century, when the financial position of the treasury had improved, a new period of building began with the completion of the main defence work around Valletta and the Three Cities.

Invasion seemed imminent about the year 1669. The Venetians had concluded a peace treaty after the fall of Candia, leaving the Turks free to concentrate on Malta; but the danger passed and each year a recurrence became less probable.

Sir Harry Luke, writing on Malta, shows how the coats-of-arms, the dress, and general taste of the Knights, grew more flamboyant

---

1. Figures are from Boisgelin p.107. Murray p.457 gives the following figures: population 1530 — 15,000; 1565 — 10,000; 1586 estimated 20,000; Census of 1632 — 50,113; 1741 — 110,000; 1798 — 114,000.
2. Boisgelin p.184 notes that in 1638, when money was very short, Lascaris ordered very special coinage, inscribed with *non aes sed fides,* in order to pay the workmen on the Valletta fortifications. But Zammit, *Valletta* p.12, says that it was under Verdale that these coins, known as *patacca,* were struck,

each year. This is equally true of their architecture. When the new spate of building began, the Baroque had taken control of Europe and its influence was from Rome itself; the churches display the restrained and monumental character of the Roman Baroque, although many of the later palaces have motifs and decoration imported from Spanish dominated Sicily, and the heel and toe of Italy. This second boom period in building lasted up to the middle of the eighteenth century.

Maltese architecture and the finances of the Order are closely tied. Events which developed after this seriously cut down building. In 1768 the Order of St. Anthony was disbanded and its possessions and responsibilities shared between the Knights of Malta and the Order of St. Lazarus. This Order received the immediate benefit, and the Knights inherited debts and responsibilities which after a certain number of years were expected to turn into valuable profit. In the year 1788 the Religion had a credit of 189,216 French livres. Soon, however, this happy state of the exchequer ceased for all time. As a result of the French Revolution, the possessions of the Order in France were finally confiscated in 1792 and the general deficit grew daily. To make matters worse, the property of the Knights on the left bank of the Rhine also fell into the hands of the Directorate when this area was ceded to France under the terms of the Treaty of Campo Formio. The expansionist policy of Napoleon took further property from the Knights and soon their possessions in Helvetia, and the Ligurian and Cisalpine States, were lost.

The total income was reduced by two-thirds, and to overcome this embarrassment the Order was forced to borrow 6,000,000 French livres from abroad; but credit soon fell so low that no one could be found to advance further money. Assistance was sought from the property of the langues in Spain and Russia, but the dispatch of money was delayed.

It is little wonder then that, when the fleet of Napoleon dropped anchor off the Grand Harbour, the Knights were in no condition to withstand a prolonged siege; especially as the temper of the French Knights, who formed the largest contingent of the army, was felt to be uncertain in view of revolutionary doctrines and the nationality of the attacking forces. The capitulation followed upon a brief period of disorder when treacherous instructions were spread abroad by several French Knights, and the island was captured with hardly a shot fired.

Throughout their occupation of Malta, the Knights had maintained constant contact with all parts of Europe, their ambassadors attending the important courts, their galleys serving alongside the allied fleets, and through their possessions in the countries of the various langues. It should be noticed that, during the first half of their sovereignty over Malta, most Grand Masters were French, but in the second half, Spanish and Portuguese Grand Masters predominate. This may partly explain the Spanish characteristics which appear in secular architecture in the eighteenth century.

Finally, the strong indigenous character of Maltese architecture must be stressed. The sound restrained approach is evident throughout all periods, and this is all the more remarkable in view of the very soft quality of Maltese stone, and the florid treatment of Baroque buildings in nearby Sicily and Calabria, and in Spain.

CHAPTER ONE

Military Architecture and Town Planning

The military background of the Mediterranean Wars against the Turks

THE MILITARY ORDERS, which formed the backbone of the western army stationed in the Holy Land during the Crusades, were hampered from the beginning by their lack of strength. Reinforcements took many months to arrive on the long and tiresome journey overland or the treacherous crossing of the eastern Mediterranean[3]; and upon arrival their numbers had become much reduced. As the wars against the Turks dragged on, year by year it became more difficult to recruit suitable troops, and as the fascination and enthusiasm of the early exploits dimmed before their eyes, so the tendency of the western rulers was reduced toward financial assistance rather than increased vigour.

For these reasons, the Orders found themselves faced by forces numerically their superior and matching them in efficiency, along a line of battle they could no longer hold with foot soldiers and cavalry. Fortresses were therefore built of massive masonry to supplement the resistance of the meagre forces defending Palestine[4]. With a line of entrenchments and fortresses the position was temporarily held in check. The Knights clung to their belief in the might of the fortified position for ever after, until finally the very magnitude and elaborateness of their enceinte outstripped the capacity of the defenders, and the greatest concentration of masonry defences collapsed before the invading fleet of Napoleon.

After the evacuation of the Holy Land (1291) the Order of St. John refused to be despondent and, after a short stay in Cyprus,

---

3. Zammit, *Malta* p.93, refers to the raids by Moslem corsairs on merchants and pilgrims in the 12th century.
4. Fedden p.13.

they built up a fleet and sailed to capture Rhodes, an outpost placed under the very nose of the Turkish power, though at that time still tenable because the flank was held by the Emperor at Constantinople. This vigorous action carried through by the Grand Master Fulk de Villaret (1310) revitalised the Order and saved it from the disintegration which rapidly overcame the Templars.

The repulse from Palestine, though a sad blow at the time, was not in the long run a disaster to the forces of Christendom, for as a result of this reverse they began to build up a powerful navy which soon dominated the Mediterranean. The Knights on Rhodes were quick to appreciate their need for a powerful fleet[5], both to victual the island fortress and to replace the task previously allotted to the cavalry, which is, to sally out with sharp and effective raids upon the enemy and to harass any invasion concentration he had prepared.

In a similar manner the great Italian trading ports built up powerful fleets to secure and hold distant islands. At the end of the eleventh century the three cities of Venice, Pisa, and Genoa had more ships in the Mediterranean than the whole of Christendom.[6] The power of the Pisans declined after their fleet had been defeated by the Genoans at Meloria in 1284, and Genoa grew stronger year by year as her Levantine trade rivalled that of Venice. After intermittent squabbling between the two cities and a seven years' war of great strain the power of Genoa was crushed at the sea battle of Chioggia.

In contrast to the vigorous maritime action of the Knights and the Italian cities, the Turks concentrated their power in the field and allowed their early and efficient naval defences to dwindle and decline. Weak fleet action at Rhodes allowed this prize to fall from their hands in the first great assault on the island (1480), and even in 1565 the large Turkish fleet which stood before Malta shivered in constant trepidation for fear of the arrival of an allied squadron.

All the same, the Turks did realise the necessity of successful naval action in the tactics they employed after the capture of Constantinople (1453). At the height of their imperial expansion, Haji Khalifeh, the Turkish historian, wrote, 'It became necessary to build ships and make armaments in order to subdue the fortresses and castles on the Rumelian and Anatolian shores, and in the islands of the Mediterranean.'[7] In 1470, for the first time, they were able

5. Porter, p.68: the fleet was built up by the Knights at Cyprus.
6. Sismondi, *Italian Republics* p.26, London 1907.
7. Haji Khalifeh, *Maritime Wars of the Turks*, Mitchell's translation p.12.

to engage the Venetians in force and drive them from the Ionian seas,[8] and in the succeeding years their ships ravaged the coasts of Italy and Sicily. The savagery of their behaviour still lives on in the folk songs of the area.[9] As the Ottoman power at sea mounted, the importance of the Venetian fleet dwindled so that it became but one contingent in the allied sea forces, rather than the sole major representative of western sea power. The first serious check to Turkish sea power was the successful repulse of the attack upon Malta in 1565, where the Turks, forced to lay long siege to the Knights firmly entrenched behind permanent land fortifications, soon began to feel the insecurity of their position. While their captains favoured lightning raids upon Christian shores, and their Moslem crews benefited from the rich booty, all felt that a fleet lingering in the roads between Sicily and Malta, in an announced position and so far from base, was too vulnerable.

The decisive naval contest was reached in 1571 when, off Lepanto, the main forces of the two opposing navies joined battle. There, Don John of Austria struck a blow which finally crushed the westward expansion of the Turks in the Mediterranean basin.[10] Although the allied fleet was made up of combined squadrons from Venice, Malta, and the western powers, the strongest influence was that of the Spanish fleet which had had its nucleus in the Catalan navy fostered by the Aragonese Kings, and had grown to power with the exploits in the new colonies.

The advantages of Rhodes

The Knights of St. John sailed from Cyprus and captured the island of Rhodes from the Saracens in 1310. On this island there already existed reasonably sound fortifications both in the outlying country and in a circuit of walls which surrounded the main town. Soon after the initial occupation, light forces were sent to capture the islands of Nisyrus, Leros, Calamos, Episcopia, Calchos, and Cos.

8. Sismondi *op. cit.* p.234. They attacked Euboea and captured Negropont.
9. Ross, *Land of Manfred Prince of Taventum,* London 1889, p.257.
    'Li Turchi se la puozzona pigliano,
    La puozzona portano a la Turchia,
    La puozzona la Turca da Cristiana.'
    In the 1480 invasion of Otranto, out of a population of 20,000 about 12,000 were killed and the remainder carried off into slavery. See Briggs, *In the Heel of Italy* pp.322–5. Attacks also occurred on the maritime villages of Malta; Zammit, *Malta* pp.107 and 111.
10. Sir Cyprian Arthur George Bridge, article *Sea power,* in ENCYCLOPÆDIA BRITANNICA, 11th edition pp.551–2.

Controlling these islands, the Knights were able to get warning of any likely invasion by the Saracens and to prevent Turkish raiders seeking refuge in their harbours.

So long as Constantinople held out against the Turks there was no serious threat to the security of Rhodes, and the Knights' fleet was employed to convoy merchant ships through the Ionian seas and to attack Turkish corsairs. But in 1453 Constantinople fell before the armies of Mahomet II, and the Turkish forces began to encircle Rhodes from the north and the south. Attacks on the island were made in 1440, and again in 1444 when a force of 18,000 infantry with supporting cavalry, laid siege to the city for forty days. The Knights had no great difficulty in holding out against this force, and a brilliant sortie drove the Turks to their ships. Mahomet II, however, boasted upon his accession to the throne that he would take 'Constantinople first, and then Rhodes.'[11] In 1470 an invasion fleet was fitted out, but was diverted to Negropont, where the Turks overcame the Venetian defences. The Turkish forces advanced on all fronts and, in Hungary, Belgrade surrendered to them in 1527.

The final blow was struck against Rhodes on 26 June 1522, when a force of 140,000 Turks landed to oppose the 4,500 defenders.[12] For nearly six months the Knights and islanders held out against withering cannon fire and the onslaught of huge numbers of troops, but final victory was impossible and the Grand Master sued for, and obtained, honourable terms of surrender : the Knights and those islanders who wished were permitted to leave Rhodes unmolested.

This was a sad loss : for Rhodes, which had been the home of the Knights for over 200 years, was a pleasant place. The climate was mild and equable, the soil exceedingly fertile, and the whole place had the appearance of one vast garden. The local inhabitants were long famous as a race of seamen and they furnished suitable recruits for the battle-fleet of the Knights.

The advantages and disadvantages of Malta and Gozo

The expulsion from Rhodes in 1522 left the Knights of St. John homeless. De l'Isle Adam, the Grand Master of the Order, hurriedly opened negotiations with the Pope and the western powers, counting

11. Porter p.130.
12. It should be noticed that the Turks were able to land a very much larger force on Rhodes than during their later attack on Malta. This was due to the nearness of Rhodes to the Turkish mainland and the comparatively safe passage afforded to the Turkish fleet.

on the reputation he and his Knights had made in their bitter fight and the threat of a new enveloping danger which the loss of that island had opened up along the southern flank of Europe. With this reputation and in the face of these dangers, he hoped that the need for his force of veterans would turn the scale in his favour and secure a suitable headquarters for the deposed Order. Among the initial proposals, Elba was put forward as a suggestion, but this was not acceptable; nor could the powers agree to a base on the mainland, or upon a much larger island such as Corsica. Much though they feared the menace of the Turks, many also mistrusted the actions of a military order which owed direct allegiance to the Pope, flaunted national distinctions, and annually increased in power and independence. If placed upon a small island, its activities could be more easily watched and contained. They discussed Minorca, Eviza, Eres, Ischia, Ponza, and other small islands without agreement being reached.[13] Finally Malta was suggested and considered. The island would be an outpost against the Turks, protecting the southern coast of Sicily and sealing off the western Mediterranean. It possessed several incomparable harbours and in fact the Grand Harbour had been a constant shelter for the battle fleets.[14]

Although much of the land was sterile and laid waste, and the need for new fortifications a great difficulty, it was the prospect of the fine ports which swayed the arguments in favour of Malta. Most of the three French langues, as well as a part of the Italian and English ones, were against using Malta, but the two powerful Spanish langues and that of Germany were in favour and showed that equal or even greater difficulties existed elsewhere.[15] Finally it was agreed and Ambassadors were sent to the Spanish Emperor, under whose dominion the island rested, to ask for its transference to the Order. In addition, other Ambassadors were dispatched to the Kings of France and England for support and suggestions.

Amid a fervour of discussions and conferences conducted mainly from Viterbo, the Grand Master, in 1524, ordered eight Commissioners to report upon the conditions then prevailing in Tripoli, Malta, and Gozo. On their return to Italy they reported 'that the island of Malta was merely a rock of a soft sandstone, called tufa, about six or seven leagues long and three or four broad; that the surface of the rock was barely covered with more than three or four

13. Bosio II p.21.
14. Zammit, *Malta* p.99 : ' Corner, the French Commander, had his fleet of twenty-seven vessels in the Grand Harbour.' This was on 8 June 1283.
15. Bosio II p.21.

feet of earth, which was likewise stony, and very unfit to grow corn and other grain; that it produced abundance of figs, melons, and different fruits; that the principal trade of the island consisted of honey, cotton, and cummin, which the inhabitants exchanged for grain; that, except for a few springs in the middle of the island, there was no running water, nor even wells : the want of which the inhabitants supplied by cisterns; that wood was so scarce as to be sold by the pound, which forced them to use either cow-dung dried in the sun, or wild thistles, for preparing food. That the capital of the country, named Città Notabile, was situated upon a rising ground in the centre of the island; that the greatest part of the houses were uninhabited; that the circumference was not more than 1,303 paces in breadth; that there were no ports, bays, or coves on the western coast of the island; that the shore in that part was full of great rocks and shoals; but that on the opposite coast there were many points or capes, with indentures in the form of bays or coves, in which ships might anchor; that there were two spacious and very good ports in the island, capable of receiving the largest fleet; but with no other defence than a small castle named St. Angelo, which was partly in ruins, its whole artillery consisting of one small cannon, two falcons, and a few iron mortars; that the island contained about 12,000 inhabitants, of both sexes, the greatest part of whom were poor and miserable, owing to the barrenness of the soil and the frequent descents of the corsairs who, without the smallest sentiment of compassion, carried off all the unfortunate Maltese who happened to fall into their hands—in a word, that a residence in Malta appeared extremely disagreeable indeed, almost insupportable, particularly in summer. As to the island of Gozo—no port of any kind on the island; approach extremely difficult; the soil, however, appeared to be very fertile; it contained about 5,000 inhabitants, including men, women, and children, who were dispersed in different villages; that the people of the island, in order to secure themselves from corsairs, had erected a castle upon a mountain, which appeared badly fortified, and with very little importance; but, weak as it was, the Commissioners judged it would not be prudent in the council to accept the island of Malta separately from that of Gozo, since the vicinity of the latter would in that case be dangerous, as it might, at some future period, serve as a retreat for their enemies.' They also submitted notes on customs, plans of coves and bays, details, etc. 'They therefore thought, so great a number of ports being extremely convenient for the armaments of the Order, that the offers of the Emperor ought not to be rejected, provided he did not insist upon

12

the Order's taking up arms against his own particular enemies. The Commissioners were of a different opinion respecting the city and castle of Tripoli.'[16]

The Emperor Charles V agreed to grant Malta, but only if the following conditions were fully observed :—

(1) The Order should swear never to suffer its new subjects to take up arms against the King of Sicily and his states.

(2) An annual homage of a falcon should be paid to the said King or his Viceroy.

(3) A renunciation on their part, to the King, of the nomination to the bishopric of Malta. The presentation to that dignity to be made among three of their Order, of which one should be a Sicilian subject.

(4) A promise that the Admiral, or his Lieutenant, should be chosen from the Language of Italy; also that those on whom the command of the squadrons might devolve, should be persons in whom the King of Sicily could confide.

(5) Absolute necessity of the King's consent to the transfer of the Isle of Malta to any other power.[17]

And finally, it was agreed that the Knights should at the same time take over the defence of Tripoli, to form a forward position safe-guarding the Imperial possessions along the north African coast.

The Grand Master agreed to the terms offered by the Emperor and, overcoming the reluctance felt by many of the Knights, moved the Convent to Sicily. The memorial of the Grand Master and Council was sent to the Emperor in 1529, and in the following year the Convent sailed for Malta and landed on the island in October.[18]

Many of the Knights were appalled by the conditions on Malta and by the poverty of the scanty population of about 15,000.[19] It was a complete contrast to their pleasant, green, and well cultivated Rhodes; and must have seemed particularly barren at that time of the year when the summer sun had dried all colour out of the vegetation. The capital, then called Notabile, and now Mdina, was in the centre of the island protected by several miles of land from the swift raids of the corsairs, and secured upon a rocky knoll; but the Knights preferred to settle close to the sea and their ships which

16. Quoted from Boisgelin II pp.15–18. The main points only are included. A contemporary report, very similar in content, was published as an addenda to Fontanus.
17. Boisgelin II pp.18–20.
18. Bosio IV p.89. 26 October 1530, though the Procurators of the Order had previously taken formal possession of the island on 20 June.
19. Murray p.457.

lay-to in the Grand Harbour. Upon their arrival, the sole defences of this Harbour consisted of two guns mounted on Fort St. Angelo. A few dilapidated houses clustered together in the Birgu, the old town on the peninsula of land behind the Fort.

To the meagre defences, de l'Isle Adam added detached works wherever the nature of the ground permitted, repaired the existing walls of Fort St. Angelo and Notabile, but otherwise held his hand; for in his mind he planned to reconquer Rhodes, and considered the sojourn in Malta as no more than a temporary expedient. To this end the fleet of the Order was set in battle array and, as a preparatory move, dispatched to capture Modon in southern Greece. In this attempt the ships suffered a serious defeat, and all further idea of reoccupying Rhodes had to be abandoned.[20] Although Malta seemed large enough to be more or less self-supporting in food if properly cultivated, this very size of the island could also be an embarrassment, for it was evidently quite impossible to make a fortress of the whole island. The south-west coast is rocky and precipitous so that there was little fear of invasion from that quarter; and to the north a series of ridges run across the island hampering the movement of troops south toward the port.[21] It was in the area just north of the Grand Harbour, and the land to the south, that an invading force might be expected to land and concentrate its army. On the one side St. Julian's Bay afforded rocky, but nevertheless good anchorage, but the finest points of disembarkation were the great horseshoe bay of Marsascirocco with its sandy shore and, nearer to the Grand Harbour, the narrow sheltered inlet of Marsascala. These three vulnerable points were difficult to cover, and it was only after the great Turkish assault that forts were constructed to delay a landing at any of these points. These forts were, of necessity, isolated and, because they could not be given supporting fire, their role could only be to signal the arrival of the enemy and delay his landing.[22]

In 1541 the Grand Master Homedes asked for the assistance of a military engineer to advise on improving the defences against an impending Turkish invasion which, due to the increased efficiency of the Turkish navy, he feared might develop very soon. Antonio Ferramolino, a Bergamese, was sent by the Emperor to carry out

20. Crocker p.16.
21. The final ridge was not fortified until the British occupation, when the Victoria Lines were constructed along its crest and Fort Leonardo built to cover the land from the north. Nevertheless these ridges, and the Bengemma hills in particular, were deterrents.
22. These forts are respectively: Fort St. Julian, Fort St. Thomas (1614), and Fort St. Lucian, with the Fort on Comino built to cover the narrow water between Gozo and Malta. Their design is described later.

this task. His report was not encouraging : he suggested that both Fort St. Angelo and the Birgu should be evacuated and the Convent moved to the peninsula on the north side of the Grand Harbour, the high ground that is called Mount Sceberras. This is the first time that this suggestion was made, a suggestion which was many times repeated, but not carried into effect until 1566 when the new city of Valletta was founded on this site. In spite of the fact that existing defences at St. Angelo were low lying, and could be dominated by fire from both Mount Sceberras and Corrodin Hill, should an enemy occupy those undefended positions, Homedes turned down Ferramolino's proposal.[23] He did this because of the expense that another move, together with completely new defensive works, would impose upon the Order; and because he feared that it might increase the instability of some of the langues and so make an immediate evacuation of Malta necessary. In these early years of occupation this attempt to break out had to be constantly guarded against. Even the indomitable La Vallette at one time felt that Tripoli would make a better headquarters than Malta, considering the position to be strategically sounder. And when Tripoli was lost in 1551, he thought that Corsica would be safer than Malta as a base, now that the latter's southern flank was exposed. He even went so far as to negotiate with the Genoan Republic with a view to purchasing Corsica, but the Republic demanded too high a price.[24]

Homedes considered the exigencies of the moment and instructed Ferramolino to strengthen the existing works. This he did by raising a cavalier (1541) on Fort St. Angelo to as great a height as possible, so that the guns might bring effective fire to bear on the entrance to the Grand Harbour and the point of the Sceberras peninsula. In addition, he excavated a wide ditch to separate the Fort from the Birgu, so that the Fort became a citadel or final stronghold, and the landward side was secured. This ditch was useful during the siege as it provided a safe anchorage for the galleys which were then protected from Turkish gunfire.[25]

Ferramolino left Malta and was killed in action in 1550. He was replaced by the Spanish engineer Pietro Pardo, who carried forward the work of preparing the island to withstand prolonged siege. He was advised in this work by Count Strozzi the Prior of Capua. Strozzi made two suggestions of paramount importance, which were

23. Crocker p.16 and Promis p.370.
24. Curione p.19.
25. Bosio II p.198.

accepted by the Council.[26] He proposed to build a new fort to protect the peninsula (now Senglea) which lies parallel to the Birgu and St. Angelo, and so protect the southern flank of these positions and the front of the Senglea peninsula. This fort was designed by Pardo in the form of a star and quickly built.[27] It was called Fort St. Michael.

His second proposal was to replace the watch-tower,[28] which stood on the point of the Sceberras peninsula, with another star-shaped fort, in order to bring crossfire to bear on the entrance of the Grand Harbour, and bar to an enemy fleet the valuable harbour of Marsamuscetto, which lies to the north of the Sceberras peninsula. Again the work was speedily undertaken by Pardo (1551 or 1552) and the fort was called St. Elmo. According to Boisgelin, it was Strozzi who represented to the Council the need to fortify the Sceberras peninsula, stating that 'the Burgh, though fortified by Castle St. Angelo, was likewise overlooked by Mount St. Julian, a point of land jutting into the sea; and that it would be proper to build a fort upon this mount, to defend its approach from the enemy; that the port Marsa Musceit was open and undefended; and that, in order to prevent the entrance of the enemy's fleet, a *new town* must be built on Mount Sceberras, the most difficult place of access in the whole island, whither indeed, some time or other, it would become necessary to remove the Convent; and, in the meantime, a fort could not be too soon erected on the point of this rock, to defend the entrance into Marsa Musceit. The Commissioners[29] concluded their report by exhorting the Grand Master and the Council to fortify all those points of land, which, being longer than broad, formed a kind of port in the interval between each.'[30]

In 1551 the inhabitants of Malta received their final intimation that the blow was about to fall on the island. Dragut, the Turkish general, landed at Marsascirocco and marched upon Fort St. Angelo. He reconnoitred the position, but finding it too strong for immediate assault, temporarily withdrew from the island.[31] From this time on,

26. Crocker p.16.
27. Scicluna (*c*. 1551–52), p.222.
28. There is some argument about what actually existed at this point when the Knights arrived. Originally there was a watchtower which stood next to the little chapel of St. Elmo (or St. Telmo). Crocker p.63; 1488 the Viceroy of Sicily, fearing a Turkish invasion, replaced the tower with a fort. Zammit, *Malta* p.136, agrees, but Bosio XVIII p.354 states 'Strozzi built a fort . . .' and Boisgelin II p.55 says 'a fort could not be too soon erected on the point of this rock' and II p.15 Report of the Commissioners: 'no other defences than a small castle, called St. Angelo.'
29. Three Commissioners were appointed with Strozzi.
30. Boisgelin II p.55.
31. Crocker p.16.

until the assault of 1565, the Turks kept the island under intermittent observation; and, in fact, in that year two spies disguised as fishermen entered the fortress, took measurements and made drawings, and from these were able on their return to Constantinople to make models in relief of Fort St. Elmo, Fort St. Angelo, the Birgu, Fort St. Michael, Città Notabile, and the Castle in Gozo.[32]

Amid scares and alarms, the work of strengthening the defences went on. Masons and workmen were called for, and shipped over from Sicily;[33] lookout towers were built around the coast;[34] bastions were constructed along the southern waterline of Isola (Senglea) facing Corrodin Hill, and a new town founded on this peninsula (1554); and the two strategical forts, St. Elmo and St. Michael, were completed (1553).[35]

The fortress of Tripoli, although favoured by La Vallette, was not generally a popular acquisition. Its defences were poor when the Knights inherited it, and its sandy foundations formed a shifting base to any permanent fortifications. It was felt that an attacking force, with an efficient contingent of sappers, could rapidly make this fortress untenable.[36] La Vallette, entrusted with its defence, ordered the outworks to be strengthened and proposed new works to replace the obsolete defences, but the Grand Council turned down these proposals,[37] sensible only to the danger which threatened Malta.

In the face of these and other impediments it was little wonder that Gaspard la Vallier was unable to hold the Turkish assault of 1551, and the town fell. La Vallier, through the cupidity of the Grand Master Homedes, was accused of treachery and arrested; and only after strong representations had been made to the Pope was he finally acquitted.

This was the position when La Vallette accepted the Grand Mastership of the Order in the momentous year of the Turkish invasion. Rhodes had been lost, Tripoli had fallen, and a small force of Knights and local militia, without other assistance, faced an enemy force over four times their size, behind hastily improvised lines.[38]

32. Bosio XXIV p.490. 1565.
33. Boisgelin II p.56.
34. Curione p.20.
35. Crocker p.17.
36. Porter p.216: Tripoli 'seemed incapable of being much strengthened, as the sandy nature of the soil rendered the erection of ramparts and the sinking of ditches a matter of much difficulty.'
37. Curione p.20.
38. The Grand Master estimated the Turkish forces to number 40,000. *Letter from La Vallette to G. Prior of Germany, 8 October 1565,*

A detailed description of the siege has been given by numerous contemporary historians; so that I need not further elaborate their story, except to relate about the disposition of the two opposing forces and the arrangements of the permanent lines of fortification which finally saved the defenders by withstanding constant bombardments and assaults until reinforcements could be dispatched from Sicily.

The Turkish fleet appeared off the islands on the 18 May,[39] and landed the main body of the army at Marsascirocco, setting up a camp at Zabbar, facing the Birgu. After a conference, Dragut attacked Fort St. Elmo with all his forces, erecting shelters in front of the fort to protect his artillery from its guns. These shelters were small obstacles to the St. Elmo gunners, who repeatedly demolished them; and, so long as the fort held out, it was impossible for the Turks to make full use of the Heights of Sceberras from which artillery could so easily dominate the Birgu and Fort St. Angelo. Attack after attack was pressed home onto St. Elmo,[40] but the solid stone walls of the star-fort deflected many of the shots, and the ditches, largely excavated from the solid rock, made mining a slow unprofitable expedient. Withering fire from the mass of the Turkish cannon finally broke down the walls and reduced all to rubble; and when infilade fire from the guns prevented further reinforcements from being sent over from the Birgu, the infantry closed in for a final blow, with ladders, bridges, and wooden towers, whilst twenty-two huge catapults bombarded and demolished what was left of the ramparts. On 23 June Fort St. Elmo fell, and the last of its 1,300 defenders died.[41]

quoted in Curione pp.138–141. Curione also gives the defending force as numbering 8,300, of which 5,000 were Maltese levies. Porter p.231 'about 574 Knights and 67 Servants-at-arms, plus a garrison of 1,200 regular and nearly 7,000 militia. This number of Knights was eventually increased by nearly 100 through subsequent reinforcements. Thus . . . La Vallette could count upon a strength of about 9,000 men for the defence of the island.' Compare this attacking force with the 140,000 which were landed against Rhodes in 1480 (though Porter gives this force as 70,000 strong, or possibly 100,000), and the report, quoted by Porter p.202, that before the end of the siege of 1522 at Rhodes, 60,000 Turks had already fallen in battle or by disease.

39. *Letter from La Vallette to G. Prior of Germany p.139* says ' 250 ships, triremes, biremes, and other vessels.'
40. Curione p.73. The Turkish guns kept up a ceaseless bombardment for four days.
41. Curione p.87, of these one hundred and thirty were Knights.

This brave resistance seriously delayed the attack against the main enceinte on the other side of the Grand Harbour, and gave the Knights opportunity to call for assistance from Sicily, which was so slow to arrive; but with the defenders of Fort St. Elmo removed, the Turks were now able to mount their guns on the high ground facing Fort St. Angelo. The main assault was opened but, though constantly breached, the defenders' line finally held. The Grand Master was repeatedly entreated to withdraw from the Birgu, and fall back behind the strong bastions of Fort St. Angelo. This he refused to do, preferring to concentrate everything on the enceinte of the Birgu and utilize the inhabitants for its defence. The Turkish soldiers were discouraged when their repeated attacks were repulsed; and finally, wasted by disease and wounds, they felt in no condition to fight the reinforcements which arrived from Sicily.[42] On 11 September the baggage was removed to the ships, the Turkish army withdrew to the beaches, embarked, and sailed away from Malta for the last time.

The Turkish attack failed for three main reasons. At the very beginning of the siege the Turkish army, having received false information from a captured Knight, marched upon the strongest position, the Post of Castile on Mount Kalkara.[43] This set it off to a bad start. Secondly, the Turks spent valuable time in storming Fort St. Elmo, although its capture was necessary in order that they might bring their ships into Marsamuscetto Harbour and mount their heavy guns on the Sceberras peninsula. And thirdly, they made no attempt to occupy the high ground on Corrodin and Salvatore.

The defenders cleared all trees from in front of the lines so that these could not afford shelter to an attacking enemy, and demolished all suburban buildings, before the Turks landed on the island.[44] The Knights system of defence consisted of a citadel in Fort St. Angelo which, with its raised-up cavalier, provided covering fire for the rest of the fortifications; the two star-shaped forts at St. Elmo and St. Michael, which guarded the flanks, the former also preventing ships from entering the Grand Harbour and Marsamuscetto Harbour; and a continuous curtain, supported by bastions, encircling the Birgu. The layout of the defences is illustrated in many contemporary books.[45]

42. Curione p.124, Don Garcia de Toledo left Messina on the 20th of August with a fleet of seventy-two triremes, carrying 10,000 picked troops, among them 200 Knights of St. John and forty Knights of S. Stefano.
43. Crocker p.19.
44. Curione p.51.
45. Naberat, *Privilèges de l'Ordre de St. Jean,* erroneously shows the Val-

Although there are no accurate drawings of these early fortifications, it is possible to get a fairly clear idea of their design from these early prints, and from the accounts of the siege. Fort St. Angelo had an irregular enceinte, the result of constant additions to a primitive castle. Cut off from the Birgu by a ditch, it had two tiers of firing platforms facing onto the harbour, four bastions connected by curtains, two of which had an indented form. The Birgu defences on the landward side were formed by a line of ramparts broken by two complete bastions and two demi-bastions at the ends : a wide water ditch cut off the Birgu curtain from the mainland. Outworks are mentioned by two writers, but I have found no sign of them in the maps. Fort St. Elmo was constructed in the form of a star with four angles, and the land front facing Mount Sceberras was broken into a bastioned form. A ravelin covered the bridge and the entrance, and facing out to sea there was a cavalier. The design of Fort St. Michael was similar, with the exception of the bastioned front and the ravelin.

The new city of Valletta

After the lifting of the siege, La Vallette took immediate action to destroy all the Turkish works and fill in their trenches for, fearing a fresh attack in the spring, he wished to leave his enemy as little advantage as possible.[46]

In spite of the warm congratulations and promises of assistance which the defenders had received from all parts of Europe, the Council of the Order was by no means reassured about the safety of their position upon Malta, and many members wished to quit the island. Money was short for rebuilding the fortifications and there were few soldiers to man them, for the surrounding countryside had been burned and depopulated by the Turks.

It was the firm stand taken by the Grand Master which persuaded the Council to remain : a stand which was considerably strengthened by the timely destruction through sabotage of the Turkish arsenal at Constantinople.[47] In order to settle the headquarters irrevocably, La Vallette took the bold step which had been advocated before;

letta fortifications in a map of the siege. Sandys p.231 has a drawing which shows the two star-shaped forts. Boisgelin pp.xviii and xix gives a list of the principal early maps of Malta.
46. Boisgelin II, p.125.
47. *Op. cit.*

he determined to fortify Mount Sceberras and build there a new city.

The earliest proposal appears to have come from the engineers Ferramolino[48] and Strozzi,[49] before the middle of the century and before the Great Turkish attack on Malta. On 11 March 1558, the important Italian architect and military engineer, Bartolomeo Genga, arrived in Malta and, after examining the position, repeated the proposals which had been made earlier. He suggested that both the Birgu and Fort St. Michael were too low to fortify adequately, and that the only reasonable way of securing these positions was by building the new city on Mount Sceberras. He made a model of his new plan which included a larger area than that later laid out by Laparelli. The front of the new city extended forward to about the line of the present Floriana defences, so that the city guns could cover the high ground on Corrodin and the water hole on the Marsa.[50] His plan was not carried out but, instead, the existing defences were improved and strengthened. In 1559, Genga died in Malta, and his place was taken, in 1562, by another Italian, Baldassare Lanci from Urbino. He also proposed that the new city should be built, but his plan was more practical than the one prepared by Genga. The city he proposed was far smaller, and the front was therefore much shorter, and could be more easily defended.[51] In this work Lanci was assisted by Antonio Quinsani di Montalcino.[52]

La Vallette, wishing to raise money for the building of the city, sent Giuseppe Cambiano, Nicolo de Villegagnon, and Martin Rojas de Portalrubio as Ambassadors to the Council of Trent, in order to obtain indulgences. Their mission was successful, and the assistance obtained from Pius IV was most helpful. Nevertheless, the work was not undertaken, and the proposals were shelved until after the siege of 1565.[53]

After the siege La Vallette applied to Pius IV for the services of an expert architect well versed in town planning and the design of fortifications, to be sent to Malta to take charge of the preparations for the new city. For this task the Pope chose Francesco Laparelli,

48. Curione p.19.
49. Boisgelin II p.55.
50. Bosio III pp.398–455.
51. Bosio III p.454.
52. Paribeni p.82 states that he assisted both Genga and Lanci on the plans for the new city. Genga died in 1559, and Lanci did not arrive until nearly three years later. If Paribeni is correct, it would suggest that Quinsani was a link between these two.
53. Bosio XX pp.453 and 459. The city is not mentioned by name, but the request is made 'per l'edificatione della nuova città sopra il Monte di Sant'Elmo. . . .'

an assistant of Michelangelo and a man with wide experience of military defences, who had worked at Civita Vecchia and Rome in the service of the Vatican.

Laparelli arrived in Malta on 28 December 1565, at the very time that the Knights were divided in their opinion upon the advisability of remaining. Many of the precious belongings of the Order had already been packed and stored ready to leave the island. In the face of this feeling of uncertainty, La Vallette ordered Laparelli to prepare his plans with the utmost speed; and within three days of his arrival, the latter was able to lay his proposals before the Council : proposals which were not altered in any important particular in the final execution of his schemes.[54]

Laparelli considered that, because of the strength of the island, it would be an unpardonable error to retire. Instead, he proposed to repair the old existing defences which were defective and to build the new city on Mount Sceberras, which would act as a guard to the harbours and the islands. There were times when the Grand Master wavered in his resolution, deterred by the thought of the tremendous expenditure involved and the opposition from many quarters, but Laparelli's insistence was supported by the report of Gabrio Serbelloni. Serbelloni had been sent to Malta by King Philip II, and arrived there in March 1566. He had known Laparelli at Cortona, in the war with Siena, and had supported his appointment as military engineer at the Vatican and Civita Vecchia. Serbelloni's advice carried great weight, and his recommendation of Laparelli's plan to the Spanish King finally persuaded the Order to proceed with the work on the new city.[55]

On 28 March the new city was born. It was christened Valletta in honour of the Grand Master who had led the Order victoriously through the siege; and a ceremony of inauguration was held at the gate of St. George (later Porta Reale) and on the site of the proposed bastions which were to guard the landward approach to the city. As the work of construction on the fortifications began, the disputes sprang up again. The Viceroy of Sicily and Ascania della Cornia arrived on Malta, accompanied by the engineer Fratino, and

---

54. CODEX LAPARELLI p.6, Prima relazione all'Ill.mo e Rev. mo Sinor Gran Maestro, firmata Franco Laparelli da Cortona, in data tre genaro 1566.
55. Scicluna p.216 ' A wax model was also prepared (by Laparelli) and subsequently sent to Philip II of Spain, the Suzerain of the islands. The original plan of the fortress was much altered by Chev. Gabrio Serbelloni, Prior of Hungary . . . but after much discussion, a final plan was approved and adopted.' I can find no reference to a dispute in the CODEX LAPARELLI. Rather, Laparelli and Serbelloni seem to have been in complete agreement.

proposed a shorter enceinte.[56] The original plan was nearly abolished and this new proposal accepted; and Laparelli wrote of the indecision of the Grand Master and the hard task he had in persuading La Vallette not to deviate from the plans he had made.[57] La Vallette, at this stage, appears to have been frightened by the expense and to have preferred the comfort of the Birgu to the exposed position on Mount Sceberras. There was a shortage of workmen, but Laparelli offered to supply them himself in order to speed the building of the defences.

Opposition was overcome and the city began to rise on the new site. By the winter of 1568 things had progressed so well that Laparelli could apply for leave to go back to Italy. In that year La Vallette died and was succeeded by Pietro del Monte, an Italian Grand Master with a tremendous enthusiasm for the new project. At the end of the year Laparelli returned to Malta and gave full instructions for the final completion of Valletta to his assistant, the Maltese engineer Gerolamo Cassar. In the following year, Laparelli, thirsting for active service and his task virtually ended, applied to be released from his duties on the island, and joined the Pope's fleet in the eastern Mediterranean. On 26 October 1570, he contracted the plague, which was already manifest in the ships upon their arrival at Suda Bay, and died at Candia. He was only 49.

The peninsula, upon which Valletta was built, consists of a plateau of land lying about 140 feet above sea level (called Mount Sceberras)[58] and a higher point, the Castile Heights, which rises to 180 feet, placed south of the plateau. The Camerata saddle joins the plateau to Fort St. Elmo, and around the peninsula five valleys indent the high ground. Of these, the Manderaggio valley is by far the most pronounced, and it was here that Laparelli planned a small creek to protect the Order's shipping from the storms.[59]

There was a ready belief at that time that a peninsula provided the most easily defensible position, and many of the contemporary writers on fortifications refer to its suitability as the site of a city.[60]

56. Occhini p.13.
57. CODEX LAPARELLI p.4.
58. The site of the Magisterial palace and church of St. John.
59. Zammit, *Valletta* p.24. Excavated stone was used for work on Valletta. A good start was made and a considerable quantity of stone quarried, but the stone of the lower strata was found to be unsuitable for building purposes and the work of excavation was abandoned before sea level had been reached. Finally, the Order decided to use the Grand Harbour as its naval harbour, instead of Marsamuscetto, and the Manderaggio was never completed. The same fate fell on the Arsenal Creek adjoining Fort St. Elmo.
60. Machiavelli, *L'arte della guerra* VII.1. Porroni II,v ' De siti in peninsula, e suoi vantaggi. . . .'

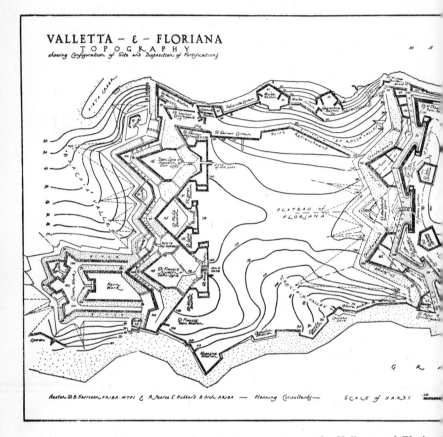

1. *Valletta and Floriana*

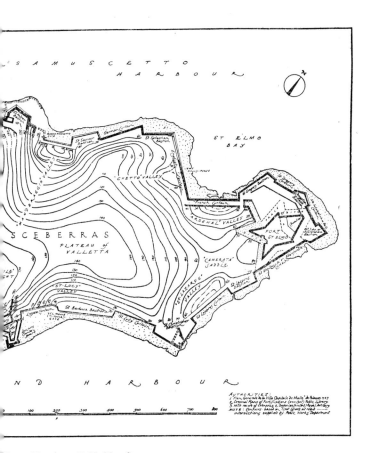

(from Harrison & Hubbard).

During the year 1566 practically all work was concentrated upon the fortifications in order to make the peninsula secure from the impending attack of a new Turkish force then being got ready.[61] The most obvious position for the line to be taken across the peninsula was from the Castile Heights at the south, along the ridge which separated the Manderaggio valley from the St. Rocco valley. Here the natural lie of the land allowed the defenders to command the 'Plateau of Floriana,' as it was later called, about twenty feet below their level. Along this suitable line Laparelli designed four bastions with counterguards.[62] By October 1567 this work had been completed.[63] Laparelli laid out four further bastions along the northern waterfront and three facing the Grand Harbour, all being connected by curtains. The reconstructed star fort of St. Elmo guarded the point of the peninsula. The most massive bastions and the shortest curtains were built on the landward front, and here the ditches were to be excavated to a depth of forty palmi below the string course of the curtains : it was only from this quarter that Laparelli feared an attack.

In spite of the fact that the first year was mainly spent in building fortifications, it seems clear that the rectangular street pattern was laid out at the beginning. There are several indications that this was indeed so. In the first place we hear that the church of Our Lady of Victory was begun in 1566, the year of the foundation of the city. It was not orientated to face the west, a disposition which would surely have been adopted if there were no other overriding factors to influence the siting of the building. Instead, it faced north-east, in line with the general grid pattern of the city.

Laparelli himself refers to the expense he had incurred between 21 October 1566 and 22 March 1567 in the construction of a house in Valletta,[64] and with the expense sheets he included plans, and drawings of a room, a window, and a door 'well proportioned,' showing that this was no mere temporary structure such as the stores he had built to accommodate provisions and ammunition at an early stage in the work.

On 21 October 1566 Laparelli commented upon the fact that the streets of the new city often led away from the bastions so that it

61. Crocker p.34.
62. Occhini p.25. He wished to make his defences on the slope of the highest part of the hill, by direct line 500 canne from the front of St. Elmo, going over the backbone of the hill.
63. CODEX LAPARELLI p.54r. Laparelli refers to the bastions as cavaliers. They function more as bastions and the two cavaliers of St. James and St. John were built in 1582 to support them.
64. CODEX LAPARELLI second file in the appendix.

was difficult for the workmen to go from one bastion to another, or to move artillery from place to place, nor could the night watchmen go comfortably round the walls. This surely is a clear indication that the street pattern existed, at least in part, at that date, and that Laparelli then found it necessary to add a perimeter road just inside the line of the curtains.[65]

Finally, before leaving for Italy in the winter of 1568, he left instructions with Gerolamo Cassar, who was to take his place during his leave of absence, informing him of the work which was to be done on the 'building and the fortifications' whilst he was away.[66] Therefore, at that time, the streets must have been laid down, and considerable building work being undertaken for Laparelli to have referred to it first in giving his instructions.[67]

The plan of the city provided for a rectangular pattern of streets, running along and across the peninsula, twelve in the length and nine in the breadth, excluding the perimeter track. The main street ran from the gate of St. George, in the centre of the curtain lying between the bastions of St. James and St. John on the land front, direct to the gate of Fort St. Elmo : there the axis of the fort turned more to the north. The principal square of Valletta was placed about half-way between the main gate and the fort, and another square opened off the south side of the street in which the Conventual church was built. It is difficult to tell if the site for the main square was decided upon at the beginning, for we know that the Council of the Order wished to build the Magisterial palace upon the Castile Heights, and was only later persuaded by Grand Master del Monte to buy and enlarge his nephew's house in the centre of the city. One thing is certain, a square upon the Castile Heights, exposed to the land which lay beyond St. Peter's curtain and isolated in a corner of the city, would never have made a convenient or suitable square for the ceremony and pomp which surrounded the civic life of the Order of St. John.

At first the engineers proposed to level the whole site for the new city and Laparelli reported on 15 October 1567 that 'in the high

65. CODEX LAPARELLI pp.43v and 44r 'in many places it is now necessary to fly back into the city and by passing through the city, go to find new places. It being a great defect to be unable to go from emplacement to emplacement.'
66. CODEX LAPARELLI pp.70–71.
67. Miege, *Histoire de Malte,* Paris 1840 (quoted in Lavedan II p.87) must therefore be wrong when he states that only under the Grand Master 'Pierre de Monte que furent arrêtées le dessins de la division des rues. . . .'

parts the work of cutting had started, to acquire stone for walls, and in the lower parts, the building of walls filled with earth behind' was progressing. But he complained of the shortage of donkeys to move the earth. Finally the work was found to be too costly, and it had to be abandoned and all the streets laid out to follow the natural terrain of the site.[68]

Valletta differed from the two previous capitals of the Order in three major respects. The new city was laid out on a rectangular grid pattern.[69] The idea of having a citadel containing the Magisterial palace, capable of making a final stand, was abandoned, and instead the palace was built in the city. The Collacchio, an area set aside for the exclusive privileges of the Knights and in which all the public buildings of the Order were situated, was not used in the new city and the auberges of the Knights were dispersed throughout Valletta, each being built near the bastion defended by its respective langue.[70]

When designing their 'ideal' cities in the sixteenth century, Renaissance military engineers usually preferred the radio-concentric plan, in which roads radiate from a central piazza; and ideal cities were designed in this manner by Filarete, Francesco di Giorgio, Fra Giocondo, and G. Maggi. Even Scamozzi and Pietro Cataneo, although they made a rectangular grid of their streets, emphasized the central square, and bound their cities within a regular figure of eight or twelve sides. This ideal was, however, rarely carried out in practice, and most of the cities which were actually built in the sixteenth century were laid out within a rectangular perimeter of fortified walls, with the main street running down the middle of the length, and with the other streets laid out on a rectangular pattern, parallel to, or cutting across, this main street. The new cities (such

68. Granting Byron an excuse to write 'Adieu, ye cursed street of stairs! (How surely he who mounts you swears!) Adieu. . . .'
69. The new city of Senglea was founded in 1544, but when the street pattern, which is in the form of a rectangular grid, was laid out I do not know.
70. Although there was not the clear distinction at Birgu which there had been at Rhodes, where a wall separated the collacchio from the Lower Town, part of the Birgu is referred to as the ' Collacchio Area ' in the Malta Archives. ARCHIVES 288 p.29v. relate to a law made by the Reverendi Domini XVI which refers to ' houses both inside the Collacchio as well as those outside.' Zammit, *Malta* p.158 ' The Knights being ecclesiastical, were supposed to lead a claustral life, and their seclusion had been as strictly maintained at the Borgo as previously in Rhodes. The proposed division of Valletta was very unpopular among the people and the young Knights, so that few came forward to buy the land. The opposition finally became so acute that the proposed division had to be abandoned.'

as Puebla de los Angeles 1531), which sprang up throughout the Spanish colonies in Mexico and South America, were planned in this fashion, and instructions for their layout came from Spain itself. On 3 July 1573 the Spanish King issued his Ordinances for the Building of New Towns.[71] These Ordinances, like most of the contemporary work on town planning and fortification, were the result of the researches of Italian military engineers.[72]

Vitry-le-François, built after 1545 to the designs of the Bolognese engineer Girolamo Marini, is another rectangular plan similar to Valletta though smaller. It has the same arrangement of a gate at one end of the main street and a fort at the other end, with the main square equidistant between the two. A somewhat similar arrangement was made at Zamosc, built near Lublin in 1578 by Bernardo Morando of Padua; but here a further wide street cuts across the main square at right angles to the one running from the fort, and the town gate was placed at one end of this shorter street.

Valletta falls into the middle of this period of the building of rectangular planned cities, and it is difficult to see what other plan could have been adopted on that rocky peninsula. In the last quarter of the century, the radio-concentric plan, which had been the ideal of the Italian designers, was popularly practised throughout Europe, and this type tended to supersede the rectangular plan. Palma Nuova was begun in 1566 and completed in 1593, Coeworden in Holland was begun in 1583, and concentric planning was carried out at Genzaro in 1621, and after 1693 at Granmichele. But in Malta the rectangular grid plan continued to be used at Floriana, a suburb built behind the defences of 1636, and at Pawla, the summer resort founded by the Grand Master de Paule in 1626.

71. *Real Ordenanzas para Nuevos Poblaciones,* ecc. NAT. ARCHIVES MADRID, MS. 3017 ' Bulas y cedulas para el govierno de las Indias ' translated in Nuttall.
72. Many of the ideas in the Ordinances were first suggested in Renaissance times by Alberti

In 1634 the Grand Master de Paule, having received information of an impending attack, sought the services of an Italian engineer. In answer to this request Urban VIII chose Paolo Floriana and sent him to the island. After studying the layout of the ground, Floriana reported that he considered the land front of Valletta was weak because it was overlooked by high ground on each side and by a plateau in front of the position. To remedy this defect he proposed to build a new land line further out upon the escarpment of this plateau, raised up to such a height that it could not be overlooked by any other position. The proposal surprised many of the Knights, who considered an enlargement of the enceinte would be a further strain on the garrison rather than an asset to the defence of Valletta.

1   Floriana's plan provided three bastions on the land front. The centre bastion of St. Philip took the place which was occupied by the main gate and curtain wall in the earlier front to Valletta. His plan, which cut out the vulnerable curtain wall except for two short sections immediately behind the demi-lunes of Our Lady and St. Francis, made the front immensely stronger than the old one. There were two gates in the depth of the line. The outer one was covered by a lunette and supported by infilade fire from two *fausse-braie*; and this only opened up the path to the second, or main gate, which lay directly behind the powerful demi-lune of St. Francis. But the most powerful defence of all was the great horn work which lay alongside the ridge in front of that demi-lune. To storm the gates the enemy would have to advance up the Brachia valley constantly faced by fire from the long parapet of this horn work.

This front was a masterly design, by an architect who had given considerable thought to the disposition of horn works, but the critics condemned the treatment of the flanks where, they feared, an enemy might infiltrate between the main Floriana defences, which faced outward only, and Laparelli's land front of Valletta. These critics suggested that a few comparatively inexpensive additions to Laparelli's work would be sufficient to render Valletta impregnable.

An envoy, who had been sent to the courts of Europe to ask the opinion of the leading military engineers, returned to Malta in February 1636 and reported that the general opinion of these engineers was opposed to this new project and preferred to add new works to the existing enceinte. In spite of this opposition, Floriani's plans were sanctioned by the Council and work began on the fortifications.

The defences of the Grand Harbour

In 1638 Firenzuola visited the island and reported upon the condition of the defences. He viewed the existing trace of the Valletta enceinte favourably and joined those who had opposed the Floriana lines. He was of the opinion that the centre of Florian's front was too strong and the flanks too weak, an opinion already held by other experts; and that the bastions had been made too acute in plan.

Firenzuola felt that the major threat to Malta would come from the hill called St. Margherita, just east of Vittoriosa (Birgu). This hill dominated the town and an enemy in possession of it could command the Grand Harbour and blockade the Three Cities.[73] He therefore submitted a design to the Council for a new enceinte enclosing both the hill and Cospicua.[74]

94
95
97

This plan having been accepted, work came to an end on the Floriana Lines, and the workmen were moved over to the other side of the Grand Harbour.[75]

The existing fortifications on the south bank of the Grand Harbour consisted of the main fort at St. Angelo, separated from Vittoriosa by a ditch; and a land front of two bastions, with supporting cavaliers and intervening curtain walls, covering the city of Vittoriosa. The Senglea peninsula was guarded by the star fort of St. Michael, which was reformed into the bastion of St. Michael, and at the other end of the land front the Sheer bastion.[76] These defences virtually provided two lines of defence.

To these fortifications the military engineers added in the seventeenth century two further enceintes on the landward side. The first

73. The Three Cities are Vittoriosa (Birgu), Cospicua (Bormla), and Senglea (Isola).
74. Crocker p.36.
75. Work was resumed in 1640 with a slightly altered plan, after the visit of Giovanni de' Medici. Further alterations were made by Valperga (1670) when 'la Gadiana,' the two falsa braca and two bulwarks on the flanks were built. Work was carried out by Blondel. Scicluna p.217, and completed by Grunenberg and de Tigne.
76. The waterfront of Vittoriosa facing Calcara Creek, and that of Senglea facing French Creek, were also defended with extended bastions, ravelins, and curtains, but because of the rocky coast and comparatively deep water, these fronts were not very vulnerable.

of these, the Margherita lines, were designed by Firenzuola in 1638, with an amended plan prepared in the following year. The designer envisaged a semicircular sweep of defences around Cospicua, with six radiating bastions and a ravelin where the junction was made with the Vittoriosa front at St. James' bastion.[77] These first three bastions and the demi-bastion were begun immediately[78] and completed, but the remainder of the work was held up until 1716 and not finally completed until 1736. During these years there was a constant threat of invasion. In the year 1641 the Turks actually landed a force of 5,000 men in Gozo and in Malta, but their advance was checked by the Maltese cavalry, and 100 galleys were driven from the beaches by the guns of Fort St. Lucian. In 1645 there was another scare, and in 1670, with the fall of Candia, the fear of invasion was revived. To counter this threat, the Grand Master Nicholas Cotoner called for a new line of fortifications to girdle the Three Cities. Maurizio Valperga, the chief military engineer to the Duke of Savoy, was invited to the island to prepare a scheme. He arrived in February 1670 and proposed to complete the Margherita lines by adding new bastions, and to strengthen the front across the hill of St. Margherita, utilizing as much as possible of Firenzuola's work. This solution did not satisfy the Grand Master, who had conceived the idea of a vaster and more noble work : and his opinion carried considerable weight in view of the fact that he himself was paying for the project.

Valperga accordingly drew up a second scheme providing for a vast semicircular ring of eight bastions and two semi-bastions, with a circumference of 5,000 yards and capable of sheltering 40,000 people together with their belongings and their livestock.[79]

The foundation stone was laid by the Grand Master on 28 August 1670, and a flowing inscription recording the gift of the works by **102** Cotoner was placed over the arch of Zabbar gate, which leads the main road into the Cities. The Grand Master announced his undertaking to the princes of Europe and received, in exchange, their disapproval of his extravagance and criticism of the size of the new fortifications. Despite this, building was carried on for ten years until funds ran out. By that time the main body of the Cotonera **103–105** lines was complete, but the ravelins which should have guarded each curtain had not been built : the work was never finished.

77. The Vittoriosa front was also strengthened by the addition of the St. Lawrence demi-bastion and the St. Ursula platform which mounted five guns to sweep the western ditch of the Post of Castile.
78. The foundation stone was laid 30 December 1638.
79. The trace followed Vauban's ' First System.'

To complete the defences of the Grand Harbour, Fra Giovanni Francesco Ricasoli paid for a fort to be built on the most eastern peninsula,[80] which marks the entrance to the Grand Harbour. The **118** narrow strip of water was then covered on one side by the guns of Fort St. Elmo, and from the other by those of Fort Ricasoli, which was named after its benefactor. The fort was designed by Valperga and begun in 1670.[81]

Eighteenth century defences to Marsamuscetto Harbour

With the land defences of Valletta secured by the Floriana lines, and the Three Cities safely girdled by the Margherita and Cotonera lines, the only quarter that remained vulnerable was the north. From that direction the long flank of Valletta lay exposed to an attack mounted from Sliema, Gzira, or the large island which lay undefended in Marsamuscetto. Two major works were commissioned in the eighteenth century to seal this quarter : a powerful fort was built on the island, and a small fort laid out on Dragut Point opposite Fort St. Elmo.[82]

Grunenberg first proposed a fort on the island in the last decade of the seventeenth century, but no definite steps were undertaken until the Grand Master Manoel de Vilhena instructed the two French engineers, de Tigne and de Mondion, to carry out the work. Owing to the shape of the island, de Tigne, who prepared the designs, was forced to restrict his trace to a square. He proposed **99** several outworks which would have covered the whole island with fortifications, but these were not built.[83] It is an indication of the cheapness of building material and labour at that time that the whole fort cost only £2,500. The fort, which was named Manoel, is a remarkably fine design and was extremely powerful with its garrison of 500 men.   **115**

The fort on Dragut Point was the last important building erected **95**

80. Scicluna p.218. This had been the site of troublesome Turkish batteries in the siege of 1565. A small fort was built there after the siege and completed in 1629. It was called the ' Torre Orsi ' after Cav. Alessandro Orsi who paid for it.
81. Grunenberg considered it too weak and proposed further additions. These were not carried out.
82. In addition Grunenberg strengthened the northern face of Fort St. Elmo when he carried the flank of the Valletta Lines around the point, building the Bastions of St. Gregory, Conception (Ball's), and St. John (Abercrombie's) in 1687.
83. Scicluna p.223, is of the opinion that de Mondion was the designer of the fort.

by the Knights before their capitulation to the French army in 1798. In 1761 the Grand Master Emanuel Pinto invited several French engineers to inspect, and report upon, the fortifications. It was one of these engineers, the Cavalier Tigne, who designed the fort which took his name.[84] Fort Tigne was built in 1793 and consisted of a simple casemated redoubt of low silhouette, capable of withholding the entrance of an enemy vessel to Marsamuscetto harbour, but not designed to withstand prolonged siege. In this event, its guns could be spiked and the fort confidently abandoned without the fear that it could be turned to advantage by an enemy engaged in the bombardment of Valletta.

A French manuscript in the office of the Chief Engineer of the Garrison[85] gave the strength of the defences on the eve of the capitulation to Napoleon. Valletta and Floriana were held by 3,000 regular soldiers and 5,000 militia, with a cavalry force of 150 men. These were deployed so that 2,000 guarded the lines, a similar number were held in reserve, and 2,000 rested and formed the artillery, did fatigues and general duties.

The Three Cities were garrisoned by another 3,000 regulars and 5,000 militia, and 2,000 men were stationed at Fort Ricasoli.

The outer defences of Malta

Towers have been built to watch the coasts of Malta from the earliest times, and there are many references to Megalathic[86] and Arab remains,[87] but it was during the suzerainty of the Knights that the majority of those now remaining were built.

These are of three types : the first type was built to watch a harbour, inlet or vulnerable landing place, and for this reason had to be designed to dominate the view; the second type formed a refuge for the villagers against the attacks of the corsairs,[88] and were thus placed in or near a village; and the last type was the lookout tower built to dominate other lower lines of defence. It was

---

84. He should not be confused with the other de Tigne who arrived in 1715, and designed Fort Manoel. See Biographies p.222.
85. Crocker p.46.
86. Torri-tal-Giganti and Torri-tal-Mramma.
87. Torre-tal-Ghassieli near Zabbar referred to in Abela lib.1 not.viii,53. It was built on a circular plan with carefully jointed pieces of stone set in lime mortar.
88. They served a similar purpose to the small village churches and the fortified houses which are found on the outskirts of many Maltese villages.

from a tower like this, the 'Torre dell'Orologio' at Vittoriosa, that the Grand Master La Vallette conducted the defence during the siege of 1565, and was able to obtain information of the disposition

2. *Gauci St. Paul 'Tat-Torga' Tower.*
4. *Gozo. Guorgion Tower.*

3. *Comino Fort.*
5. *Delimara Tower.*

of the Turkish forces. This tower, which had its origin in Sicolo-Norman times, was built on six floors. The Knights must have made modifications soon after their arrival, for the fourth floor balustrade bore an inscription with the date 1549. An old map of 1565 shows the tower in virtually the same condition as it was until it was destroyed in the last war.[89]

Of the towers built before the advent of the Knights, the lookout posts were usually circular in plan, but the larger fortified houses which gave refuge to the surrounding population were often square or irregular. The Guorgion Tower in Gozo is a typical example of this type. 4

In the early years of the seventeenth century the Knights, under the leadership of the Grand Master Wignacourt, began the erection

89. Mifsud, *La milizia e le torri antiche di Malta* in ARCHIVUM MELITENSE IV No. 2, 1920 pp.70–71.

of a number of powerful forts. In 1610[90] the Wignacourt Tower at St. Paul's Bay was built. It became the prototype for the other forts of this period. Square in plan, it was internally provided with two

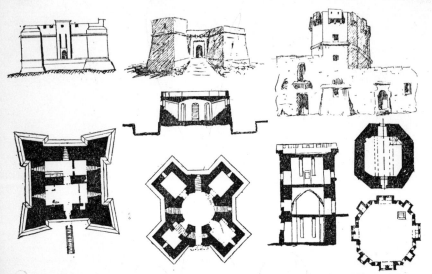

6–7. *St. Thomas' Fort.*   8–10. *Mamu Tower.*   11–14. *Qrendi. Cavalier Tower with first floor and terrace plans.*

rectangular barrel-vaulted chambers on each of its two floors. The lower floor was strongly battered and divided from the upper floor by a bold torus moulding : there were four corner towers looking out across the countryside and the bay, and a central doorway approached by a flight of steps and a drawbridge. The two powerful forts of St. Lucian, guarding the vulnerable bay of Marsascirocco, and St. Thomas, watching over the entrance to Marsascala and St. Thomas' Bay, were built respectively in 1610 and 1614.[91] Vittorio Cassar designed a similar fort on Comino in 1618, which was called St. Mary's Tower. This tower guarded the narrow strip of water between Malta and Gozo.

The Xavia Tower near Zabbar (1620) and the Orsi Tower (1622), built on the point opposite St. Elmo and now occupied by Fort Ricasoli, followed in the reign of this Grand Master. The stately Red Tower near Mellieha was built in 1649;[92] and there are many other towers which, though not specifically dated, were erected in this period.

90. Braun, *Works of Art*. But Mifsud *op. cit.* p.79 gives the date 1609.
91. Both were probably designed by Vittorio Cassar.
92. Dated by an inscription on the tower.

Subsequent Grand Masters strengthened the outer defences and Lascaris in particular should be mentioned, for it was he who on 13 January 1647, by an order in Council,[93] decreed that further towers should be built along the shores. As a result of this a number of square lookout towers were built in the last half of the seventeenth century. These were modelled on earlier designs and were remarkably uniform in style. They consisted of a square plan enclosing a single room on each of the two or three floors, and a flat roof protected by a parapet. The staircase arrangement was not always identical, but it usually consisted of an external stone stair leading to the first floor, with an internal circular stone staircase leading from the main floor to the cellar, and an internal iron ladder mounting to the second floor and the roof. The late seventeenth century Delimara Tower is a typical example, and the Vincenti **5** Tower (1726) at Mqabba is a later tower of almost identical design.

15. *'Ta-Wied Znuber' Tower.*   16. *15th century tower.*

This type became the 'torre dello standardo' of the eighteenth century : a two-storey structure built on a base of thirty-nine piedi and a height of fifty piedi, it had heavy walls constructed of choice materials, and a further strengthened scarped base. The ground floor formed the guard room and the first floor contained one large hall connected to the ground by an external stone staircase and to the roof by a spiral staircase. The tower which was built on the flank of the entrance gateway to Mdina is a typical example of the 'torre dello standardo.' It was erected during the Grand Mastership of Vilhena (1722–36).[94]

93. Mifsud *op. cit.* p.79.
94. *Cabreo Università Notabile 1750* vol.304, fol.9, No.6. Described by Mifsud *op. cit.* p.70.

There are two important and unique examples which do not follow the plan arrangement of the towers already described. The

11–14 first, the Cavalier Tower at Qrendi, is the only octagonal tower on the island. It has three storeys containing octagonal rooms on the first two floors and a square room on the second floor. The terrace is octagonal, with eight drop boxes; four double and four single.[95]

8–10 The other unusual tower is the Mamu Tower, dating from the seventeenth century. It was built in the form of the cross of St. Andrew, with a circular room covered with a shallow vault occupying the crossing of the arms. It is on one floor only, with the exception of the arm on the left of the gate which has two floors. The tower is surrounded by a ditch excavated from the solid rock, and the walls of the ground floor are scarped.

With the exception of these last two examples, the towers, which are very numerous on the island, are remarkably uniform, though many have later buildings attached to them which vary in size and design. These towers are by no means unique to Malta but occur along the shores of the Mediterranean wherever the corsairs were likely to raid the countryside. There are numerous examples in Sicily, Calabria, and the heel of Italy: in Corsica, Sardinia, and the coasts of Spain.

The fortified villa

Most of the important houses which lay on the outskirts of the villages had some form of fortified wall or tower to provide a refuge

4 against the raiders. The Guorgion Tower in Gozo is a typical example dating from the fourteenth century, and there are others still remaining outside old villages like Zebbug.

But in Malta, there are two important houses which, although they are fortified, are something more than mere fortified houses. The design of their fortifications has been used to create a systematic work of architecture and the result is a building which is close in conception to such fortified villas as the Villa Farnese at Caprarola. In function too these houses were villas and formed the country residences for use in the summer.

17,122 The first is the Summer palace at Verdala, a few miles from Rabat. It is built on high ground to benefit from the cool sea breezes and is laid out with an elaborate garden and a boschetto.

95. Mifsud *op. cit.* p.73, suggests that the design was influenced by the San Michele Tower at Ostia designed by Michelangelo in 1560 and executed by Nanni di Baccio Biglio between 1567 and 1570.

The villa was designed by Gerolamo Cassar in 1586. It is almost square in plan,[96] three storeys high, with bastioned corner towers rising a further storey. The villa is approached by a flight of steps

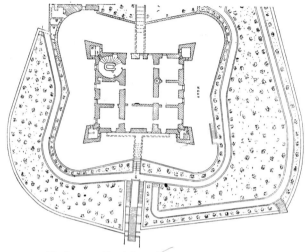

17. *Rabat. Verdala palace, ground floor plan.*

to a fine door in the centre of one side on the first, or main, floor. The only other door is on the opposite side and leads to a terrace. The main door has a crisp quality and is beautifully proportioned, showing that Cassar's work is not always marred by Mannerist distortions.

The plan is straightforward and almost symmetrical. An entrance lobby has an oval staircase on one side and an ante-room opposite. The lobby leads directly to a fine vaulted hall which has two square rooms on each side.

Cassar's peculiarities appear at several places in the building : the uncertainty with which he handles the relationship between the internal and façade symmetries resulting in many compromises in the placing of the windows is typical of his work. The panels below[97] the side windows on the first floor acting as pseudo-balconies to repeat the pattern of the main balcony; the small piece of rustication above these windows; and finally, the main cornice topped with an ovolo moulding over a cavetto, these are all signs of Cassar's handiwork.

96. 176ft. by 188ft.
97. He also uses these on the first floor of the auberge d'Italie in Valletta.

The Selmun palace at Mellieha is nearly two hundred years later but its plan is almost identical. Here the decoration is Baroque

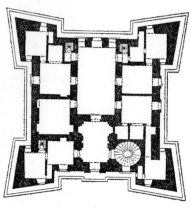

18. *Mellieha. Selmun palace, first floor plan.*

19. *Drawing of a fortified villa (after Francesco di Giorgio).*

and the angles of the bastions thrust forward more acutely : all the lines are more exaggerated at the Mellieha palace. The architect was Cachia (1700–90?), who also designed the auberge de Castile at Valletta.

18,125,126 The Selmun palace was undoubtedly influenced by Verdala,[98] but what of the origin of the Verdala plan? Like so many of the buildings of this period in Malta, its origin can be traced in the first place to Italy, and more directly from the French architects who gathered their knowledge from northern Italy. Francesco di Giorgio's

19 scheme for a villa with bastions,[99] though larger in scale, has the same basic plan as Verdala, with a central hall and porticoed balconies; but du Cerceau's project,[100] obviously inspired by this Milanese example, is smaller and nearer the Maltese arrangement of a central hall with three rooms on each side and a portico at one end. Du Cerceau's drawing was not produced until after Verdala palace had been built, but there can be no doubt that this plan type for a fortified villa was in general circulation among the architects working in France in the sixteenth century and, further, it should be noted that the Grand Master Verdale, for whom the palace was built, was himself a Frenchman.

98. It is interesting to note that Cachia had come in contact with Cassar's planning when he remodelled the latter's auberge de Castile in 1744.
99. Uffizi 336. A.v.
100. *Livre d'Architecture* xviii.

CHAPTER TWO

Churches

Early churches in Malta

THROUGHOUT the mediaeval period there was only one important church on the islands of Malta and Gozo. This was the Cathedral at Mdina, the ancient hill capital of Malta which lies in the centre of the island. Legend holds that this church was built on the site of the old palace of Publius, 'chief man of the island.' Publius, the Roman Governor, was converted to Christianity by the Apostle Paul in A.D. 58.[101]

In 1090,[102] Count Roger, the youngest son of Tancred the Norman and brother of Robert 'the Cunning,' crossed with his fleet the narrow strip of sea from Syracuse, which he had captured five years earlier, and occupied the island of Malta. In order to celebrate the release of the islanders from the yoke of the Mohammedan Saracens he set about to rebuild the Cathedral church at Mdina, and before his death in 1101 he dispatched masons from Sicily to carry out the work. This is evidence of the paucity of architectural works on Malta at that time, and the inexperience of the local masons in designing and erecting a large building : for it is one of the few occasions when Maltese designers and craftsmen were not felt to be competent to erect their own building. The new church, though important at that time in Malta, was small in comparison with the fine works carried out by the Normans in neighbouring Sicily.[103] It had a basilican plan with three aisles, the nave and the two outer

---

101. For details of St. Paul's shipwreck and the conversion of Publius : *Acts of the Apostles* xxviii, 7.

102. Braun, *Maltese Architecture* p.11, states that work was begun about 1090.

103. There are no mediaeval buildings in Malta which compare with the great abbey of Monreale or the classic villa ' La Cuba,' built by Roger's grandson William near his capital at Palermo.

aisles being separated by two rows, each of eight Corinthian columns,[104] and the five bays in its length made it a church of modest dimensions.[105] The church was extended in an easterly direction during the period of the Castilian domination when, in 1419 in the reign of Alphonse I, transepts and a short choir were built across the east end of the basilican nave. This method of enlarging an existing church, being easy to carry out, was adopted throughout Europe during the mediaeval period and in Malta there are several later examples of this treatment.[106] The cost of the Cathedral extension may have been defrayed by the 'Count of Malta,' Don Consalvo Monroi, who is said to have reduced the people to utter misery by the year 1425 as a result of his extortionist practices. Certainly no money for building could have been forthcoming from the inhabitants in the succeeding years when Barbary corsairs plundered and invaded and when an epidemic of the plague raged fiercely in 1427 and 1428. In addition to these discomforts the Maltese were exerting every effort to raise the sum of 30,000 florins in order that they might persuade King Alphonse to confirm their civil freedom.[107]

The old remote churches of this period have received very little study in Malta. Many of those which still survive lie in isolation from the modern villages: sometimes marking the site of an old deserted village, sometimes built in splendid isolation. All of those which were built during the Saracenic and Norman periods of occupation, with the exception of the Cathedral at Mdina, appear to have been troglodytic, and even the important little church of St. Mary was cut into the solid rock of Fort St. Angelo in the year 1409. This church, sometimes referred to as the church of St. Angelo, was dedicated at first to the 'Mother of God' and, after the siege of 1565, to the 'Nativity of Our Lady.' It should not be confused with the chapel of St. Anne, which lies on higher ground in the fort and which is fully described later. This church of St. Angelo was destroyed in the last war. In addition, the following

---

104. One capital is preserved at Rabat.
105. Abela III Not.II p.94 states there were eight columns. Thus allowing four on each side and springing the arches of the nave arcades from corbels or direct from the east and west walls of the cathedral, we arrive at the five-bay nave described by Braun, *Maltese Architecture*.
106. St. Gregory at Zejtun and old parish churches at Lija and Siggiewi. Braun, *Maltese Architecture* p.12: 'In 1584 Qormi church was turned back to front by adding a large cruciform east end at the west end of the old nave of 1456, which was, however, pulled down soon after and an aisled nave erected in its stead.'
107. Zammit, *Malta* pp.106–107.

rock-cut churches still exist: St. Mary 'Tal Minsija,' Birkirkara, Mellieha (now lying beneath the later parish church), Msida (beside the church of the Immaculate Conception), the church beneath St. Paul's, Rabat, St. Mary Magdalene and 'Tal Virtù' both at Rabat, and St. George at Siggiewi.[108]

Traditional Maltese churches with longitudinal plans

The churches so far mentioned had little effect upon the design of buildings erected during the period of the Knights of St. John, but in the fifteenth century a church plan was being worked out which was to become a standard building type constantly used in the erection of small churches in Malta up to the end of the seventeenth century. The little chapel of Our Lady of Victory at Ta 127 Qali in the parish of Mdina is one of the simplest and, at the same time, one of the earliest examples of this plan. The plan is a simple rectangle a little longer than it is broad and the walls are constructed of faced ashlar on both the inside and the outside with stones nearly square in shape. Between the inner and the outer courses there is an infilling of rubble : this is the Maltese mason's traditional method of constructing a wall. The chapel is now severely damaged and the roof has fallen in, so that it is easy to see the construction of the

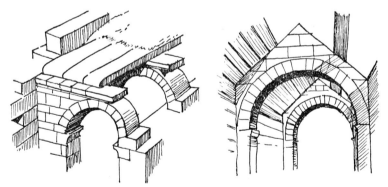

20–21. *Syrian system of roof construction (after Milani, 'L'ossatura murale'* III, *Pl.18).*

walls. Originally three arches bridged the nave dividing the space longitudinally into four bays. These bays were then sufficiently narrow to allow the masons to lay thin slabs of stone from arch to

108. This list is taken from Braun, *Works of Art,* and there are other examples.

arch and so roof the chapel. This type of construction appears to have originated in the Hauran, in Syria, where, because of the lack of wood, the builders replaced the timber roof by one composed of stone slabs supported upon rib-arches, and so produced a church, which, in contrast to the usual Mediterranean type, is remarkable for its breadth.[109] The eastern wall of the nave still stands intact and from it one may judge that the pitch of the roof was comparatively flat and probably not more than fifteen degrees. The only light which penetrated the interior was from the open door at the west end and a small window opposite on the eastern wall.[110] The windows in Maltese churches are always cut very small so that the interiors offer a cool respite from the scorching heat of the sun in summer and a haven of peace from the icy blasts of the *tramontana*[111] in winter. The 'Gothic' door is that in name alone. An impressive drip mould is so amply shaped that the pointed head is barely perceptible, whilst the opening itself is square-headed, bridged by a flat arch of masonry, and indented with the mere suggestion of an ogee. The drip curves to form the capital of a wide pilaster, today much weathered and disfigured. The western gable is now shattered, but from the remains it seems clear that there was no window over the door, though in most churches in Malta and among them those dating from the fifteenth century, this place is commonly pierced by a small circular or oval window.[112] Before the western end of the church there is a small atrium surrounded by a stone wall about three and a half feet high.

The characteristics of Our Lady of Ta Qali, save one, were those which were later used with a surprising regularity in the small churches on the island. Severe simplicity of the well-proportioned block shape of the building, a largely indigenous plan consisting of a plain rectangular cross-ribbed form, usually three projecting pilasters inside, a low pitched roof, and an atrium standing before the west end. Only the small circular window, which usually is pierced above the door, is here omitted.

109. Strzygowski, *Origin of Christian Church Art* pp.55 and 67–68.
110. For the sake of simplicity and convenience I shall always refer to the parts of the church as though they were correctly orientated. In actual fact, many Maltese churches do not lie on the east-west axis.
111. A wind which often blows from the north in January and February and is frequently accompanied by hail.
112. Perkins p.172. The origin of the circular window over the doorway is Sicilian. He illustrates the little church of St. Basil at Mqabba (Pl. XIXb) and compares it with similarly treated façades in Taormina. However, the Sicilian examples are nearly always circular, whilst many in Malta are almost elliptical, as though pressed down by the weight of masonry lying above.

Undoubtedly the best preserved example of a parish church of this early period is St. Mary ' Ta Bir Miftuh ' at Gudia, which dates back to 1436. It has a plain rectangular plan of the type described above and on the outside it measures approximately thirty-six feet by forty-eight feet. Externally it appears as a plain cube, for what slight pitch there is to the roof is here concealed behind a low parapet and the rain water is thrown off each side of the nave roof by means of projecting spouts. These spouts will be found only on churches and other ecclesiastical buildings, for regulations required all private house owners to collect the rain water from their roofs and lead it to cisterns or wells in the courtyards, where it could be conserved for use in the dry weather.

The main façade has a square-headed entrance surmounted by a Gothic drip mould giving it a noble border, and a small deep eye inserted in the bold face of the masonry above. A triple-arched campanile crowned by a cushioned pediment, a lofty ball and a crucifix, is placed upon the cube, whilst consoles roll down across the two lower arches and are held, weighed down by cannon balls.[113] A low-walled atrium in front of the church is considerably wider than the west front of the church and originally embraced a building which adjoined the north-west corner of the church. Of this only the entrance door and part of the walls remain, but it is still possible to trace the line of the rectangular plan.[114] Braun[115] suggests that, following the practice already carried out in the cathedral, the church authorities added transepts to this church in the sixteenth century, which have since been removed. Certainly an examination of the ground and the eastern end of the church reveals the existence of considerable additions, but these appear as an elongation of the nave in an easterly direction rather than any form of transverse building. The present nave wall, at the north-east corner, contains remains of a Gothic hood mould which may mark an earlier doorway. The eastern wall itself is constructed of masonry which has been used before, and one stone bears a crude carving of a man on horseback placed on end. Further to the east the lines of the wall can be traced continuing the nave for a further sixteen yards until

113. Braun, *Maltese Architecture* p.15, talks of a restoration in 1512. This could account for those floral additions, although stylistically the whole bell-cot seems to be not earlier than the end of the 16th century.
114. Braun, *Works of Art* p.6 : ' The ancient church was once flanked by two others dedicated respectively to the Nativity and the Assumption. The workmen, on their own initiative and for their own interest, carefully excavated the site of the former, the plan of which may thus now be seen.' This would account for the abnormally wide atrium.
115. Braun, *Maltese Architecture* p.6.

they reach the boundary wall of the field which may have been the eastern termination of the church. No foundation stones are visible in the next field. Within the ruined walls portions of the flying arches which spanned a crypt pierce the ground level at several places. If this is correct, then there must have stood here a church of unusually long proportions : of proportions far longer than those found in Maltese parish churches, and with the sides bearing the relationship of about 8 to 3. But this long narrow nave would not have been without precedent in Malta : the nave of the great Con-

153 ventual church of St. John in Valletta, excluding the extended choir, has a proportion of about $7\frac{1}{2}$ to 3, and a similar tunnel-like appearance must have been imparted to both alike, but on a smaller scale at Gudia.

130 The old parish church of St. Gregory at Zejtun is one of the finest churches of this period. It was later enlarged by the Knights. Like ' Ta Bir Miftuh,' it dates from 1436, the year in which Malta was divided into ten parishes and many of the parish churches begun; but its design is more elaborate. In roofing the rectangular nave the masons have shown a decided advance on their earlier methods, for instead of laying their roofing slabs across the tops of

21 arched cross walls, the slabs are carried on the backs of masonry arches. In this way the ugly upper portion of the cross wall is concealed inside and the vault and rib harmoniously follow the same arc of a circle. The Knights added transepts to the east end of the mediaeval nave and vaulted these with a true Gothic quadripartite vault where the roofing slabs are set into the groined ribs, these having been rebetted to receive them.[116] The true Gothic vault is rare in Malta; this example and a similar extension of the old parish church at Siggiewi being the two best examples, for the Gothic vault had already been superseded by the architecture of the Renaissance in many parts of Europe when the Knights set foot on Malta. One has only to glance at these churches to see how far Malta lagged behind the current fashion in Italy. Few condescended to drop their architectural recipes on this barren shore : and the Knights too, after their expulsion from Rhodes and during their fervent hunt for a new home, seem to have had little time to indulge in the delights of the new fruits of the Renaissance. For when this new vault was building, some 600 miles to the north Giuliano da Sangallo had

116. Braun, *Maltese Architecture* p.4. Calleja, *Works of Art* p.114, states that this extension seems to have been built by Gerolamo Cassar, in view of its fair proportions and simple plan. I have not fully investigated this possibility. Panelled pilasters occur, similar to door of St. Augustine, Rabat, but the Gothic vault is strange.

completed S. Maria delle Carceri at Prato and the Cancelleria was contemplated in Rome; while by the time the Knights had added their Gothic transepts, Michelangelo was working on the Basilica of St. Peter's.

The façade has the usual shallow-pitched gable end which **128** straightens out on each side to receive the low parapet wall. This feature is found in Lombardic Romanesque and may have been introduced into Malta by the Normans.[117] It lightens the sombre façade giving it a grace and elegance which would otherwise be wanting, while the charm which is imparted by the addition of the bell-cot and the sixteenth century Renaissance doorway[118] make this façade one of the most delightful of the early ones in Malta. And the traditional west light is there, a round hole set deep above the centre of the portal. The entrance is interesting : tall and graceful, two fluted columns step forward, breaking with the entablature and cornice. These rest on a bracketed keystone and two attenuated pilasters with deep-set panels done in a manner we shall see presently many times. The impost mouldings too are deeply panelled.

The nave is buttressed externally, the only example[119] of this prac- **130** tice in Malta, where land was always precious and the maximum space was required inside the churches. The closely spaced wall piers, which could be no further apart than the effective span of the roofing slabs, were also found to constitute an obstruction in the nave and later masons tended to thicken the whole line of the nave walls to take the transverse thrust from the arched ribs. In St. John's, Valletta, however, where the span was great and the developing thrust enormous, buttresses had to be provided, but these were successfully contained within the church by the simple expedient of adding an aisle chapel between each pair of buttresses.[120] **158**

The early nave roof of St. Gregory is raised up in the third bay toward the east and an intersecting vault is inserted so that its gable

---

117. This horizontal treatment of the gables is found as early as the 6th century B.C. in the 'Temple of Ceres' at Paestum (see Robertson, *Greek and Roman Architecture*, Cambridge 1929, p.79), and are common in mediæval Italy in such churches as S. Maria in Strata (Monza), S. Giusto at Lucca, and S. Francesco d'Assisi at Palermo.

118. The door was added about the middle of the 16th century when the Knights were altering the east end of the church.

119. Braun, *Maltese Architecture* p.11, is in error in stating that there are four buttresses. There are three on each side making the usual four compartments in the nave.

120. A method used in Rome on the Baroque churches of S. Caterina dei Funari, the Gesù, and S. Andrea della Valle : to quote but three. It was, however, common in Gothic and is found in some Renaissance churches. After about 1560 most of the Baroque churches were built in this manner.

end raises the level of the nave walls in this bay. The great wedge block of the transpets, which lie across the east end of the old nave, wraps its stone walls around the nave so that only part of the fourth and most easterly bay is visible on the exterior. The transept walls are nearly a third higher than those of the nave and yet appear incomplete. Bold corner pilasters buttress these later additions. Rising from a plinth, they have sculptured bases but no capitals or entablature. Over the middle of the transepts there rises a low saucer dome on a squat drum;[121] a gay little dome in shining pink. This appears to be the earliest example of the dome remaining in Malta, and it shows all the uncertainty of an early design : a robust solid drum and a dome pierced by an eye in the centre to light the dark interior. The only other light comes from small segmental-headed windows with a military cast which hang in the opposite walls of each transept. The military character of this east end is heightened by a great sloping face of masonry which lies against the south-east wall of the church like the battened lines of the Valletta defences. All the early works of the Knights show this stamp, an austere character which was symbolic of the life of the religious and military Order which had fought its way back from the Holy Land.[122] Their early works of architecture are simple and grave where the indigenous architecture of the island is simple but carefree, and it is the Maltese character, rather than that of the Knights, which shows itself in the churches of the succeeding centuries. No building demonstrates this strange difference more clearly than St. Gregory, which exhibits a complete *volte-face* between its west and east ends.

Strangely enough, the next church to be discussed is the exception
131 to the rule. The little chapel of St. Anne, which lies within the precincts of the Castle of St. Angelo and looks out across the waters of the Grand Harbour, is reputed to rest on the site of the ancient Phœnician Temple of Juno. This is the chapel in which the Knights first worshipped upon their arrival on the island as it lay adjacent to their new city, the Birgu. The building which stands today dates from the fifteenth century, but has been much altered.[123]

121. Added in the middle of the 16th century when the new transepts were built.
122. Perkins p.173 : 'Seven years had intervened since the Order had been expelled from Rhodes and it would seem that during that period it had mislaid the craftsmanship and something of the tastes which had inspired its former works.' Nor had it gained new tastes.
123. Braun, *Works of Art* p.44. Perkins gives the date of rebuilding about 1534. Braun, *Maltese Architecture* p.6 : 'The old chapel had six five-foot bays, and it would have been absurd to have merely cut narrow

Its façade displays a lightness of touch and a grace which is absent from contemporary buildings erected or altered by the Knights, and it owes this character to the graceful additions commissioned by that stern old warrior, Philip Villiers de l'Isle Adam, the Grand Master who led the Knights to their new homes after his valiant defence of Rhodes. A round arched doorway leads into the nave and above it is placed the traditional single light, a horizontal ellipse here almost circular. Above this, the work of the Knight's direction is evident. The clear-cut cavetto cornice rests on cyma reversa brackets which bear evenly on a simple but deep string course. In this passage from the plain masonry block of the main nave wall through a succession of mouldings which become more delicate as they ascend, we are prepared for the crowning piece, a small bell-cot flanked by thin playful consoles which buttress it. Though the orders have not been used on the bell-cot, the proportion of pilaster to entablature has been approximately preserved and there is a cornice above. The bell hangs in a semicircular-headed arch which is set back from the face of the bell-cot, so that though the orders are omitted, the composition is still a descendant of the architectural form of the theatre of Marcellus so beloved by the architects of the Renaissance in Italy. The whole triangular composition rests upon a stone base which is a better expedient than applying it to the cornice of the building. We do not know the name of the architect who was responsible for the reconstruction of this chapel.[124] The mouldings and the general detail are by no means pure, but the building has a crisp vitality which is missing in many of the other buildings put up by the Knights at this time, in the years between their occupation of Malta and the great Turkish siege.[125] Elsewhere the mouldings are usually blunt and bulbous, and their ' fat ' Melitan mouldings become a feature of Maltese architecture until the turn of the sixteenth century. But there is no sign of them here at St. Angelo : the main cornice has a slim cavetto. Inside the chapel, upon the centre free-standing column, a torus moulding rests upon a cavetto in a manner

arches between these. So he (de l'Isle Adam) took the bull by the horns and ripped out three of the flying arches converting the six narrow arches which he then roofed with Gothic vaults.'

124. Bowerman p.45 : ' In August 1947, Mr. J. Darmanin accompanied me in an inspection of the Chapel and Crypts of St. Anne. There we found . . . in the crypt, the stone with dates 1647, 1658, 1647, and the name MOLINO.' Now it is known that Ferramolino was sent to Malta in 1541, and that he did work on Fort St. Angelo. Is it possible that the dates had been wrongly read? Whilst 1547 would seem more reasonable, 1558 would not, for again it is known that Ferramolino left the island before 1550. However, it is worth pursuing the suggestion that he was the architect of the chapel.

125. 1530 to 1565.

reminiscent of the profile of the fortifications[126] of Castle St. Angelo.

We have seen the effect of additions to the plain rectangular nave of the Maltese church. Elsewhere, transepts, with or without a choir and apse, have been added, and at Gudia the nave itself was extended to form an elongated rectangle. Here only, on the chapel in Fort St. Angelo, do we find the conversion of the plain rectangle into a double nave church in a manner often found convenient by mediaeval builders. This is the only example in Malta and the whole chapel is a throw up of Gothic architecture. Compared with the ponderous Mannerist buildings which grew up at the end of the century in the new city of Valletta, this building is designed in a lighthearted and straightforward manner.

Small traditional churches of the late 16th and succeeding centuries

Before discussing the major churches of the late sixteenth and early seventeenth centuries it would be well to show how the traditional Maltese church retained all its main characteristics in the smaller chapels which were built in the three centuries of occupation by the Knights of St. John. Whilst the larger buildings took on a sophisticated air, these little chapels altered little from year to year, and only in their details and mouldings is any change apparent.

129   For reasons of comparison we shall take 'Ta Bir Miftuh' at Gudia as our prototype.

134   Our Lady of Sorrows (*Pietà*) at Hamrun, built in 1590, follows the tradition set by St. Gregory at Zejtun where the line of the roof is not fully hidden by a parapet, but emerges in the centre part of the western façade in the form of a pediment. At Hamrun the little chapel was influenced by the more advanced work which had just been carried out on the new churches at Valletta and Rabat, and the pediment was capped by a cornice moulding. The apex of the pediment supports a pedestal and a tall sculptured figure of the *Pietà*. Because of this, the bell-cot was placed on the flat parapet wall and cornice moulding, and to prevent any conflict with the

126. This occurs many times in Renaissance fortified walls and was a favourite moulding of Sanmichele. It was also used by Gerolamo Cassar on numerous occasions though there is no reason to associate his name with this chapel. De l'Isle Adam died in 1534 and the chapel was probably completed about that time. The first reference to a building by Cassar is after his appointment as engineer to the Order in 1565. ARCHIVES 1579–80–81, fol.270.

piece of sculpture it was made taller than is usual with these churches in Malta. There can be no doubt that the Baroque doorway, with its broken pediment which mischievously curls up at the corners, the little corbel brackets which support the lintel, and the elaborate cartouche above, is later in date than 1590 and an addition to the façade. The broken pediment occurs several times in Malta before the close of the century,[127] but never in this assured manner nor in conjunction with such flowing heraldic escutcheons. The window over the door is made up of two half circles with a rectangle lying between them, thus stretching the proportion horizontally. There is the usual open courtyard in front of the façade this time peacefully planted with a few shady trees.

St. Roch at Balzan (1593) has the usual rectangular nave with a **136** lower and narrower choir built on the east end, about half as long as the nave and contemporary with it. Six water spouts throw the rain water clear of the nave and choir walls. The sides and the east end are severely plain except for a rectangular window with a moulded architrave and a flat detached cornice on the middle of the south wall of the nave, and a circular opening with a plain circular architrave at the east end, but the west end, being the façade, is treated with more elegance. It is a well proportioned block with the usual central door and circular window above, crowned by a shallow pitched raking cornice built up of several mouldings and overhanging at the eaves where it is not returned down the sides of the nave. The door architrave consists of flat planes and a shallow cyma reversa and, with its detached canopy, is similar in arrangement to the south window of the nave. The circular window is treated with novelty: it has a graceful latticed infilling of overlapping semicircles and its flat masonry frame is enclosed in a square moulded panel. This square is, in turn, surmounted by a form of triangular pediment enclosing a circular flower in its field, but the naïve pediment is far too small for the square frame which it crowns and its extremities barely overlap the inner mouldings of the square. This church has not the usual atrium in front of its west door, but the road widens there forming a little piazza, which may have at one time been an enclosed atrium of the Maltese type.

St. Anthony the Abbot, in the grounds of Gerolamo Cassar's **138** Verdala palace a few miles from Rabat, dates from the end of the sixteenth century. Although it follows the traditional Maltese church

127. The old parish church at Lija; St. Ursula at Valletta; the Great Hospital, Valletta; St. Augustine, Rabat; and St. Anthony the Abbot at Verdala palace near Rabat.

in general design, there are many peculiarities in its details. Almost adjoining one corner of the fortified villa of the Grand Masters, it may have been designed by Cassar himself.[128] The massive corner piers are typical of his work and they are used here for the first time on a small church in Malta. The entrance door, with its peculiar Doric order and spidery pediment, could also be his, but the details of the main cornice, cavetto upon a double torus moulding separated from an astragal band by a deep frieze, are not typical of the entablature Cassar has used to cap his buildings; neither do these mouldings occur on the villa itself. Nor again do I know of any other work by Cassar which has a panelled façade. Panelling later became very popular in Malta and was used to give a feeling of recession to Baroque façades. Here is an early example of this motif and four distinct surfaces are evident : the thrusting forward of the corner piers, the slight projection of the central window, the general surface of the façade, and the recessed surface of the four panels which flank the main door. The facial expression of some of the earlier churches, such as St. Gregory at Zejtun, has been repeated here with the addition of more complex mouldings but, at the same time, with less happy results. The raking cornice echoes the gable end of the chapel, and the cornice is broken across the line of the corner piers, but instead of turning up into a horizontal cornice (like the Zejtun church) at Verdala it is swallowed up by the strong horizontal band of the cornice which engirdles the building just below the parapet level, and the roof seems to be wedged uncomfortably between sturdy pedestals. This Mannerist feature is typical of Cassar's work.

The following points suggest that Cassar could have been responsible for this design : its proximity to Verdala palace; the advanced character of the work in comparison to the other small chapels of this period; the large corner piers; the Doric order on the main door; and the Mannerist treatment of the pediment. However, there is no documentary evidence to connect his name with this chapel; the system of panels used here does not appear to have been used by Cassar elsewhere; and finally, the details of the mouldings are not typically his.

Four other small chapels built before the close of the sixteenth century, and varying considerably in quality, will serve to show a continuance of tradition in plan and façade arrangement.

128. This chapel, which is probably contemporary with the villa dating from 1586, is not referred to in the testimonial of Cassar in ARCHIVES MS. 439 *Liber Bullarum,* fol.270 verso.

'Tal Ingrau' at Zejtun is a small lonely church about a mile 137 from the casal along the road to Marsascala. It is dated 1597. A plain rectangular block of a building with a slightly pitched roof, it has the usual small atrium before the west front surrounded by a low stone wall and with an opening opposite the door. There is the usual bell-cot and an absolutely plain door; in this case the opening over the door is replaced by a small rectangular hole while two larger windows flank the door. This variation on the original becomes frequent in the next century, but this must be one of the earliest churches to show it.

St. Roch at Zebbug, built in 1593, is a typical example. The 138 church measures externally about twenty-four feet by twenty-two feet. This nearly square nave is divided into three bays by two masonry arches, and the ceiling slabs span just under seven feet.

St. Mary's church at Qormi, dating from the end of the sixteenth 139 century, has its roof concealed behind a horizontal parapet in a manner similar to the century earlier 'Ta Bir Miftuh' at Gudia. 129 There is an ornamental doorway with a small plaque above and a small window on each side of the door.[129] The bell-cot is later. It is strange to find this richly carved and well proportioned doorway on the very plainest of plain churches, and it can only be accounted for by the fact that the church is in Qormi, a village rich in delicately carved masonry dating from this period. Qormi has one of the most important unattributed monuments of the sixteenth century in Malta—the tall graceful parish church of St. George (1584). There 166 are certain things which call to mind the architecture of the church of St. George in this little door at St. Mary's. The tall linear quality of the design, the deep-cut panelling of the impost pilasters are reminiscent of the parish church, but the personal style of the frieze carving is particular to St. Mary's and her close neighbour, the coeval church of St. Peter. Notice here how the water spouts jut 140 forward over the atrium like two projecting cannons. Strzygowski[130] describes the church of St. Gospa at Vis (Lissa) in Croatia as being 22 circular with similar small windows each side of the door, and suggests that these features were to assist in defending the church. This may be the origin of the Maltese windows.

The desecrated church of St. Peter in the old capital Mdina, was 141

129. A type of church very similar to these Maltese examples (with windows low down beside the door, a circular window above, and a bell-cot) was designed in the 15th century under the influence of L. Laurana in Verpolie in Dalmatia. Illustrated in Venturi, *Architettura del Quattro-cento* I p.677.
130. Strzygowski, *Early Church Art* p.29.

built in 1617. It has a curious trio of blind windows on the façade, the remains of a diminutive bell-cot hiding behind a massive raking cornice and, most unusual of all, a semicircular-headed doorway.

22. *Vis (Lissa). St. Gospa (after Strzygowski).*

But Mdina is a law unto itself, and we cannot tell what influence the old Sicolo-Norman cathedral may have had upon its neighbouring churches. St. Peter's has one thing in common with its contemporaries; an increased height. From the turn of the century, very broadly speaking, the proportion of the façade tends to be vertical rather than horizontal.

142 St. Catherine ' Tat Torba ' at Qrendi is another old church which was rebuilt in 1625, when no doubt this new façade was added to an existing nave. The severe box-like nave with a slightly pitched roof
144 is screened by this later façade. The façade is split into two storeys by projecting vertical strips at the corners supporting two horizontal bands of masonry. These are substituted for the architectural orders and merely suggest their function. The ground floor is broken down into three units, a central doorway crowned with a canopy supported on scalloped brackets and two side windows bounded by heavy stone frames projecting to the face of the corner strips. On the first floor the same arrangement, but in a simplified form, is repeated. The bold blocks of rectangular masonry echo the lower theme, the centre block giving added prominence by being increased in size. The parapet resembles a crenellated tower, for the corner strips are carried above the entablature (as at St. Anthony the Abbot at Rabat) and is crowned by carved terminals. Three other projections break the skyline above the three panels. This strange façade, which has an oriental appearance, is really no more than the final outcome of a long system of simplification where a building is broken down into

easily digested dimensions in the very way that the architects of the High Renaissance used the column and entablature, but here all reference to Classical orders has been avoided, and plain bands of masonry, either projecting or receding, repeat the same process.[131] The culmination of the application of this formula was reached in Rome a few years later when between 1647 and 1649 Borromini built the wall that is beneath the Torre dell'Orologio on the Convento dei Filippini.[132] 71

Both St. Anthony the Abbot and St. Catherine ' Tat Torba ' are important for their influence. No other churches are so extreme, but few are without some mark of an influence derived from these two. St. Saviour at Qrendi (1658), whilst conventional in most other respects with its two flanking windows and its circular window crowning the door, shows signs of the new fashion in the blocking-out of the jambs around the south door, in the pinnacles and vases on the eaves, and in the block-like character of the bell-cot. This church is also much taller than its predecessors and is approached by a monumental flight of steps.[133] 135 142 143

The features of the small church had then been formed and from the middle of the seventeenth century, when it became usual to apply the giant order to the façade, the only variations are those of complexity or simplicity.

St. Angelo at Zejtun (1670) is typical of this development. Large pilasters define the corners and are topped with pinnacles. These in turn are linked to a pedimented bell-cot. The circular window is replaced by a Baroque segmental-headed window.[134]

The church of the Immaculate Conception at Zebbug was built in 1677, but is now desecrated. It accepts all the new fashions and 145

131. Panelling of the façade, an idea inherited from Rome, is common among secular buildings in Malta, but is unusual on the façades of churches. St. Anthony the Abbot started the fashion and here it is taken up with great gusto. For a fuller description see Quentin Hughes, *Church of St. Catherine, ' Tat-Torba '* in ARCH I, 1954.
132. Donati p.174. Portion of the convent toward Monte Giordano was begun in 1647 and the clock tower was completed in 1649.
133. Alberti VI, cap. 3 and 5, called for churches to be raised up and approached by a monumental flight of steps, and the Council of Trent further emphasized the need for this treatment. Cf. Borromeo's opening remarks on p.5 require three or five steps. Cf. also Wittkower, *Architectural Principles* pp.7 and 45–46.
134. This segmental window appears as a free-standing unit as early as the 15th century in the Po Valley, Palazzo del Comune at Jesi by Francesco di Giorgio; court of S. Maria delle Grazie, Milan; great cloister of Certosa at Pavia; and Villa Mirabella near Milan. But its most popular use is during the Baroque period. See also its use at St. Gregory, Zejtun, on transept.

absorbs them with an academic grace. Its details are precise : well formed and well proportioned panels, pedestals, links, and segmental windows are all there, but refined by a master who has studied the Academic school of seventeenth century Rome. The double pediment of the doorhead, the graceful roll of the arched opening to the bell-cot, and its fine cornice raking in the centre, are the studied work of a competent architect. Only the two flanking windows seem obtrusive, called for by tradition and perhaps provided with regret by the designer.

146,147   The lovely secluded little church of ' Tal Hlas ' near Qormi was designed by the Maltese architect Lorenzo Gafà in 1690.[135] The façade is rather similar to the last and the two windows still appear as an afterthought unrelated to the general design, but now incorporated by a band of whitewash which covers and protects the base of the building. The atrium to this church is more developed than elsewhere and the façade is flanked by porticoes;[136] beyond the atrium there is a small irregular piazza shaded by pleasant trees. It is this quality of the forecourt which makes this church so very attractive rather more than the designs of the details which are of a poorer quality than those on the nearby church of the Immaculate

145   Conception at Zebbug. The subdivision of the nave is marked by pilasters on the outside of the nave wall, and the interior is further lit by three ample windows on each side of the nave. It is curious that, whilst the façade has one giant order, the sides are broken into two storeys by a string course which acts as a capital to the pilasters. These capital mouldings suffice on the side elevations : there are no entablatures.

148   St. Catherine's church at Qormi is a plainer and more crude version of the last two and is contemporary.

This form of church persists right into the eighteenth century, as

149   the Oratory of the Holy Crucifix bears witness; this latter was built in 1720 and severely damaged during the last war. It has a tall façade with superimposed pilasters and a small flight of steps leading to the west door. An armorial cartouche replaces the usual window, and in fact no windows are required on the main façade as the chapel has an intersecting barrel vault roof of three bays. Six large

150   windows light the nave from the cross vaults. The oval window,

---

135. ANCIENT MONUMENTS COMMITTEE, *Report to Viscount Gort.*
136. This is called by Borromeo p.11, 'an Atrium, proportioned to the space, and in keeping with the structure of the ecclesiastical edifice. It should be surrounded on every side with porticoes, and adorned with other suitable architectural work.'

omitted from the west front, is inserted in the east wall over the High Altar.

The type of church I have described is not unique to Malta for I have found a church façade in Sicily which is similar to the seventeenth century versions. Though the type is the rule in Malta, it is the exception in Sicily, and many of the Maltese features, such as the atrium, the window grouping, the single bell-cot, panelling, and the oval centrepiece, are not included in this design. The church is that of S. Anna in the town of Caltagirone and it was built some time after the disastrous earthquake of 1693.[137]

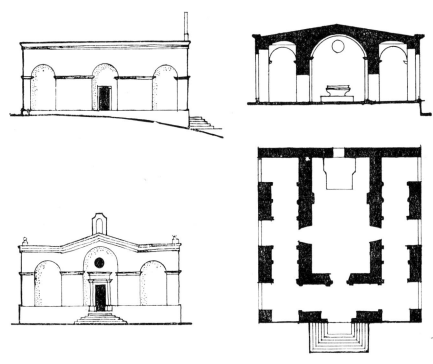

23–26. *St. Paul's Bay. St. Paul's church.*

There is a variation in Malta which seems to have had no influence upon any of the other churches on the island. The nucleus of the church of St. Paul at St. Paul's Bay is old : it was built some **23-26** time about the end of the sixteenth century and is situated on the coast by La Scaletta on the Bujebba road where a spit of rock runs

137. Fichera p.37.

out into the bay. During the Grand Mastership of Alof de Wignacourt (1601–22), the original rectangular plan was much altered,[133] and later these additions were again changed in a few minor ways. The church was badly damaged during the late war and is now being restored as it was after the rebuilding under Wignacourt.[139] The original building which forms the nucleus of the later church was a plain rectangular block measuring eighteen feet by thirty-seven feet with walls four feet thick. The chancel was divided from the nave by a pair of plain pilaster strips which supported a vaulting arch.[140] The old church had the usual plain flat-headed western door and circular window above it, with another one at the same height on the eastern wall. The alterations carried out under Wignacourt consisted of the addition of a charming arcade round three sides of the church, increasing its overall size to sixty-five by fifty-three feet. Each side of the arcade was punctured by three arched openings, the centre ones leading to doors in the church : two new doors having been cut in the north and south walls of the nave. The arcade has flat roofing slabs laid upon arched ribs but, in addition, flat saucer domes occur over six of the arched openings. These additions, plus the fact that the arcade is raised up on a podium and approached from the west by a flight of seven steps, makes the façade more interesting than those of the contemporary small churches. Corner escutcheons and pinnacles, together with a naïve cornice, the usual bell-cot, and an eight-pointed Maltese cross resting on a ball, complete the decoration of the church.

The development of the longitudinal plan in Maltese churches

As one would expect from a religious order like the Knights of St. John, the first building they erected in the new city of Valletta was the small church of Our Lady of Victory,[141] built to commemorate the defeat of the invading Turkish army. Work was begun in either 1566 or 1567,[142] a year after the foundation of the new city. The church lies south-west to north-east and is thus not correctly orientated. In view of the fact that a virgin site was selected and

138. Braun, *Works of Art* p.22.
139. This description is based on the Malta Ministry of Works and Reconstruction's drawings for the reconstructed church.
140. This simple way of defining nave and chancel was later used by Gerolamo Cassar on the Conventual church in Valletta.
141. Braun, *Works of Art* p.28.
142. Zammit, *Valletta* p.17, gives the date of the building as 1667, but this must surely be a misprint.

the line of no earlier church had to be followed, it seems reasonable to suppose that before building was commenced the grid layout of the city streets had been planned by Laparelli and Gerolamo Cassar.

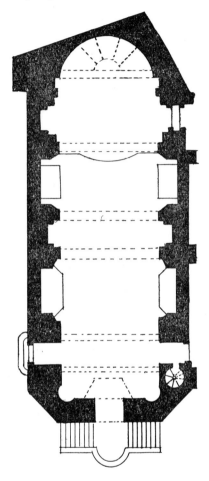

27. *Valletta. Our Lady of Victory.*

This church and the Magisterial palace, the next building to be erected, both lie correctly with the lines of the new streets, though the cavalier of St. John,[143] placed obliquely to the street pattern   1 and abutting this church, has distorted the layout of the buildings and some of the streets around the church.

This church has a plain rectangular nave with a ribbed barrel   27,67,68 vault, a semicircular apse, and a bowed west front. The general

143. Built 1582.

shape of the nave is probably original[144] but otherwise the church shows few of its original features. In 1752 it was enlarged by the Bailiff of Majorca, Fra Gerolamo Ribas Montelieu, but this enlargement probably only consisted of the addition of a campanile on the north-west wall of the nave, for the main features of the façade must have been fixed when Fra Ramon Perellos y Roccafull placed[145] a dedicatory bust of Innocent XI (Odescalchi) above the central window in 1690 on account of the Pope's successful intercession in a dispute between the ecclesiastical authorities and the magisterial court.[146]

243
151,152
In 1571 Gerolamo Cassar began the Augustinian church at Rabat, on the east side of the town toward the walls of Mdina. In its arrangement and many of its details it was to form the prototype for his more important Conventual church of the Order which he began two years later. In plan it has a nave of three bays continued eastward to form a choir from the fourth bay. The distinction between the two parts of the church is marked by raising the level of the floor of the choir and thickening the arched rib between the third and fourth bays.[147] The pilasters are massive and their cap mouldings support the springing of the shallowly coffered barrel vault. This vault, though almost semicircular, has a perceptible pointedness at its apex as though the architect feared for the stability of his structure and played for safety. The massiveness of the whole church design suggests an architect inexperienced in constructing large spans and without the example of immediate predecessors in the vicinity to guide him. But the sombre weightiness of this design characterises all Cassar's work and symbolises the austere military character of the Order at whose appointment he did his life work. Unlike his succeeding architects in Malta, he worked almost exclusively on the instructions of the Knights, save for the design of the five monastic buildings which he made. He does not appear to have been responsible for one parish church.[148]

The first two bays of the side aisles are cross vaulted with semicircular ribbed barrel vaults let into the nave wall and supported on even more massive supports, half columns naïvely capped and nearer to Norman Durham in style than to their Tuscan prototypes in Italy.

144. Zammit, *Valletta* p.17.
145. He was made Grand Master of the Order seven years later.
146. Inscription on the façade.
147. A principle Cassar adopted on St. John's in Valletta.
148. Though Calleja, *Works of Art* p.114, makes an unsubstantiated claim that Cassar was responsible for the alterations to the old parish church of St. Gregory at Zejtun.

The façade is an enigma because its design is strange in Malta. It is different from the design of the rest of the church which is by Gerolamo Cassar. The façade shows a bold attempt to link the high central nave with the lower side aisles, and the solution is obviously influenced by Renaissance church façades in Italy.[149] As Cassar travelled to Rome in 1569 he would surely have known the executed design for S. Maria dell'Orto (1567) and the prepared design for the Gesù in Rome, both of which were by Vignola : the latter was one of the most-talked-of buildings of that time, and both these façades have a tall nave adopted on this church in Rabat. Both the Gesù and the Rabat façades show Mannerist characteristics, though not of the same type. The flat paper-like quality[150] of the Rabat façade stamps it as a product of the Mannerist school and thus plausibly connects it with Gerolamo Cassar's name; the proportion of the doors and windows are not those we normally associate with his work. The main porch is flanked by Corinthian columns, but Cassar almost invariably used the Tuscan order[151] with all its solemnity, and the columns on the Rabat façade, instead of being squat, are decidedly elongated. However, it is important to remember that this is an early work and the architect might have tended to exaggerate the difference in proportion between the masculine Tuscan column and the maidenly Corinthian,[152] in using the latter order. The light quality of the raking cornice broken upward into a rectangular panel containing stiff little statues sparsely spaced, immobile, on a plain background, is nearer to Quattrocento work in Tuscany[153] or to Platteresque in Spain. In fact, all the decoration : the long pilasters with their

149. The first bold attempt to tackle this difficult problem of linking nave and aisles was made by Alberti at S. Maria Novella in Florence (1456). (See Wittkower, *Architectural Principles* p.38.) Later examples, many less successful, but foreshadowing the simple concave links later used by Vignola, were built at S. Maurizio, Milan; S. Benedetto, Ferrara; S. Maria in Vado, Ferrara; and S. Caterina dei Funari, Rome (*c.* 1560).

150. Pevsner, *Architecture of Mannerism* p.124, mentions the paperiness of the Mannerist façade of the Palazzo Massimi, Rome (1535). I shall show later that Cassar makes use of a strange motif on his auberge d'Aragon in Valletta, and the only other example of it I know occurs on this Roman palace.

151. He used the Ionic order on the façade of the auberge de Provence in Valletta.

152. Vitruvius IV,i, likens the various orders to human beings, stressing the robust quality of Tuscan and Doric and the graceful qualities of Ionic and Corinthian. John Shute, *The First and Chief Groundes of Architecture,* London 1563, fol.IV and XI, illustrates them with an accompanying sketch of Atlas against the former and the figure of a young maiden against the latter.

153. Stokes, *The Quattrocento,* London 1932, pp.111–126.

hollowed out grooves and thin raised panels, the graceful detailing of the circular window,[154] the running pattern of rectangular panels in the frieze of the side doors, and the delicate flower patterns in the spandril and frieze of the main portal, do not suggest that Cassar was responsible for this part of the design. In proportion, it is akin to the doorways of the anonymous parish church at Qormi (1584), and in quality it foreshadows the work of Tomasso Dingli at Attard (1613) and the old parish church of Birkirkara (1617), though it is not so fine. Gerolamo Cassar rarely used the panelled pilaster, although he has done so on the two western pilasters inside the nave : Dingli invariably used it, and in its elongated form.

To conclude then we may surmise that : (a) the façade is the work of Gerolamo Cassar who had designed the remainder of the church and here was advised by someone with a knowledge of Spanish architecture,[155] advice which he avoided later on his other buildings; or, (b) the details of the façade were carried out by another hand, perhaps the Master of Qormi, or by Gerolamo's own son Vittorio working with his father; or again, (c) the façade was completed at a later date possibly by Dingli and was precursory to his more famous church façades.

On 22 November 1573,[156] work began on Cassar's most important building, the Conventual church of the Order, dedicated to St. John its patron saint, in the new city of Valletta. This church replaced the old Conventual church in Birgu (Vittoriosa). The Grand Master La Cassière,[157] assiduous in pushing forward new building work in Valletta in an attempt to make the new city popular and to complete the evacuation of the Birgu, paid the entire initial cost of the new building and in addition provided a large endowment for its upkeep.

Gerolamo Cassar had schooled himself in the church of St. Augustine at Rabat and now he repeated the formula on a larger scale. The plan is a plain rectangle 189 feet long, including the apse, and measuring 118 feet across the inside of the chapel walls. Roofed with a tunnel-vault, it gives the effect of gigantic suction from the

154. Giovannoni p.185 states that the rose window in S. Caterina dei Funari, Rome (c. 1560), is the last survivor of the great rose windows of the Middle Ages. This motif however is used repeatedly throughout the Renaissance and Baroque in Malta.

155. Note the strange resemblance to the façade of the church of Montserrat in Madrid (illustrated in Contreras IV Fig.173 p.174), where nave and aisles are similarly linked, the link also stopped by a sculptured terminal; and the architect employed grooved pilasters resting on a single pedestal, its double function indicated by a separate panel below each of the coupled pilasters.

156. Flower p.36.

157. 1572–82.

west door onto the High Altar at the east end and is, probably, one
of the most successful churches of the Early Baroque in its effort to
produce this concentration and eastward drive.[158] The horizontal

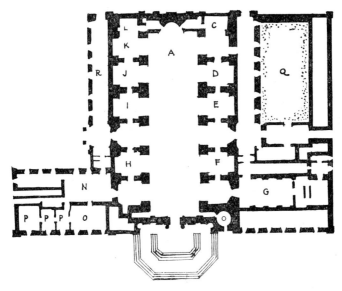

28. *Valletta. Conventual church of St. John.*
References to plan :
A. High Altar.   B. Chapel of the Baptism of Christ.   C. Chapel of the
Blessed Sacrament and Our Lady of Philermos.   D. Chapel of St. Sebastian
of the langue of Auvergne.   E. Chapel of St. George of the langue of
Aragon.   F. Chapel of St. James of the langue of Castile et Leon.
G. The Oratory.   H. Chapel of the Adoration of the Magi.   I. Chapel of
St. Catherine of the langue of Italy.   J. Chapel of St. Paul of the langue
of France.   K. Chapel of St. Michael of the langue of Provence.
L. Chapel of St. Charles or of the Holy Relics.   N. Large sacristy.
O. Small sacristy.   P. The Sacred Treasury.   Q. Campo Santo.
R. Fattened rib of nave vault.

lines are further emphasised by a very slight pointedness applied to
the great semicircular arches of the tunnel-vault, and the lack of
entablature and cornice between the capitals and the springing of
the arches produces a long low building of unusual proportions. The
great span of fifty-one feet only rises to a moderate height of sixty-
four feet three inches above the level of the floor. The slight point-

158. Blunt p.128, and Fokker pp.24 and 28.

ing of the vault has been the cause of much argument in the past.[159] Though, in truth, the Knights had ample precedent for this feature in works both witnessed and commissioned during their stay on the island of Rhodes. They had left Rhodes fifty-one years before this church was begun and it seems likely that some Knights still lived who remembered the architecture of that island. In Rhodes, there are numerous examples of this treatment from the fourteenth century church of Kadi Mesdjidi[160] to the early sixteenth century church of Babou-Mestoud Mesdjidi,[161] where the slightly pointed arch with a barely perceptible point is placed in conjunction with the semicircular arch of the apse and a similarly shaped head to the window over the west door. The Knights' own chapel of St. Demetrius has a slightly pointed vault resting upon a semicircular arch.[162]

Cassar's failure to provide an entablature and cornice has also been attacked by purists.[163] The capitals of the sixteen pilasters form a continuous running architrave set back to be related to the nave wall in the intercolumniation. Ferres[164] has suggested that because of the weight of the main vault the design was modified during the course of construction and the vault made to spring direct from the capitals, thus lowering the centre of gravity and the line of thrust and correspondingly increasing the stability of the whole structure. He further relates the tradition that this reduction in height was made after an objection had been raised by the military authorities that the defending guns on the cavalier of St. James would have their field of fire restricted seaward, to the south-west, and that the guns could not be depressed to their necessary limit.[165] In spite of these suggestions, which carry with them no authentic literary evidence to support their claims, it is possible to suggest that Cassar

159. Flower p.36 suggests it may have been used to increase stability and suggests influence from Sicilian-Gothic, Rhodes or Cyprus may have had some effect; Bonnello, article on *Valletta* p.933 adopting the partisan attitude of pre-war fascist art-criticism, says that 'it contained motifs indigenous to Sicolo-Norman architecture'; Flower p.46. In the discussion which followed Flower's paper, Bedford suggested that the Church of St. Angelo, where de l'Isle Adam was buried, formed the prototype for the roof of St. John's. He must have been referring to the old crypt in the Chapel of St. Anne in Fort St. Angelo which has a barrel vault of slightly pointed profile, and which must antedate St. John's by many years.
160. Gabriel p.184.
161. Gabriel pp.199–200.
162. Gabriel p.176 : 'est voûtée d'un berceau brisé; le chœur, demi-circulaire, s'accuse a l'exterieur par une abside a trois pans.'
163. Apart from the lack of an architrave, it is surely quite logical to omit the cornice on the interior of a building.
164. Ferres p.73.
165. Ferres p.73.

adopted this arrangement because he liked the result. He had done the same sort of thing before, in his church at Rabat, and he constantly omitted the entablature, as the whim took him, on portions of the façades that he elsewhere designed. Added to this, it must be said that he had considerable precedent, both in Malta and elsewhere. The designer of the early church on Fort St. Elmo,[166] at the tip of the Valletta peninsula, in many ways foreshadows this treatment and has no elaborate cornice. A far more influential source may have been the roof of the library in the Escorial monastery[167] near Madrid, built to the designs of Juan de Herrera between 1567 and 1584, and thus almost contemporary with St. John's, Valletta. Here are the same widely spaced pilasters with unconventional capitals from which springs, directly, the immense barrel vault. The design is less masterly handled than that by Cassar; the ceiling has a distracting division into large compartments made by two horizontal ribs which run the length of the library on each side of the apex, and windows in small intersecting vaults break up the smooth passage of the eye from end to end of the hall. Throughout the seventeenth and eighteenth centuries it was no unusual thing to omit the entablature in buildings both in Italy and elsewhere. Michelangelo had done it on the top floor of the exterior of the apse 71 of St. Peter's, Rome, Borromini again in a similar position on the façade of the Collegio dei Propaganda Fide in Rome, and internally it occurs between drum and dome at S. Tommaso di Villanova at Castel Gandolfo.

The rhythm of the bays inside the church is peculiar and worthy of note, for it raises a problem. From the west, Cassar started by placing a third of a pilaster against the inside of the façade wall, and then a small bay about a third of the size of the normal bays. Four normal bays and arched ribs followed, punctured low down with oval windows which light the body of the nave. The fifth rib is thickened[168] to about double the normal width and projects into 153 the nave a little more than the others : this pronunciation marks off the nave from the choir, which then continues for a further two bays and is concluded at the west end by a full rib. Thus, there is

---

166. Prendergest in Flower p.46. This church was built in 1553 and restored, or more probably redecorated, by the Grand Master Lascaris in 1649.
167. Illustrated in Contreras III Pl.xxxii facing p.498. In this hall, as at St. John's, the last rib but one is thickened to cause the eye to pause before it is finally stopped at the end wall. In St. John's this pause denotes a change of function in the parts of the church, as between nave and choir.
168. As at St. Augustine's, Rabat.

no repeat of the opening third of a bay, nor is there any finality about the rhythm of the bays. This may be a Mannerist idiosyncracy, and the church is full of them; or again it may suggest that Cassar at one time intended to extend the church in an eastward direction.[169]

If it were extended eastward as a prolongation of the longitudinal line of nave and choir it would have made the church disproportionately long for its width, for its proportions are already longer than is usual in Malta or elsewhere. In addition, the east end would have crossed and blocked one of the crossing streets in the grid plan of the city, for the east façade as it now exists lies as far east as the street will permit. This difficulty was not unsurmountable : St. John's was the most important building in Valletta, after the fortifications, and the crossing street, of no great importance, could have been sacrificed. Also, relief from the excessive length of the church could have been achieved if Cassar had planned transepts and a dome springing[170] from the fattened rib which now marks the division of the church into nave and choir. This rib now appears to be no more than decoration, but on examination we find that its buttress is also fattened to the double width, suggesting that it was required to take some added load. To support this suggestion there exists a print[171] of the City of Valletta which shows a bird's-eye view of St. John's church with transepts and a monumental dome.

A far easier way of overcoming the broken rhythm of the nave bays would have been for Cassar to extend the church westward so that the façade would be in alignment with the face of the present towers. Had he still wished to project the towers in front of the façade, there would still have been ample room without in any way blocking the street, for there is a piazza in front of the church at present. In this way he could have increased the western bay to its full width. Evidence is scanty and these must remain hypotheses until further written evidence can be brought forward.

Finally it should be noticed that the form of construction, as well

93

---

169. This idea is suggested by Ferres, p.73.
170. This would have made the church in the form of a Latin Cross. The church was completed in 1577, and it is possible that the directive of the Council of Trent drawn up in 1563, and still fresh in the minds of all bishops, might have influenced the design here. At the last moment Cassar's confidence in spanning this large area with a dome may have failed him and he completed the church as it is today. Cf. Borromeo, *Acta Ecclesiæ Mediolanensis* Bk.1 chap.34, and *Instructions* p.9.
171. In the Valletta Museum, by Pierre Mortier, Amsterdam n.d. The dome also appears, rather half-heartedly, in Plan VI Royal Malta Library, where it is perched on a sloping roof. Engraving entitled *Cité de Valete de Malthe, c.* 1600.

as the shape of the chapel windows, bears a close resemblance to that used in such Roman buildings as the Basilica Nuova of Maxentius, evidence of Cassar's visit to Italy[172] The way in which he has transmitted the thrust from the vault to the sloping buttresses contained within the thick walls of side chapels was proposed by both Michelangelo (1554)[173] and Vignola (1568) in their plans for the Gesù, Rome, and became a regular feature in Baroque churches : but Cassar was early to use the device.

Although this great church shows much influence from the Mannerist movement in Italy it is, as well, a monument of the Early Baroque.[174] The long drive eastward of the hollow arched vault, the perspective breaking down of the lines over the concentric archivolts at the chancel end, drive the eye on to the altar. What tendency there is for the arches of the side chapels to draw off the eye is minimised by great tapestries which drape down from the capital mouldings toward the floor, and the line of the steps which separates nave from chapels. True to the practice of the period, painter and sculptor have been pressed into the service of architecture, and few churches can rival St. John's in their controlled magnificence.

The giant Belgian tapestries were ordered by the Grand Master Ramon Perellos in 1697. Fourteen large panels and many smaller adorn the nave walls, their designs being based on paintings by Rubens and Poussin and executed by Judocus de Vos.

The painting of the great vault was commissioned by the brothers Rafael and Nicholàs Cotoner who held the Grand Mastership in turn from 1660 to 1680. Mattia Preti, then resident in Malta, starting in 1662, carried out the murals in less than five years, painting in oils straight onto the primed stonework of the vault.[175]

Each chapel contained between the buttresses which support the nave was allotted to one of the langues of the Order,[176] except the corresponding space in the western bay, which was made into lobbies

158

153

154

---

172. ARCHIVES MS. 432 *Liber Bullarum* fol.253. Cassar was issued with a passport dated April 1569, to visit Rome and other places in Italy in order to study architecture. I am indebted to Dr. E. Sammut who has favoured me with a copy of this passport. See also Quentin Hughes, *Influence of Italian Mannerism* p.4. Although the possibility should not be overlooked that Cassar got the idea of this window form from Palladio, by way of Laparelli who was in constant touch with the Venetians. Palladio had used it on his Venetian churches: S. Francesco della Vigna façade (1562), S. Giorgio Maggiore nave, and Il Redentore nave (1577).
173. Illustrated by de Rochis.
174. Bonello article *Malta* p.45: 'sebbene eretta verso la fine del'500, per colore è forse il monumento più significativo del Barocco italiano. . . .'
175. Sammut, *Co-Cathedral* p.14.
176. Zammit, *Valletta* p.35. Allotted at the General Chapter held in 1604.

at the entrances to the sacristies and the oratory, and those in the third bay which lead off into the two covered loggias later added to the side walls of the church.

Mattia Preti had the small doorways, which broke through from one chapel to the next, considerably enlarged and arched over so that a passage way was formed between the chapels running parallel to the nave and functioning as an aisle.

The first langue chapel on the right aisle was allotted to the Knights of Castile, Leon and Portugal, and dedicated to St. James.[177] The altarpiece and two lunettes are by Mattia Preti, and so is much of the rich carving and gilding which is a characteristic of the church.[178] This chapel also contains two rich tombs dedicated to the Grand Masters Manoel de Vilhena (1722–36) and Emanuel Pinto de Fonçeca (1741–73) : the former tomb was executed in 1729 by the Florentine sculptor Massimiliano de Soldanis Benzis.[179]

The chapel of the langue of Aragon is in the next bay. All the paintings here are by Preti and the chapel contains two important tombs : the first, to commemorate the Grand Master Nicholàs Cotoner, has been ascribed to Domenico Guidi; the other, a monument to Ramon Perellos, is by Guiseppe Mazzuoli.[180]

The fifth bay holds the chapel of the Knights of Auvergne dedicated to St. Sebastian. The two lunettes are by Arena and the altarpiece is usually attributed to him.[181] The chapel also contains a monument to the Grand Master de Clermont de Chattes Gessan (1660).

At the end of the church, the chapel of the Blessed Sacrament opens from the chapel of Auvergne. It was formerly known as the chapel of Our Lady of Philermos, so named after the painting saved from Rhodes and brought to Malta by the Knights. Tall gates of silver, elegantly turned and mounted on a richly coloured balustrade of marble, sweep out in a double curve gently modelled, and a projecting step echoes the line of the plan. The gates, and the flank-

---

177. Sammut, *Co-Cathedral* p.27.
178. The decoration was largely paid for by Fra Thomas de Hozes, Bailiff of Llosa.
179. Sammut, *Co-Cathedral* p.29. If this is true, Vilhena was taking no chances with his memorial to posterity for it was executed seven years before his death. However, Sammut contradicts himself when he states that it was modelled four years earlier than the memorial to G. M. Zondadari executed in 1725. It was the practice in those days to prepare one's tomb before death.
180. Fleming attributes this work to Melchiorre Gafà.
181. Sammut, *Co-Cathedral* p.35, suggests that this work may be by Filippo Paladini (1544–c. 1614) who was exiled to Malta by the Grand Duke of Tuscany.

ing silver screen which makes up the composition, isolate the chapel into a haven of solitude.

In the left aisle, the chapel in the second bay was allotted to the Knights of Germany. It contains an altarpiece and lunettes by Eradi and a tomb sculptured for the Grand Master Marc'Antonio Zondadari (1720–22) by Soldanis Benzis in 1725.[182]

The chapel of Italy dedicated to St. Catherine, which is opposite the entrance lobby to the loggia, is one of he most important in the church. The *Mystic Marriage of St. Catherine* which forms the subject on the altarpiece is by Mattia Preti, and Caravaggio's *St. Jerome* hangs on the western wall of the chapel. The chapel also holds : two unascribed statues, to *St. Catherine* and *St. Euphemia*, presented by the Prior of Lombardy, Roberto Solaro ; the altar ' Our Lady of Carafa,' presented by Fra Gerolamo Carafa in 1617 ; and a monument to the Grand Master Gregorio Carafa dei Principi dalla Roccella (1680–90).

The chapel dedicated to St. Paul of the langue of France was remodelled in the nineteenth century and the original mural decorations have been swept away. It still retains, however, the mausoleum of Adrien de Wignacourt (1690–97), nephew of the French Grand Master Alof de Wignacourt, and a stately monument to Emmanuel Marie de Rohan-Polduc. An impressive sarcophagus emblazoned with the winged coat-of-arms of the dead Grand Master rests on a panelled pedestal containing the inscription. The bust of the Grand Master stands out darkly, raised up upon a support on the lid of the sarcophagus, and is thrown into relief by the light stone of the draped flags which fork out from behind him. The paraphernalia of cannons and shields and spiked halberds completes the radiating composition which is set before a bold flat obelisk, sturdy in shape, resting upon the back of the pedestal. The light line of its edged moulding confines a richly matched mottled panel of marble.

The last chapel is dedicated to St. Michael, patron saint of the langue of Provence. It contains monuments to two Grand Masters : Antoine de Paule (1623–36) and Jean-Paul Lascaris Castellar (1636–57), and an altarpiece which is a contemporary copy of the painting of *St. Michael and the Dragon* by Guido Reni.

The chapel which opens out of the chapel of Provence, and lies against the east end of the church, is now dedicated to St. Charles and sometimes referred to as the chapel of the Holy Relics. In 1784 it was allotted to the Anglo-Bavarian langue, a composite langue

182. Sammut, *Co-Cathedral* p.55.

made up of the remnants of the langue of England, which had lost most of its former glory through the confiscation of its property by Henry VIII during his dissolution of the monasteries, with that of Bavaria. In 1540 an act for the dissolution of the Order of St. John in England, Wales, and Ireland received royal assent on the final acceptance by England of the Protestant religion. This sealed the fate of all projects set afoot to revive the English langue to its former strength.[183] The altarpiece was designed by Agostino Masucci.

The crypt, containing the tombs of many Grand Masters, is entered from a stairway leading down from the chapel of the langue of Provence. It is a shallow-vaulted room with the sarcophagi set deeply into rectangular niches.[184]

The room is low and the vaulting springs from squat sturdy pillars with painted panels. The transverse arches are painted to represent panelling with foliage intertwined between macabre subjects representing skeletons and bats. All the fresco decoration covering the crypt was the work of Nicolò Nasini. The tombs of the Grand Masters—de l'Isle Adam, Pietro del Ponte, Juan d'Homedes, Claude de la Sengle, La Vallette, del Monte, La Cassière, Hugues de Verdale, Martino de Garzes, Alof de Wignacourt, and Luys Mendez de Vasconcellos—are all placed in the crypt along with that of the Englishman, Sir Oliver Starkey, secretary to the Grand Master La Vallette; his is the only tomb there of anyone below the rank of Grand Master.

Above, in the chancel of the church, the great eastward movement resolves onto the radiating marble group of the *Baptism of Christ,* set in the recessed apse, the work of Giuseppe Mazzuoli. The original designs were made by the Maltese sculptor Melchiorre Gafà, but although the designs were approved, the work was not carried out because of the death of Gafà in Rome in 1667. The High Altar was completed in 1686 to the designs of Lorenzo Gafà, Maltese architect and brother to Melchiorre. The low stately lines of the altarpiece, with the *Baptism* rising above, complete the climax of the church.

On each side of the west end of the church large wings were later added projecting the façade from Kingsway on one side to Mer-

183. Rees pp.85–86.
184. Sammut, *Co-Cathedral* p.45. Cassar has again used the slightly pointed arch in the close vaults over the niches, with the exception of the large end niche which has a four-centred arch. This shape, though a favourite in late mediæval work, has many precedents dating from the Renaissance in Italy and Spain, so that Cassar cannot be accused of consciously aping Gothic work.

chants' Street on the other. Gerolamo Cassar died in the year 1586 and work began on the northern wing,[185] containing the two sacristies and the treasury, in 1598.[186] This wing was for the safe keeping of the sacred relics and vestments. The northern wing contained the residence of the Prior of the Order and, behind this, the Oratory of the Decolation[187] built in 1603 at the expense of Fra Stefano Maria Lomellini.

The first and more important sacristy approached from the nave of the church, is a rectangular room vaulted by a semicircular ceiling pierced by shallow coffering and running at right angles to the nave. Though these wings were erected after Cassar's death we have no knowledge of what hand he had in the design. Nor do we know if he intended to extend the church laterally. Certainly it could not have been visualised by him from the start of work on the church, for inside the sacristy we see the crude grafting of this room to an earlier part of the church : the sturdy pilaster which marks the end of the buttress, and which supports the first rib of the nave, projects boldly into the sacristy and pierces one side of its coffered vault. The doorway, whilst being centrally placed in the lobby in the first bay of the nave, enters one side of the end wall of the sacristy and the arched line of the original lobby window, now filled in, shows clearly in the sacristy, playing uncomfortably against the line of the larger curved vault, both of which spring on the north-west corner from the same point. The main sacristy contains paintings by Preti and Stefano Pieri; the latter's *Scourging at the Pillar,* painted in 1572, was taken there from the chapel of the langue of England in 1631, when the chapel was transferred to the langue of Germany.

Matteo Perez de Alesio, Antoine de Favray, Francesco Potenzano, and Scipione Pulzone, have paintings in the sacristies. There is also a contemporary copy of Danielle da Volterra's *Descent from the*

185. All compass references to churches are on the assumption that the altar is at the east end and the entrance in the west front. Actually St. John's runs approximately from north-east to south-west, with the altar at the south-west end.
186. Zammit, *Valletta* p.35. But Sammut, *Co-Cathedral* p.11 says 1604.
187. Sammut, *Co-Cathedral* p.11 states 'the plain, two-storeyed buildings on either side of the façade were built toward 1667.' This seems inconceivable. It would mean that the oratory and the two sacristies were built with their façades set back from the face of the towers to two different levels. The character of the two-storey façades now existing seems to contradict this. It is close to Cassar's style and certainly earlier than 1667. The same mouldings are used and the windows and doors are similar to other early 17th century examples in Malta. Finally, the use of a large pilaster at the corner, its cap moulding a repeat of the cornice, shows clearly the influence of Gerolamo Cassar.

Cross[188] and a triptych of *La Pietà* by an anonymous Flemish painter of the sixteenth century.

The oratory was erected so that the Knights might have suitable accommodation for their devotions and so that novices might be conveniently instructed. In addition : its size, pleasant proportions, and magnificent decoration, made it a room most suitable for public assemblies and certain official functions. Unlike other important rooms in the church, this one has a flat wooden ceiling of large proportions. The ceiling follows the development which had taken place in Italy as a result of Michelangelo's new creation in the Ricetto ceiling of the Laurentian Library at Florence. In his design he had broken away from the traditional coffered ceiling of the Late Mediaeval and Early Renaissance periods[189] and had treated it as a field of moulded shapes more complex and more integrated than the chequered pattern used before. Both the decoration of the walls and the design of the oratory ceiling suggest a date considerably later than 1603, the date of commencement of building.[190] The tall graceful pilasters of the Corinthian order, the segmental-headed windows of croce Guelfa design, with painted representations in false perspective on the opposite wall, are certainly in advance, decoratively, of anything else erected in Malta about the year 1603. The three canvases in the ceiling, *Crucifixion, Ecce Homo,* and *The Crowning with Thorns,* which fit panels prepared in the ceiling, were painted by Mattia Preti, who did not arrive in Malta until 1662. It seems inconceivable that either the oratory should have taken at least fifty-eight years to build and decorate or that it should have been decorated soon after 1603 and fields of canvas prepared in the ceiling in the hope that years later a painter would be found to decorate them.

Therefore we must conclude that either the date 1603 for the commencement of the building is incorrect or that the oratory was completely decorated or re-decorated, perhaps under the supervision of Mattia Preti, between 1662 and 1699, the date of his death, by which time the canvases must have been completed.[191]

188. The original fresco of the *Descent from the Cross* is in the chapel of Lucrezia della Rovere in La Trinità dei Monti, Rome. Vasari IV,77.
189. Wittkower, *Biblioteca Laurenziana* p.195.
190. Zammit, *Valletta* p.35 and Sammut, *Co-Cathedral* p.23.
191. It should be noted that Mattia Preti was able to make architectural alterations to the nave of the church. He had the window on the west front altered to his suggestion and enlarged, Bonello, *Bulletin of Museum* p.161. So there is nothing unreasonable in suggesting that he may have proposed the theme of decoration in the oratory. Bonello states that he actually prepared the designs for the western window. A comparison of the mouldings might reveal something !

The oratory contains an altarpiece attributed to Stefano Algardi[192] and behind it *The Beheading of St. John* by Caravaggio, done during his short stay in Malta in 1608. If the painting were commissioned for its present position it would suggest that building work on the oratory was, at least, nearing completion by 1608, but I think this unlikely.

29. *Valletta. Conventual church of St. John, west front.*

If the interior of St. John's (the long drive of the nave and its rich decoration) is Baroque, the façade is certainly not. It is the work of Cassar and contains all the elements of a Mannerist composition. **155** Its bleak and rather forbidding appearance is characteristic of his work in Valletta and far removed from the Humanist architecture of the first half of the sixteenth century in Italy. Cassar has constructed a screen façade of two storeys with a centrepiece to face the high arch of the nave, and wings to screen the buttresses from the nave clerestory wall. The façade repeats, in a modified form, one of the proposals made by Michelangelo for S. Lorenzo in Florence[193] and is flanked by three-storey towers and octagonal spires.[194] This mediaeval idea, the practice in most Gothic cathedrals, became a characteristic of Maltese church architecture. It is rare in Renaissance and Baroque Rome,[195] though a favourite arrangement in

192. Sammut, *Co-Cathedral* p.24. 'On the altar there is a striking group of the *Crucifixion with the Madonna and St. John* carved in wood from the models of Stefano Algardi (?) (17th century).'
193. 1515.
194. The spires were found to be unstable as a result of bombing and were pulled down in 1941.
195. Though by no means unknown. The following projects have western towers: Bramante's design for St. Peter's, designs by Giuliano da Sangallo and Serlio. Churches which were actually built with western towers include: S. Agnese in the Piazza Navona, St. Peter's (begun and removed), and SS. Trinità dei Monti, Rome.

Spanish churches: the idea spreading from Spain to the Spanish possessions in Europe and the Spanish colonies in the Americas. This accounts for its continual use in Sicily and, possibly because of its proximity, in Malta.[196] Squat pyramidical spires are also found in Spain,[197] and there are examples in Sicily.[198]

The following points are clearly Mannerist in conception and suggest also that Cassar's work is a mixture of naïveté due to his late training and practice in architecture, and of contemporary influences from Italy, often half appreciated.[199] The lack of a clear rhythm in the intercolumniation is a Mannerist feature. In the central arch of the façade, the intrados of the arch is formed from the capital mouldings of the ground floor order whilst the extrados is made up of the base mouldings of the superimposed order. This double-function shows a lack of clear articulation in a motif which essentially forms part of the upper storey and rests upon the ground floor order. The high semicircular arched niches and the lower arch of the main portal create an anticlimax at the very point where, according to Early Baroque practice, a great elevating concentration is needed.[200]

Cassar has omitted the entablature from the ground floor order[201] (as he had already done on the interior of the nave), and the cap moulding is formed into a running cornice in the intercolumniation. The wings, which were added later, repeat this moulding as a cornice. In the centrepiece of the superimposed order he does the same thing, but at the end of the façade, where the towers rise, he adds a full entablature. Because of this, the raking cornice rises directly from the capital mouldings of the superimposed order. The top order of the towers again has no entablature, but is surmounted by a balustrade. He uses the pseudo-Tuscan order throughout, although the sizes of the various orders are dissimilar.[202]

196. The use of western towers is further discussed and illustrated in the summary of Maltese churches on p.119.
197. The church of the Escorial de Abajo; Nuestra Señora del Puerto, Madrid; and numerous secular buildings.
198. Cathedral at Cefalu; S. Lucia del Mela; the Santuario di Gibilmanna; the Matrice Vecchia at Castelbuono.
199. For evidence of Cassar's Mannerist disposition see the Biography p.205.
200. See how this Baroque concentration is achieved by the use of doors at S. Maria in Vallicella, Rome (1605), by Longhi and Rughesi; and again at SS. Vincenzo ed Anastasio, Rome (1650), by Martino Lunghi junior, where the niches are purposely omitted and the plain panels make no attempt to offset concentration.
201. Michelangelo's apse of St. Peter's, Rome. Serlio VI pp.4 and 28. The top floor of triumphal archways has no entablature, but abacus and cornice are combined.
202. Palladio I Cap.xii. This is contrary to Palladio and creates the necessary disquieting effect required for Mannerism. Serlio the true Man-

The main portal has columns of the Tuscan order supporting a 156 block entablature which runs back into the wall, leaving the cornice moulding, of an unusual design, to span the width between the columns and support a stone balustrade, assisted only by two scrolled consoles. This is a confusion in the function of the structural members of, the order, where the architrave should support the weight and the cornice throw off the rain. This confusion of function is again shown in the way Cassar has broken the entablature over the pilasters in the tower leaving the portion over the intercolumniation apparently unsupported.

Finally, the windows in the top storey of the towers show a lack 155 of clear articulation which is very similar to that found in the great arch over the portal. Intrados rests on panelled pilasters[203] and extrados is supported upon small projecting corbels.[204]

Over the main door Cassar had originally placed a low window, a croce Guelfa, surmounted by a disproportionally high entablature and raking cornice.[205] This has the appearance of being squashed down almost below the level of the top of the balcony balustrade by the heavy mass of entablature and mass of wall above as well as the large plain mass of wall area over the main arch. This old window is shown in a contemporary print, very accurately drawn, now kept in the Valletta Museum. Mattia Preti suggested several alterations to the church so that his proposed murals and decorations might be better lit. At a council meeting[206] it was decided that to enlarge the oval eyes in the vault and convert the chapels on both sides of the apse into two smaller apses might imperil the stability of the structure, but the Commissioners agreed to carry out Preti's suggestion for enlarging the western window to its present shape and size. 156

The bells, pillars, and supporting scrolls on the right hand tower were added at the beginning of the seventeenth century. The bronze bust of *The Saviour* in the main tympanum is by Alessandro Algardi.[207] The church was completed in July 1577 and consecrated

nerist in his Book IV 'on the Doric Order' uses the same order in superimposition.

203. Cassar has here used tall narrow pilasters with recessed panels in them. Though the mouldings are different, the idea is similar to that used on the doorways of the church of St. Augustine at Rabat. It should be noted that Cassar was familiar with this motif and therefore it is conceivable, though still unlikely, that Cassar designed the doorways at Rabat.

204. For a further description of this Mannerist façade see Quentin Hughes, *Influence of Italian Mannerism.*

205. Bonello, *Bulletin of Museum* pp.159–161.

206. ARCHIVES 260 (*Liber Conciliorum Status* 1657–1664).

207. Sammut, *Co-Cathedral* p.11.

by Archbishop Ludovico de Torres of Monreale on the 20th of February in the year 1578.[208]

We have shown that the two wings containing the sacristies, treasury, and the residences of the Grand Prior and Vice Prior are later than the main body of the church, but these were certainly completed by about 1664 when the Venerandi Commissarii approved of the removal of Cassar's western window and the substitution of the new design by Preti. The print in the Valletta Museum which shows the west front as it was before the removal of Cassar's window also shows the two wings complete as they are today. The proportion of the side windows, their proto-Tuscan pilasters and excessively deep entablatures, the large corner pilasters, and the construction of both base and cornice moulding of the main order, all characteristics of Cassar's work, show that the wings were either designed by Cassar before his death in 1586 (and in which case he probably contemplated and designed the sacristies and the oratory) or that the work was designed by a student of Cassar and erected during 1603–04, the date attributed to the sacristies and the oratory.[209]

The sacristy which leads off the side of the high altar in the oratory is later than the two wings. Here there are two doorways placed alongside each other : and their design and workmanship are more gentle than anything we normally associate with Cassar. This elevation onto Merchants' Street has an untidy appearance, mouldings cease quite arbitrarily and the two doors just mentioned are too closely spaced to lie comfortably together.

The balcony above is also later, similar in character to those added to the façade of the Magisterial palace in Valletta,[210] and strongly flavoured with Spanish influence. The two covered loggias which run parallel to the side chapels were built in 1736,[211] and are entered through doors in the lobby formed by the third bay of the nave and from the doors at the east end of the church which lead directly into the street. Two other doors, one from the cemetery and one from Kingsway, lead into the loggias opposite the lobbies which are made wider to allow a change of direction.

159,160

280

208. Zammit, *Valletta*, p.35, and Flower p.36.
209. Sammut, *Co-Cathedral* pp.11 and 23, and Zammit, *Valletta* p.35. If these extensions are not by Gerolamo Cassar, who then could have designed them? His son, Vittorio, does not show these characteristics in his work and the proportions of his buildings are different.
210. In detail they differ. Those on the church are supported on winged cherubs and clusters of robust fruit whilst those on the palace are held by large ornate consoles. However, they have resemblances and appear to be about the same date, and probably done by the same mason.
211. Zammit, *Valletta* p.35.

The loggias, rising as they do to the foot of the semicircular 161,162
windows which light the chapels, form the major part of the elevations onto Kingsway and the cemetery. Tuscan pilasters are laid
upon each other and against large recessed panels which repeat the
pattern of support and entablature. The windows are typically
eighteenth century, in particular the type which is made up of a
rectangle with a half-circle at top and bottom of a diameter a little
less than the width of the rectangular opening. This pattern was
seen on the ceiling of the oratory, but all examples of this shape as a
window date from the eighteenth century in Malta; such as those
in the loggia at Rabat, clerestory windows of St. Augustine's church
at Valletta, the west front of Zabbar parish church (1738) and St.
Bartholomew at Zurrieq (1774). The doorways are robust and
stately, with restrained carving kept small in scale, and show that
the restrained work of the Academic school in Italy and the Neo-
classical school in Spain was then being felt in Malta.[212]

Two other churches in Valletta show signs of the work of Gerolamo Cassar.[213] They are the church of St. Catherine of the langue
of Italy, which will be discussed fully in the chapter on centrally 38,233
planned churches, and the Carmelite church which he built in 1573.

The latter has been much altered since Cassar left it. It was
repaired and redecorated by Giuseppe Bonavia[214] and to him must
surely be ascribed the Academic screen façade of two storeys, with
the centrepiece crowned by a raking pediment. The walls are plain,
with large panels repeating the arrangement on the side elevation.

The model seems to have been Giacomo della Porta's façade of
S. Luigi dei Francesi in Rome (completed 1584), or one of its later
derivations.[215] However, the two windows in the centrepiece of the
first floor are not a usual Italian motif nor, fortunately, is it used
elsewhere in Malta.[216]

---

212. This is very pronounced in Lija parish church (1694), St. Barbara in
Valletta (1739), and the façade of the Carmelite church at Valletta.
213. He also designed St. Paul Shipwrecked, the Augustinian church, the
Dominican church, and the church of the Franciscans: all in Valletta.
These have since been entirely rebuilt and show no discernible trace of
his influence.
214. Zammit, *Valletta* p.39.
215. Giovannoni gives a list of these related façades on pp.228–229. Sum-
marised under his sixth type of church façade and variations in types
7a and 7b.
216. The idea of placing two windows each side of a central axial mass
comes from Serlio, but he and his French followers use it for planning
reasons. However, it is also used on the façade of Turin Cathedral and
in a palace design by Leonardo da Vinci (Institut de France, MS.B.
16recto).

In the plan Cassar has followed the usual Maltese pattern of a
163 plain longitudinal church. The four-bay nave has massive pilasters
supporting a full entablature and a barrel vault with slightly pointed
arches. The side chapels, similar to his church in Rabat, have cross-
barrel vaults, but the passage ways between them are wider, nearly
transforming them into side aisles. The decoration, the design of
the clerestory vaults, and the intersecting vaults which have been
cut into the barrel vault for the windows, all seem later.

The square crossing, dome, choir, and segmental apse are probably Bonavia's work. If we suggest that the square crossing is by
Cassar we must also conclude that he designed the dome. But the
information available is not sufficient to permit us to draw this
conclusion. However, if the square plan of the church of St. Cather-
38 ine of Italy was originally by Cassar (and it seems likely that it was),
then he must have spanned that with a dome.[217]

It is at least possible that Cassar built a dome both here and on
the church of St. Catherine and, unless we have evidence to the
contrary, we should not exclude the suggestion that Cassar at one
time contemplated adding a dome and transepts to the Conventual
church of St. John.

163 The interior of the Carmelite church today has a character which
is strongly Sicilian : largely due to the decoration, the alterations to
the nave roof, and the gallery over the west door. The cross vaults
from the clerestory windows, in making the main barrel vault seem
flatter than it actually is, strengthen this resemblance.

164 The side elevation may well have been designed by Cassar. The
architectural orders are omitted in the definition of the shapes and
replaced by plain posts and slabs giving an uninterrupted wall surface. Semicircular-headed arches are set in the upper recessed panels
and the upper storey of the façade is a pierced screen hiding the
buttresses which support the nave wall and the thrust of the vault.
This seems coeval with the rest of Cassar's work on the church : for
the general disposition of the post, lintel, and recessed-arched
304 opening closely resemble St. Anton's palace stables[218] built near

217. The one piece of evidence which seems to support the theory that the
     dome of the Carmelite church is by Cassar, is that the large pilasters at
     the crossing rise higher than those in the nave, and the cornice mould-
     ing of the nave runs into the capital moulding of the crossing pilasters.
     The crossing arches then rise directly from the capital moulding with
     no further entablature interposed. This is not the sort of thing a 17th
     or 18th century architect would do, but to Cassar it would not seem
     unusual.
218. Braun, *Works of Art* p.1. It also appeared on the church of the Minor
     Observants, Floriana (1588, destroyed 1941).

the end of the sixteenth century, and the courtyard of the Hospital of the Order built soon after 1575. It must be the first use in Malta **290** of the aisle screens disguising the nave buttresses.[219] This became a feature of most of the later parish churches throughout the seventeenth and eighteenth centuries.

An inscription on the tower tells that it was rebuilt in 1924 to the **164** original design. It is similar in arrangement to that Gerolamo Cassar designed for the west front of St. John's, but the proportion is **155** more slender, and it has a deeper base to the top storey order and

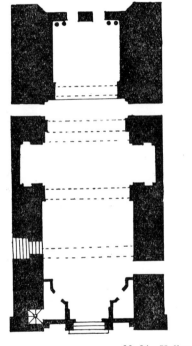

30–31. *Valletta St. Ursula.*

stone vases on the corners of the balustrade. There are full entablatures on each order, with the portion over the intercolumniation unsupported by pilasters. The intrados of the belfry arch rests on a panelled pilaster and the extrados upon supporting corbels; but this, again, is a feature copied in most of the belfry windows on the island.[220]

219. Note that Sir Christopher Wren used this idea on the aisle walls of St. Paul's.
220. For example the parish churches of: Zebbug (1599), Qrendi (1658), and Zejtun (1692), etc.

There is a façade of a church which exhibits all the Mannerist tendencies of this period, but its thin crisp character does not suggest the hand of Cassar. The monastery of St. Ursula was founded in Valletta in 1583 and the little church begun in that year.[221] The church was badly damaged in the late war but appears to have been rebuilt to the original design.

It is one of the first examples in Malta of the use of a super-imposed order on the façade of a church, though St. John's is a little earlier. It has not the excuse here that the higher order suggests a high nave and the lower order the wider-spreading lower aisles, which is the reason for its original use at such churches as S. Miniato al Monte at Florence and later at S. Maria Novella at Florence, and its adoption by the Jesuits still later. However, both in Italy and near-by countries strongly influenced by Italian thought, the façade has always been considered as a completely separate work of art unified in itself and often divorced from the church it faces, by time, proportion, and style.[222] It may be the early date of the façade, or the current influence of the Mannerist architects or, again, a combination of these two factors, which has produced a strange rhythm. The orders are applied in three planes. The first has coupled pilasters for the lower order supporting a pilaster capped by a pyramid and alongside another free pilaster throwing off a short length of raking cornice. The second plane, a quarter pilaster set back from the face of the first plane, which supports a superimposed quarter pilaster. A third plane is again set back and consists of the capital mouldings of the superimposed orders and cornice and cap mouldings of the raking cornice applied to the ashlar face of the church façade. Nor is the rhythm the only disturbing factor. The super-imposed order has no entablature, and capital mouldings and cornice mouldings run into one. Whilst the lower of the first plane has a coupled base, the pilasters above stand each on its own base. The tall doorway has a broken pediment repeated in the centrepiece which lies within the break, and the attenuated Doric columns are grotesquely echoed in the flanking window frames. A central eye and two small windows beside the door are traditional Maltese features.[223]

221. Braun, *Works of Art* p.28.
222. Giovannoni p.196.
223. Braun, *Maltese Architecture* p.21, states 'toward the end of the period 1580 to 1660 an attempt was made to introduce a refinement by dividing all buildings, even churches, into two architectural orders.' That this tendency began much earlier is shown by St. John's, Valletta

The larger parish churches

From the end of the sixteenth century a large number of parish churches were built in Malta as a result of the increased prosperity which had come to the island with the advent of the Knights of St. John. Whilst the earlier churches had been without exception planned as single-cell rectangular buildings, and the great Conventual church of St. John had followed that pattern but with the addition of side chapels to the nave, the new parish churches deviated from it. They were all comparatively large and they were all built in the form of a Latin Cross.[224]

With transepts and apse all flat ended and with the very shallow pitch of the church roof concealed behind a low parapet they have a curiously box-like appearance from the outside. The arms of the transepts and the apse are invariably of equal projection. Decoration is cut to a minimum on the exterior, the façade being made the main field for display with the western door the centre of that attraction.[225] Nave, transepts, and choral apse are usually divided into two floors by a string moulding and capped with a cornice at the parapet level. In construction the masons followed methods to which they were accustomed. The churches were spanned with semicircular ribbed barrel vaults, the line of the vault following the line of the rib but set back slightly. Above the arch of the vault the area was filled in to the level of the shallow-pitched roof. The aisle walls were raised to the full height of the nave and concealed the nave buttresses. In the early parish churches the external wall gives no indication of its task but later architects follow the pattern set by Gerolamo Cassar at the Carmelite church in Valletta and pierce the top floor of the aisle walls to form an arcaded screen. **164**

The crossing was usually spanned by a dome[226] expressed quite simply at first, but later with the designs of Lorenzo Gafà, becoming a complex work of art.

This brief introduction to the parish churches is necessary because the first of these new churches, the church of St. Paul at Rabat the **175**

(1573) and St. Ursula (1583). The giant order continued to be used on some churches to the end of the period of the Knights of Malta. See the summary of churches using the giant order p.123.
224. Shape laid down by the Council of Trent for all Catholic churches, where it was at all possible (Borromeo, *Instructions* p.8).
225. Also as proposed by Borromeo, *Instructions* pp.10–11.
226. The exception is Gozo cathedral.

suburb of the old capital in the centre of the island, has been so altered and added to at later periods that its early characteristics are hardly discernible. It appears to have been built over the ancient Grotto of St. Paul[227] where, it is suggested, St. Paul was imprisoned during his stay on the island. The present church was begun in 1575,[228] and so is one of the first examples of the new parish church. In 1600 Giovanni Beneguas came from Cordoba to join the company of the Knights, but upon his arrival on the island he became a hermit instead and dwelt for some years in the Grotto of St. Paul. In 1617, with the aid of money he had collected and privileges granted to him by Paul V, he was able to begin work on a chapel, the Sanctuary of St. Publius, which he built above the grotto in the church of St. Paul. Under the Grand Master Lascaris this chapel was enlarged and in 1692 entirely rebuilt by Lorenzo Gafà.[229]

All the interior of the church has been remodelled and a later façade partly obscures the lines of the old nave wall.

The façade is an attractive sober composition of three equal bays on the lower floor, joined by recessed panels, and the centre bay is emphasized by a superimposed storey. Recessed and sweeping scrolls, modelled on the Vignola pattern,[230] lie above the recessed panel and join the centrepiece to the two wings. Information is scarce upon this façade, but one reference[231] ascribes it to the Italian architect Filippo Bonamici (1705–80), who had been called to Malta to carry out alterations to the Jesuit church in Valletta.[232] This façade, with its triple-segmental pediment, is certainly unusual in Malta, and it has particular details which are shared, or at least suggested, in the work on the façade of the Gesù in Valletta. On both façades the architect has used Doric pilasters for his ground floor order and their mouldings are very similar; the proportion of the triglyphs and metopes are the same and so is the use of a half-triglyph in the corners of the recessed planes with no related half pilaster below. For the superimposed order St. Paul's church has the Ionic style whilst the Gesù has Corinthian capitals.

The Vignola type of link[233] between the upper centrepiece and the lower wings occurs on both façades, though the one on the Gesù

238–240

227. Rutter p.125.
228. Braun, *Works of Art* p.20.
229. Rutter pp.125–126.
230. Design for Gesù façade and S. Maria dell'Orto, Rome.
231. Inscription on photograph in Valletta Museum.
232. Bonello article *Valletta* p.933.
233. I use the term 'Vignola link' for convenience, for his designs which incorporate it are most widely known. But it had been used before.

is more elaborate and its side is decorated with the head and shoulders of a woman. Both façades have the same windows set back in panels, both have the same arrangement of a recessed plane between wings and centrepiece, and upon doors and windows the exaggerated guttae mouldings are used, either singly or in groups of three.[234]

At the same time it must be pointed out that Lorenzo Gafà (1630–1710) had been employed to rebuild the Sanctuary of St. Publius which forms part of St. Paul's church and was therefore engaged upon work on the church after 1692;[235] the very fine seventeenth century dome seems to be by his hand.[236] The façade, though it is not typical of his work, has many elements which are used by him elsewhere : the Vignola type links,[237] the carved terminals and vases,[238] the segmental-headed window in the centrepiece,[239] and the pinching-in of the door architraves beneath the pediments.[240] Certainly on stylistic evidence the façade should be accredited to Bonamici, for the resemblances are far closer between St. Paul's and the Gesù in Valletta than between it and the façades known to have been designed by Gafà. This would mean : that the original façade existed until Bonamici added a new one in the middle of the eighteenth century, or that his façade replaced earlier work, perhaps by Gafà, of which we have no evidence, or that (and this is unlikely in view of the usual practice in Malta) the church remained from 1575 until the middle of the eighteenth century without a façade.

The interior has Ionic pilasters with half Ionic columns set against them. These are raised well clear of the floor, placed upon boldly moulded pedestals. The general character of the nave decoration does not conform to that found in the other churches by Gafà, with the exception of a deep attic, or decorated band which runs between

---

234. This is in common use in 18th century Rome, but occurs elsewhere, especially in Sicilian work of the School of Vaccarini.
235. Rutter p.126.
236. The high drum, the coupled pilasters and straight broken entablatures, the powerful folding scrolls which relate dome to drum, the double ribs which carry up the lines of the pilasters, and the tall clear-cut lines of the lantern, are features found in his other domes at Siggiewi, Zejtun, and Mdina cathedral.
237. St. Lawrence, Vittoriosa (1681); 'Tal Hlas,' Qormi (1690); the Matrice, Gozo (1697).
238. 'Tal Hlas' at Qormi, and the Matrice, Gozo.
239. Nave clerestory of the Cathedral at Mdina, St. Lawrence, and 'Tal Hlas,' but common in late 17th and 18th century Malta.
240. Sarria chapel, Floriana (1678); St. Catherine, Zejtun (1692); the Cathedral; and the Matrice at Gozo. However, Gafà never uses the double pediment, that is, one contained within the other, on any of his buildings.

the springing of the vaults, the apse semi-dome and the line of the entablature, and the use of segmental-headed windows set in small cross vaults which light the nave, transepts, and choir. These last two features are common in Gafà's designs and the exaggeratedly high band is peculiar to his work.[241] It seems possible then, that Lorenzo Gafà was responsible, not only for the dome, but for a new vault to the nave, transepts, and choir, and for the semi-dome of the apse; and that someone else, perhaps Bonamici, was called in later to complete the decoration of the nave or to redecorate portions of it. This could be done without affecting the structure of the building.

The parish church of St. Julian was begun next, in the year 1580. It was considerably enlarged in 1682 and further alterations took place later.[242] The parish church of Our Lady of Victory in Senglea was begun in the same year. A portion of the church was rebuilt in 1650 and a considerable amount of the decoration dates from that period.[243] The church was almost completely destroyed by bombs when the city of Senglea was devastated on the 16th January 1941. The barrel vault of the old nave, which had existed until then, was coffered and had a slight point at the apex similar to the vault of St. John's in Valletta.

166 Alterations were made to the old parish church of St. George at Qormi in the year 1584, when a large cruciform addition, consisting of choir and transepts, was built on to the western end of the old nave which had been built in 1456. This was however pulled down 'soon after' and the present cruciform church built in its stead.[244] We do not know the exact date of the final rebuilding but from the style of the building it appears to date from the end of the sixteenth century. It is large, and strangely graceful when we compare it with contemporary work being erected by Cassar in Valletta, and it has none of the ponderous qualities we usually associate with his work. Undoubtedly there were other architects[245] at work in Malta at this time, though none is well known and no one has received credit for the design for this fine and important church.

241. Braun, *Works of Art* p.21.
242. Braun, *Works of Art* p.21.
243. Braun, *Works of Art* pp.24–25 contains photographs of the damaged building.
244. Braun, *Maltese Architecture* p.12.
245. As well as several military engineers, Maltese and Italian, there were various Maltese architects working in the late 16th century whose names we know: Giovanni Attard, Paolo Burlo, Andrea Cassar, Matteo Coglituri, Evangelista della Menga, and Paolo Micciola. It is also possible, though unlikely, that this church was designed by one of the visiting Italian military engineers.

The façade is tall and with superimposed Doric pilasters. The **166** centrepiece has a steep raking cornice, the sides are topped with balustrades. The wings, with their narrow intercolumniation, are carried up to form graceful western towers each crowned with a balustrade and a spire. Though the treatment is that used by Cassar on St. John's, Valletta, the effect is decidedly different. The feeling **29** is more akin to Gothic, though no Gothic tradition exists in Malta; and the tall proportions of the orders, emphasised by deep panelling in the pilasters, is not that used by Renaissance architects in Italy. Serlio produced two drawings[246] which are rather similar in feeling **167** if not in detail, but these he did after he had visited France and seen examples of French mediaeval cathedrals. The architect may have seen a copy of Serlio though this façade is no slavish imitation.[247]

The main portal with its tall coupled Corinthian columns on **168** combined pedestals, its broken cornice, its unsupported intercolumniation, decorated centrepiece, and the arched opening of the door, are all features found in the main door of St. Augustine's church at **151** Rabat. The line of the portal entablature forms the line of the main entablature of the lower façade order : an unusual feature. This makes the superimposed order considerably taller than that upon which it is supported. This external subdivision is purely arbitrary and has no relationship to the interior of the church where the coffered barrel vaults are supported upon a giant order of Doric pilasters and a bold triglyph and metope entablature. The aisle doors echo the treatment of the main portal, except that because **170** they are less important, their coupled columns are replaced by single ones; but the door leading to the north transept is more sturdy in appearance, lintel headed and bound by pilasters with recessed panels,[248] and a semicircular-headed light is inserted between cornice and relieving arch above.

All the main pilasters of the church façade are also panelled in **171** an elaborate fashion. This method seems probably to have been

246. Serlio V ed. Vicenza 1618, fol.212 and more particularly fol.216 (Fig. 167). See also Giuliano da Sangallo's design for S. Lorenzo at Florence (Fig.165).
247. Numerous books on architecture were collected by the Knights and these finally found their way into the library. They include : Alberti, two editions (1546 and 1580); Palladio, four editions including the 1570 edition; Vincenzo Scamozzi, three works from 1583; Serlio VI books of architecture 1584; and six editions of Vitruvius dating from 1556.
248. The side doors of St. Augustine are built like this and their pilasters rise from the ground and not from pedestals as do the other doors.

derived from work in Spain, though it does occur in Italy.[249] But in Italy the panels are rarely deeply cut and their centrepieces do not return to the surface of the pilaster. The aisle walls are carried up to screen the buttresses of the nave in the usual Maltese fashion. Here, although the treatment is similar to the Carmelite church at Valletta, the detailing seems later. A balustrade fills the lower part of the arched opening; the string course which marks the springing of the arch is carried across the intervening wall surface, and the cornice is more elaborate. We must discount the possibility that this screen at Qormi may be later than the main fabric of the church.

173
164

Braun[250] has suggested that Qormi may have been designed by the architect who was responsible for Senglea and Zebbug parish churches. He noticed a resemblance in the workmanship. The architect, he suggests, may have been Vittorio Cassar, the son of Gerolamo. It is feasible to think of Vittorio working with his father on the Augustinian church at Rabat and adding the later embellishments. The naves of Zebbug, Qormi, and Senglea have points of resemblance. All have the single order of Doric pilasters with slightly recessed panels, all have the full Doric entablature, and all have the semicircular arches of the aisle cross vaults carried up toward, but not quite touching and supporting, the main Doric architrave. At Qormi this weakness is most pronounced because the Doric pilasters occur only at the crossing and the ends of the nave, leaving a length of apparently unsupported entablature.

180,174

This was obviously felt to be a weak point in the design, for it was later disguised by decorative patterns. The architect may also have felt the inadequacy of the supports, for at the later church at Zebbug (1599) he included a pilaster between each opening to the aisles.

180

Undoubtedly Gerolamo Cassar was responsible for the interior of the Rabat church and there he used rectangular windows piercing the vault and resting on the nave cornice. At Rabat these windows are large[251] and a little clumsy, but in the later churches, although

249. In Quattrocento palace architecture in Rome; Bramante's S. Maria delle Grazie, Milan; Lombardo's S. Mari dei Miracoli at Brescia (1480); drawings by Serlio; and in France as early as 1508 at Blois; 1515–23 at Chenonceaux; and 1526 at Chambord.

250. Braun, *Maltese Architecture* p.19. Unfortunately I have not fully examined the one church we know is by Vittorio Cassar: the old parish church of Birkirkara (*c.* 1600). If the details of this church are similar to those of Qormi, Zebbug, and Senglea, and the façade of St. Augustine at Rabat, it would make the attribution of these churches to Vittorio Cassar fairly secure. However, it must be remembered that much at Birkirkara is over sixteen years later, for Tomasso Dingli completed the design for Vittorio Cassar.

251. Large ones are needed because there is no dome to light the interior.

the same idea is again used, the window openings are made much smaller, almost apologetic intrusions in the line of the vault.

Qormi has a fine dome with console buttresses springing from its surface and running down to the cornice of the drum.

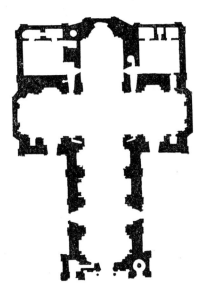

32. *Zebbug. Parish church of St. Philip.*

The parish church of Zebbug followed soon after Qormi was begun : work starting in the year 1599.[252] The church is designed in the usual form of the Latin Cross with western towers.[253] The walls of the apse and the transepts are projected slightly to form three distinct faces of masonry, and these are separated by pilasters which are broken across the corner.[254] This treatment allows the architect greater depth in the arrangement of the transept chapels and the high altar. The nave is divided into four bays, with north and south **180** doors opening out of the second bay, and spanned with a semi-circular barrel vault resting on ribs, large ones over the nave pilasters and two thinner ones to each intercolumniation. The windows which light the nave are cut into the vault between the two centre ribs. The coffering of the vault is a variation on the earlier examples

252. Braun, *Works of Art* p.45.
253. Added later, in 1660. Braun, *Works of Art* p.19.
254. It may be pertinent to note that the drum of S. Eustorgio in Milan (*c.* 1462), by Michelozzo, has both pilasters which are panelled and broken in profile across the corners of the drum. I do not suggest that there is any direct point of contact between these two drums, which are separated by more than a hundred years. There must be an intermediate influence somewhere.

with the pattern made up of cruciform shapes surrounded by smaller squares treated alternately with different patterns. The transepts are also barrel vaults. Much of the decoration is later, in particular the ornate altar in the north transept, while the domed aisles are later still.

There are many features in this church which show strongly the influence of Gerolamo Cassar: but though the motifs are similar to his, in all cases either the proportion or the usage is slightly different, suggesting the work of someone fully conversant with the style of Gerolamo Cassar. And who is more likely to be familiar with his work than his own son, Vittorio Cassar? The main portal is a replica of Cassar's design for St. John's, Valletta: the same Doric columns, the entablature running back to the wall, the long span of the cornice supported on rolling consoles, the same balustrade, and the same semicircular headed opening to the doorway. But at Zebbug the details are more refined: the column bases are smaller, triple guttae and a triglyph appear on each entablature, the cornice moulding and the consoles are more orthodox, and the edges of the balustrades are chamfered. Whilst the window, with its segmental cornice resting above the portal, may be contemporary, the upper portion of the façade is definitely later. The robust pilasters of the lower order, with their pseudo-Doric caps formed into a string course across the whole width of the façade, are like Gerolamo's work; but the spacing of the columns and the intercolumniation is much more orderly than his arrangement on the Conventual church. A semicircular-headed window is placed centrally in each upper storey of the end walls of the transepts and the apse. The one in the apse is now filled in, but originally it must have resembled those which light the side chapels of the Conventual church and those lighting the interior of St. Catherine of the langue of Italy in Valletta: the original work is attributed to Gerolamo Cassar.[255] The transept windows are similar but the side lights are now filled in and a segmental cornice and frieze rest upon the centre light.

In the nave a third of a bay is added to the most western of the four complete bays. This seems justifiable in plan, for its supporting pilaster forms the corner pilaster of the tower; the arrangement is similar to that used at the Conventual church, but at Valletta there is no such excuse for its use. The vaulting ribs at the crossing are considerably fattened and projected, but at Zebbug this treatment has structural significance whilst at Valletta it merely indicates a

255. Paribeni, *Malta* p.90 and Braun, *Maltese Architecture* p.19.

transition from nave to chancel. It is strange how the architect of the later church has found structural justification for some of the Mannerist idiosyncrasies of the earlier designer.

The dome over the crossing is a fine example of the type of dome used on the earlier parish churches. It is raised upon a high octagonal drum, pierced by eight rectangular windows proportioned to to the wall area. The full entablature is supported on Doric pilasters broken across the corner in the same way as those on the transept and apse walls. The dome itself, a single shell construction forming a semicircular surface inside the church, does not therefore rise very high above the cornice of the drum. It is surmounted by a lantern buttressed with scrolls and crowned with a simple cupola. The clean lines of the dome and the careful proportions of the drum and its austere mouldings form a sombre climax to the simple line of apse and transept. These qualities make early Maltese churches stately buildings, especially when seen from the east. They contrast well with the turbulence of Platteresque Spain and the disordered use of Renaissance motifs in many of the Early Renaissance designs in England and France. When this church was being built, the effect of the Italian Renaissance had been felt for only about thirty-three years in Malta.[256]

The church of the Annunciation at Birkirkara[257] was designed by Vittorio Cassar about the year 1600. In 1727 the church of St. Helen was built, and this replaced the earlier church as the parish **227** church of Birkirkara. After that the church of the Annunciation was allowed to fall into disrepair and now a large part of it has collapsed. This is a great pity, for it is one of the finest examples of the period in Malta. The vaults of the nave and transept have fallen, and only one campanile remains.[258] This is traditional in **181** design, based on the prototypes on the Conventual church, but the details are different. The pilasters are Corinthian and the entablatures are complete. The wall surface between the pilasters is panelled and the circular window cuts into the edge of the panel. The main belfry window is unusual and more like the work of the eighteenth century.

256. Before leaving this church it should be noted that according to the writing on the photograph in the Valletta Museum it was rebuilt by by Dingli between 1621 and 1632. The stylistic evidence does not support this claim. Why should the church have been rebuilt after only twenty-two years? Dingli assisted Vittorio Cassar at Birkirkara; he may have also helped on parts of this church.
257. A very full description of this church appears in E. B. Vella, *Storja tà Birkirkara*.
258. There may not have been another. I was unable to get inside this church, nor was I able to examine the full perimeter of the walls.

In plan, the church is laid out on the Latin Cross; planned as seven squares with three squares for the nave bays, one for each transept, a square crossing and a square choir.[259] It has simple proportions simply used, and a dome at the crossing now destroyed.

182,183   The finest part of this building is the façade which was designed by Tomasso Dingli and begun in 1617. It is a fine rhythmical façade richly carved and decorated. Though the Corinthian capital has been used before in Malta, this is perhaps the first example there of the use of the giant Corinthian pilaster on the façade a church. The church is based on the temple front,[260] and the rectangular frame of the pilaster and entablature is broken down in a rhythm to the smallest common denominator, which is the shape of the door.

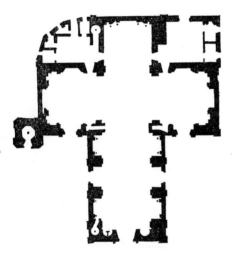

33. *Attard. Parish church of St. Mary.*

As the rhythm ascends from the door to the outline of the façade, it ascends in the same way up the front in three ripples in the six carved niches which flank the door. Many of the details found in earlier churches are repeated : panels on the pilasters, a great circular window over the nave, and small oval windows over the door; but they are more maturely used and their decoration confidently handled. The carved centrepiece has a Spanish quality and the superimposed arrangement with the carved escutcheons reminds me of Santi Spiritus at Salamanca and the Pellejeria door of Burgos cathedral.[261,262]

259. Braun, *Maltese Architecture* p.12.
260. An early example is S. Andrea, Mantua (1470). Cf. Giovannoni p.199. He calls it the 'Vitruvian expression.' The orders are used *altitudinibus perpetuis* as opposed to orders in *altitudine duplicis*.
261. Illustrated in Contreras pp.4,5,7,and 9.

The parish church of St. Mary at Attard, begun in the year 1613,[262] **184**
was the first church known to have been designed by Tomasso Dingli.
It is the best example of his work and, at the same time perhaps the
best Renaissance monument on the island, for Malta's period of
prosperity came too late for the pure influence of Bramante to take
root. By the time the Knights had landed on the island the seeds
of Mannerism were being sown in Italy; and during most of the
period of their occupation, Baroque was the prevailing style in
Europe. Dingli's work is the one important remnant from the past,
though the purity of his design is constantly affected by Spanish
influences.

34. *Attard. Parish church
of St. Mary.*

The plan of Attard church is appealing in its simplicity. The **33**
triple-bay nave with cross doors in the centre bay creating centres
of focus, draws off the longitudinal effect usually associated with the
Latin Cross plan.

The nave and chancel is barrel vaulted with a coffered ceiling, **34**
while the transepts are spanned with saucer domes. Over the crossing there is a tall drum and a semicircular dome springing from the
cornice moulding above the gallery of windows. In section the
triplet of domes and their crowning lanterns form a calm composition. The nave pilasters, both supporting the cross arches of the
nave chapels and the main ribs of the nave vault, are of the Doric
order and, following Gerolamo Cassar's tradition, have no entablature. Their capitals continue as a running moulding along the
wall surface from the springing of the arches. This church was
designed when Dingli was twenty-two years old, and because of the
size of the project it is understandable that he should seek the

262. In 1610 the parish church of Tarxien was started; the architect is unknown.

inspiration of erected buildings on the island to build up his confidence.

184,183 The main façade, like in his later design for Birkirkara, is in the 'Vitruvian expression' designed like a temple front.[263] In proportion it is a pedimented square but, although he uses the niches filled with statues and a rather finer portal than the one at Birkirkara, the whole rhythm of the façade is much simpler and far more static. The doorway is round headed and there is no build-up of square 185 shapes to the outline of the façade. Whilst the design of the door- 151 way is clearly derived from such earlier models as St. Augustine's church at Rabat and the aisle doorway of Qormi parish church, the proportions are more correct and the details more delicately carved. Carved foliage is introduced in the recessed panels of the Corinthian 186 pilaster each side of the door and on the door of the east transept. 187 The south aisle door, more slender in proportion, has carved rect-angular panels set in the frieze : a mode of decoration favoured by Dingli but used earlier in the nave ribs of Qormi church. The side doors have oval lights above them. This seems to continue early Maltese practice such as at the chapel of St. Anne in Fort St. Angelo and is commonly found over house doors throughout the period of the Knights. Here at Attard, as before at the church of the Annun-ciation at Birkirkara, the pattern of the oval windows is repeated down the nave walls in the intercolumniation with rectangular win-dows above which pierce the barrel vault and light the nave. The pilasters are repeated down the side walls of the nave, echoing those on the inside and, because of the extra depth required for the façade and the organ loft at the west end, coupled pilasters are employed. In the junction of nave and transept, Dingli has managed to fit a quarter pilaster to give apparent support to the entablature at the corner : always a difficult problem to overcome. The entablature 189 forms a low parapet and conceals the shallow pitch of the nave roof. 188 The dome over the crossing is placed on a high, severe type of drum pierced by four windows which are exactly proportioned to the sides of the drum and lie on the diagonal lines from corner to corner; the only decoration consisting of a small cornice moulding and a traditional Maltese roll moulding at the corners of the drum and around the windows. At the corner, the moulding continues

---

263. Giovannoni pp.179 *et seq*. The two-storeyed Jesuit façade was more usual in Italy at this time. Before this, Galeazzo Alessi, Vignola, and Palladio had used the 'Vitruvian expression' and later Maderna, Borromini, and Galilei were to use it, but in a more complex manner than on this façade at Attard.

down the wall to a point on a line with the bottom of the window and then abruptly stops. We do not know whether Dingli thought this an architectural embellishment or whether he realised that the lower part of the drum would be invisible from the ground. The campanile, which adjoins the north transept, was added to the church in 1718, and the line of the balustrade which encloses the precinct area in front of the church also seems to be later.

The parish church of Our Lady of Victory at Naxxar was begun **193** by Dingli in 1616, while work was still in progress on his earlier church at Attard.[264] The Naxxar design could never have been as attractive as that at Attard; and now its original façade has been replaced by a later one and the plan shape marred by the addition of aisles and aisle chapels. Where at Attard he has made a straightforward statement of architecture, at Naxxar he has experimented; being probably more confident after his earlier success. If one ignores the later aisles, the plan at Naxxar is leaner and has none of the ample simple proportions of the earlier plan. And the interior of the nave has not received the bold treatment that he gave to his **192** nave at Attard. Here he has used coupled Corinthian columns with disproportionately smaller composite columns superimposed above.[265] To stiffen this unstable effect he has applied these to panelled pilaster strips and repeated the pilasters to support the cross arches of the aisles. But although the pilaster strips rise from bases at floor level, the columns, in contradiction, rise from pedestals, and both columns and pilasters share a common entablature. The same restless feeling is apparent in the design of the nave and transept vaults, where the simple rectangular coffering is replaced by an elaborate pattern of large and small crosses combined with circular and star decoration. The inside of the drum has stunted Corinthian pilasters between which are twelve niches with scalloped arches, similar to those on the façade at Birkirkara and Attard. The remaining four **183,184** intercolumniations hold rectangular windows. The church also receives light from the usual rectangular windows which pierce the vault between the smaller ribs, large circular windows in the end walls of the transepts, and oval windows in the later aisles.

Externally, Dingli's work can be seen on the dome, transepts, and **194** the apse. The dome, approximately similar to his earlier designs, no longer has the traditional Maltese mouldings at the corners of the

264. One of the side doors at Attard bears the date 1616.
265. The use of superimposed orders inside a church is unusual. Bramante proposed it in one of his designs for St. Peter's Rome, Geymuller p.143, also S. Francesco della Vigna, Venice; S. Paolino, Lucca (1517).

drum; instead, coupled panelled pilasters and a full frieze have been added. The transepts and east end have the usual square shapes set with superimposed pilasters at the corners. These pilasters are panelled with mouldings, an arrangement much favoured by Dingli. The west front, with its two towers, and the aisles were added to the church in 1912.[266]

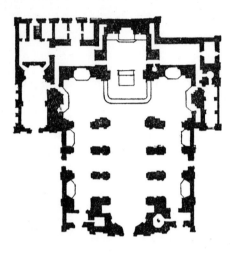

35. *Zurrieq. Parish church of St. Catherine.*

197   The parish church at Zurrieq (the architect's name is unknown), though begun in 1634, has had many later alterations and additions. The original church probably had the usual three-bay nave with transepts and a square apse. The aisles, which were added later, may have replaced the usual aisle chapels which led off the nave. The proportions of the plan are similar to Naxxar parish church and **199** less ample than at Attard, but in the nave the architect has returned to the giant order of Doric pilasters, with smaller ones supporting the cross arches of the aisles. Here, these rise to support the entablature and this support is emphasized by a corbelled keystone. While the barrel vault is still supported on large ribs over the nave pilasters, with two smaller ribs between them enclosing the rectangular window which pierces the vault, the coffering is made up of very much larger units. The enlarged pilasters at the crossing are stepped forward with their accompanying entablature to take the weight of the thickened ribs which support the drum. The dome may be a little later. It certainly shows a transitional stage between the early simple dome part hidden behind a plain drum, a characteristic example of which is Attard, and the later use of a crowning dome,

266. Inscription inside the west door.

94

with ribs and buttresses, of which the designs of Lorenzo Gafà are the finest on the island. The dome at Zurrieq has little projection above the cornice of the tall drum, but ribs now show on the surface running down to the corners of the octagon where the junction is weighted with decorated stone vases. The powerful shape of the drum is emphasized by panels in the light surfaces and light semi-circular-headed windows, with deep reveals, set well down in the drum. The dome is here developing that dynamic quality which characterizes the later examples. The main dome and drum are supported by three saucer domes, one over the apse and one over each transept.

Our Lady of Grace, the parish church of Zabbar which Dingli **201** started when he was fifty years old, was his last important church. Only the architecture of the nave and the exterior of the aisles and transepts show his mark; the rest of the church is later. The nave barrel vault is supported on fluted Corinthian pilasters resting on **202** panelled pedestals. These pilasters and the cross arches of the aisles support a full rich entablature carved with dentils and modillions. There is a clear distinction between the function of the Corinthian pilasters and the Doric pilasters which support the aisle arches. Though both are approximately the same height, the first are raised to their necessary height by the pedestals, and in this way there is no conflict at the bases. Whilst the handling of the parts is more competent in the work of his old age, the details are more mannered. The bays of the barrel-vaulted nave are decorated with a lineal pattern developed from his earlier coffered work, and to get the maximum effect of the pattern he has omitted the two intermediate ribs of each bay. The main ribs are carved with long narrow rectangular patterns set in pairs to contrast with the surface of the barrel vault, and a feeling of added strength is given to the crossing by using double ribs clearly divided by a space of roof. The apse and transepts have corner pilasters reaching their full height and a full entablature broken forward over the corners. The pilasters are panelled in Dingli's usual manner. Not content to leave the bold outline of these wings he has added corner vases and a crowning centrepiece to each wing.[267]

The dome is Baroque and clearly not the work of Tomasso Dingli. Stylistically it seems to belong to the work of Lorenzo Gafà (1630–1710) and therefore can hardly have been built before about 1660. The tall drum pierced by bold semicircular-headed windows set in

267. These may be later additions put up with the dome.

panels, the coupled pilasters with their entablatures broken straight across the corners, the attic between dome and drum, and the bold curling scrolls working down with coupled ribs over a tall dome, are all characteristics of Gafà's work.[268] If he designed the dome of Zabbar, it seems unlikely that he did it before 1675,[269] which was the year he designed St. Nicholas parish church at Siggiewi.

The façade was built in 1738 and the towers in 1742.[270] The aisles are probably about the same date. The façade is ornate and has many eighteenth century characteristics in its details.[271] The discoloration of the stonework and the large mortar joints make it appear more fussy and more broken up than it actually is.

Santa Vennera parish church was begun in 1647. Luqa church, which has been ascribed to Tomasso Dingli,[272] was begun in 1650. The façade and steeples are later. The church was almost destroyed by bombs and is now being rebuilt. The parish churches of Ghaxaq and Gudia date from 1655[273] and 1656.[274] Balzan church, dedicated to the Annunciation, has a rich and unusual façade with elongated pilasters and was built during the years 1669 and 1695.[275] Here is a façade with a strongly Spanish flavour. The disproportion of the members and the lace-like quality of the decoration are characteristic, and it is the exception which proves the generalisation that Maltese church architecture is predominantly Italian in character. How else would the façade stand out so markedly as of a different quality from the usual Maltese façade?

With the death of Tomasso Dingli in 1666 the late flower of the Renaissance on the island faded and the Baroque of Italy and of Sicily, where it was marked by Spanish influence, replaced it in all important church architecture which followed.

The first parish church to show the full effect of the Baroque was the church of St. Nicholas at Siggiewi, begun in the year 1675[276] to

268. See the domes of the parish churches of Rabat, Vittoriosa, Zejtun, Siggiewi, and the Cathedral at Mdina.
269. Rutter p.133 gives the dates 1676–93.
270. Inscription on the porch and upon a crest between the towers.
271. The porch windows occur on 18th century aisles to St. John's, Valletta; St. Augustine's, Valletta; the early 18th century loggia at Rabat; and St. Bartholomew, Zurrieq (1774). The spires are strongly Spanish in flavour. A type also used by Cachia and by the architect of the church of the Immaculate Conception at Msida.
272. Valletta Museum photograph gives the date as 1565 and the architect as Dingli. It also states that the side steeple was designed by W. Baker in 1858.
273. Braun, *Works of Art* p.6.
274. Braun, *Works of Art* p.6.
275. Bonello, article *Malta* p.45. Notes the fine dome of Balzan church.
276. Braun, *Works of Art* p.27.

the design of the Maltese architect Lorenzo Gafà. In the nave he 205–208
used coupled composite pilasters with a sharply cut entablature
broken forward over them. He then interposed a tall attic band,
richly sculptured, before the springing of the vault.[277] In this way the
ceiling was made higher and the interior more spacious. Then for
the ceiling itself he used a barrel vault with small intersecting vaults
so that ample windows could light the nave. This is a decided break
from the conservative barrel vault of the past and in line with
current practice in Italy and Sicily, where Gafà had studied and
travelled. The vault, now released from the rigid line of its predecessors, becomes a field of pattern and picture-making and the Baroque
painter is given full opportunity. Gafà came under the influence of
the Baroque painters during his stay in Rome, and his brother,
Melchiorre Gafà,[278] was a notable sculptor of the time. Both the
sculptured attic band and the serried rows of pilasters are more
clearly shown at the end of the south transept, and he used this
pilaster treatment to build up a massive support for the springing of
the dome at the crossing. In the dome, the high drum and the 204
central lantern windows throw two saucers of light painted panels
between the ribs of the dome.

Externally the dome is unique in Malta. It stands so proudly
aloft on an extremely high drum that it seems not to belong to the
main body of the church. Nowhere else does Gafà raise his dome so
high, and here the explanation may be that he wished to raise the
dome clear of the façade and realised the impossibilty of doing this
with a normal height of drum because the village street leading to
the façade runs uphill. The treatment of the façade is truly dynamic. 203
Like a ship in full sail, thrusting its bow forward, it is set trailing its

---

277. The imposition of a high attic course between the entablature and the
springing of the arch of the vault is carried out through a desire to
increase the apparent height of the church. This conscious desire for
verticality is surely closely akin to Gothic, and is just another mani-
festation of the strange link between the two styles. The attic course
occurs in the following churches in Naples : 17TH CENTURY—SS. Apostoli
by Francesco Grimaldi, and on La Sapienza also by Grimaldi, but here
it only occurs over each pilaster on the arch rib of the vault. Frate
Nuvolo uses it on S. Sebastiano, but the function is slightly different
here, for this is an oval church with superimposed orders, and above
the upper order he uses this band to define the drum before the springing of the dome. Cosimo Fanzago on S. Nicolo della Carità, and S.
Ferdinando. In the former it again occurs only over the pilasters, and
the intervening space between the clerestory windows is left plain. He
also uses the motif on Ascensione a Chiaia, S. Giorgio Maggiore, and la
Pietrasanta : 18TH CENTURY—La Nunziatella by Sanfelice, Concezione a
Montecalvario by Vaccaro, SS. Trinità dei Pellegrini by Vaccarini, and
Spirito Santo (1775) by Mario Gioffredo.
278. c. 1630–67.

two campaniles in the wash. The fine and powerful porch, the last important addition to the church, was added in 1864.

While Siggiewi church foreshadows later work on the island, the parish church of St. Mary at Mqabba lingers in the past, although it was not begun until fourteen years later. Its dome is similar to that on the parish church of Zurrieq, though the panels containing the windows are smaller and the parapet larger. The dome is not powerful and is low and partly hidden by the parapet.

As well as designing St. Nicholas at Siggiewi, Lorenzo Gafà designed the parish churches of Vittoriosa (1681)[279] and Zejtun (1692)[280] and the cathedrals at Mdina (1697)[281] and in Gozo (1697).[282] Because of the quantity and the quality of his work he is one of the most important architects who worked in Malta in the latter half of the sovereignty of the Knights. All his churches have the grace and good proportions which distinguish works of the Roman Baroque, and none of the efflorescence of the Spanish Baroque which is so abundant in the kingdom of the Two Sicilies. Despite the 'plastic' qualities of Maltese stone, the architects have retained a discipline in design which is refreshing in comparison with contemporary work in Palermo, Syracuse, and the rebuilt town of Catania.[283]

The parish church of St. Lawrence in the old city of Birgu (renamed Vittoriosa after its valiant stand against the Turkish invasion) was completely rebuilt in a larger form from the designs of Gafà in 1691.[284] It has the usual Latin Cross plan with three bays to the

279. Paribeni p.84 states that it was rebuilt in 1697.
280. Braun, *Works of Art* p.46.
281. Rutter p.121.
282. Zerafa p.25.
283. Sitwell, *Southern Baroque Art* p.303. Fleming p.169 is quite wrong when he talks about the exuberance of the architecture in Malta. For its time it has a remarkable sobriety. He states that 'it flourished with unparalleled gaiety and exuberance . . . barley sugar columns tried to look at home among the prickly pears (p.170) . . . although locally produced, Maltese architecture can hardly be considered indigenous and there is little or nothing uniquely Maltese about it . . . they regard architecture purely as a form of exterior decoration and grafted ornaments they had copied from Europe onto their own primitive building style as if it were some kind of low-relief wall paper.' One writer has noticed that this is not so. Luke p.78 says 'Its Baroque [Mdina] in buildings such as the graceful episcopal seminary is, in fact, more like the restrained Baroque of Salzburg and Vienna than the frenzied extravagances of the architects of the period in Sicily and Calabria.'
284. Inscription on aisle door. This was the original Conventual church of the Knights before St. John's was built in Valletta. Scicluna states that it was here that the Knights first worshipped on their arrival. Braun, *Works of Art* p.44 states that they first worshipped in the chapel of St. Anne. St. Lawrence was sometimes called St. Lorenzo a Mare and

nave and a portion of a bay added at the west end to accommodate the galleries. On the south side there are two sacred chapels which lead into the south aisle. Buildings are placed along the whole length of this side; but on the north wall there is a side door opening onto a small square with the oratory of the Holy Crucifix (1720) on one side and the eighteenth century church of St. Joseph closing the inland side and touching the north transept of the parish church.

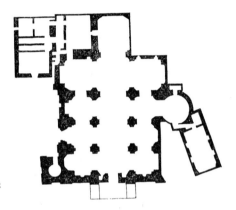

36. *Vittoriosa. Parish church
    of St. Lawrence.*

The whole site is restricted, and steps climb up from the water's edge to the west front of St. Lawrence. The interior of the church is similar to St. Nicholas at Siggiewi, but a richer effect is obtained by forming clusters of pillars, laid one upon the other, down the side of the nave. The pilaster shafts are of pink marble, their bases are biscuit coloured, and the plinth which surrounds the church has a mottled effect obtained by using black and dark green. The attic band is there, but lower than the one Gafà used at Siggiewi; and above the vault is a field of decoration, panels of painting and ribs decorated with a leaf motif picked out in gold. The apse is flat and pierced with an oval eye set vertically above the high altar : this is a distracting sight and less commendable than the oval panel with its radiating lines and the recessed apse at Siggiewi.[285] In his later work at the Cathedral he is unable to use this motif because he was forced to incorporate the apse of the old church in his new design.[286] The dome of St. Lawrence was damaged in 1942 and had

according to Bosio III pp.89a, 871e, and ARCHIVES 360 p.519, it was used as the Conventual church from 8 September 1530 until 1571.
285. This may once have been a window which has been filled in.
286. This apse was actually part of the earlier Cathedral and was incorporated into the new building by Gafà to preserve the mural by Mattia Preti.

to be pulled down. This is a great loss, for Gafà excelled in the design of domes; but each side chapel, formed in the aisles, is covered with a dome. The pendentives are carved with a delicate lineal pattern, while the surface of the dome is left unadorned to contrast the rich decoration of the church and to act as a reflector to the light which pours down from the central eyes.

The façade, because of the site, is raised on a high plinth and approached by a flight of steps. It is a powerful sturdy façade with coupled Corinthian pilasters on the lower order and block-like slabs of pilasters above. The centrepiece is linked to the wings with Vignolan scrolls, and the church has two squat towers. The unfluted pilasters, the powerful main cornice, and the block-like projections and recessions, make this a monumental façade suited to the parish church of the militant city, Vittoriosa.

In contrast to this his next church, the parish church of Zejtun begun in 1692, is much more graceful and elegant : here the full orders are used; Doric on the lower order; Ionic superimposed. This gives additional height to the façade; and to further this end Gafà has carried the superimposed order across the whole front of the church and he repeats it down the sides, forming the finest buttressed screens on the island. These are rhythmically graceful, with a larger intercolumniation pierced by arched openings. The western towers are taller and more graceful than those on St. Lawrence, and where a sturdy effect is obtained in the latter by using coupled pilasters, in the former greater elegance is achieved by building the pilasters one upon the other. This gives a tower narrower in proportion, emphasized by a stronger chiaroscuro. The centrepiece has a third superimposed storey of stumpy pilasters, spreading scrolls, and a broken segmental pediment. On the façade the pilasters are clustered to give the necessary depth to the composition, but on the side elevation this was unnecessary because of the deep wells of darkness cast in the screen walls, and the pilasters could be set either singly or coupled. The crowning magnificence of the dome is a masterpiece of dynamic design, only equalled in Malta by Gafà's later dome on the Mdina Cathedral.

Gafà was sixty-seven, and his architecture had reached maturity, when he was commissioned to rebuild the cathedral church at Mdina. The new church, which is one of the two really important works of architecture in Malta[287] worthy of comparison with anything found abroad, was built when Malta was at the height of its

287. The other building is the parish church of St. Helen at Birkirkara designed by Cachia in 1727, and largely influenced by the Cathedral.

glory, and Gafà had benefited from the work of the pioneers and from his own practical architectural experience. The old cathedral was destroyed by an earthquake in 1693 : one of the series of serious earth tremors which affected the central basin of the Mediterranean at that time, and which caused such devastating damage to Catania.

In 1697 the Cathedral was started and it was completed five years later. The consecration took place in the same year, 1702. It has not the ponderous quality of his earlier work at Vittoriosa. Gafà realised, too, that the light-hearted mood of St. Catherine, Zejtun, **215** would be inappropriate for a cathedral church. The balance has produced a monumental façade which is not oppressive.[288] The superimposed orders, Corinthian below and Composite above, are carried the full width of the façade; plain unfluted pilasters are used and Gafà, sure of his proportions, has boldly left large areas of undecorated masonry. The centrepiece, crowned with a simple raking pediment, is set slightly forward from the wings which carry two rich squat towers. The doors and the single central window were originally covered with segmental pediments,[289] but the one over the main door was recently removed and a broken triangular **219** pediment substituted. The façade is set on a plateau raised three steps[290] above the level of the city square. The side elevations are models of simple composition : coupled Corinthian pilasters on a combined high base for the lower storey, their full entablature broken forward, carry pilaster blocks above. The intercolumniation below has traditional oval windows set back into rectangular panels; and above, arched openings, set in larger panels, pierce the screen wall. The screen has no functional use. It merely hides the nave **218** buttresses and is tied into the side of the larger façade screen. Throughout there is a careful balance of horizontal and vertical, a characteristic in Baroque art which is usually associated with work only in Rome. Once again, the dome is the masterpiece. Much bolder and far more dynamic than anything he has attempted before, Gafà mounts great folding scrolls on the surface of the dome, and brings forward the eight corners of the octagon with serried rows of coupled pilasters.[291] This dome and the rich interior are near

288. This turn toward a more classical restraint is also evident in the late Baroque architecture of Rome, in the work of the Academic School under the leadership of Carlo Fontana. From that city it spread throughout Europe. It will be seen in many of the later works in Malta.
289. This may be seen in old photographs.
290. As proposed by Borromeo p.5.
291. The idea is similar to S. Maria della Salute in Venice (1630) though the effect is quite different.

the summit of Maltese Baroque art and, unlike the Conventual church in Valletta, the work is all of one period.[292] Lorenzo Gafà also designed the Matrice in Gozo, now raised to Cathedral status. The Matrice and the Cathedral at Mdina were begun in the same year, but the former was never finished. Inside it are his usual characteristics : the serried groups of tall pilasters raised on high bases instead of the more distracting pedestals, the rich entablature and the carved attic which lifts the vault higher, the vault intersected in each bay to allow adequate light from cross windows above the entablature, and the semicircular apse which had been used at Mdina. The Matrice drum was built but the dome was never added. Instead, a shallow dome has been inserted inside so that it does not show on the outside, but in the interior it bridges the crossing. The usual buttress screens are also missing and the buttresses are clearly visible as one approaches the citadel up the road from the port of Mgarr. There are no western towers, and a façade of superimposed orders is similar to Vignola's design for the Gesù in Rome and the type of Jesuit façade which spread through Europe and the Spanish colonies in the seventeenth and eighteenth centuries. Instead of towers a tall campanile is attached to the north-east side of the church.

There is one other important parish church dating from the last years of the seventeenth century. In 1694 Giovanni Barbara designed his masterpiece, the church of St. Saviour at Lija.[293] It was his first important building, started when he was about twenty-four years old,[294] and it replaced the old parish church which was too small by that time. The interior of Lija church follows the example set by Lorenzo Gafà : the same grouping of pilasters; the high attic, this time panelled; and ample panels in the vault which, along with the curved semi-dome of the apse, are fields for the painters' work. It is curious how the Maltese architects almost invariably chose a plain area of flat unfluted pilasters and a simple outline of Doric or Tuscan capital and entablature. It is impossible to say how much Barbara learned from studying the work of Lorenzo Gafà. His style is certainly his own and quite distinct from that of the older architect, and he appears to have had opportunity to study abroad.[295] Barbara

222

133

224,225

---

292. Except the old apse. Bonello, article *Malta* p.45 says, when translated, 'the massive building of the cathedral . . . does not seem built from stone laid one on top of the other, but of rocky cliffs chiselled and folded by the exigencies of man.'
293. Braun, *Works of Art* p.10 and Zerafa p.30.
294. According to Tencajoli p.2 he was born about 1670 and died in 1730.
295. Tencajoli p.2 says that Barbara studied in Rome. Galea, *Malta* p.11 says 'famous abroad as a military engineer.'

has used tall graceful pilasters on his façade. They are in the Corin- **226** thian order, and raised up on high pedestals and a running base so that he could get the necessary height for the internal effect he required.[296] The centrepiece projects forward slightly and the two wings carry graceful towers with spires modelled on the Spanish fashion. The whole treatment is plain and simple with the decoration reserved for door, window, and spires. The church is raised above the little casual square by a double plateau marked with two sturdy pyramids raised on pedestals and ball feet; and the western door is approached by three low flights of steps, of four, three, and two steps respectively. The pilasters and their pedestals are carried in an even rhythm along the aisle and transept walls, and the only windows are deeply set rectangular openings just below the main architrave, lighting through pierced openings in the cross vaults. The dome is interesting. Without the great powerful shape we **223** associate with Gafà's designs, it nevertheless has a charm, and in style seems midway between the earlier domes of Dingli and Gafà's dome on the Cathedral. The dome surface, though not pushed high above the drum, sparkles with its silver coat in the sunlight, and the rolling consoles, capped with vases, rise out of its serene unribbed surface. Pilasters are broken across the corner and not thrust aggressively forward, and the cornice is continuously bold, supported upon sharp-toothed modillions. The vases are repeated, resting on pedestals over each pilaster, along the roof of the nave and transept in order to tie the dome into the design of the whole church.

The finest parish church on the island is the church of St. Helen **227** at Birkirkara, designed by Domenico Cachia[297] in 1727[298] at the age of twenty-seven. The church was completed by 1745.[299] In

296. Although the general disposition of the façade has little in common with the inter-penetrating temple fronts used by Palladio on his Venetian church façades, two characteristics of the Lija church, the tall pilasters embracing the whole façade, and the raising up of the pilasters on high pedestals, are generally rare in Italian church design, with the exception of those façades designed, or influenced, by Palladio. Most other churches of the time have façades made up of superimposed orders. The influence of Palladio on church façade designs was lasting. Wittkower, *Architectural Principles* pp.80–87. There are at least two façades in Italy coeval with Lija church which are strongly influenced by Palladio: S. Vitale, Venice (*c.* 1700) by Andrea Tirali; and the Cathedral at Castelfranco (1723), a posthumous work of Maria Preti. See also the close connection between the design of the lantern at Lija, with its square-headed windows and scrolls, with those by Palladio on the Zittelle and Redentore (1576–92) churches in Venice.
297. Sammut, *Profili,* p.15. Born 1700 and died 1790.
298. Braun, *Works of Art* p.1. But Valletta Museum photograph gives the date 1735.
299. Rutter p.142.

325 1744[300] he was called to rebuild and decorate the auberge de Castile et Leon in Valletta, and from the style of his work on the auberge it seems clear that he had actually visited works of architecture in Italy and Sicily. We do not know whether or not he had been abroad when he began the church at Birkirkara. He had had the examples of the work of Lorenzo Gafà to inspire him, but his façade is superior to these and superior to any contemporary work in Sicily. By the time he came to add the façade to St. Helen's church he was a master of plastic design, and this is all the more remarkable as we know of no other church or important building erected by him before that date.

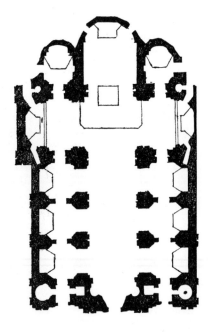

37. *Birkirkara. Parish church of St. Helen.*

37 The Latin Cross plan has the usual nave of 'three-and-a-bit' bays,
221 with aisle chapels, but the transepts are deeper than usual and
232 project beyond the line of the aisle walls. The apse, too, is more deeply set and the long eastward drive is not distracted by side entrances which normally occur in the middle bay. The interior has many Maltese characteristics such as the plain unfluted pilasters on high bases and the high attic band above the entablature, but the general effect is richer than is usual. Coupled Corinthian pilasters

300. Zammit, *Valletta* p.71.

support the twin ribs of the vault, panelled and incised with golden foliage. The vault and the apse are great fields of fresco, and the undersides of the arches leading to the aisles, and the domes and pendentives of these aisles, are richly painted and carved.

The dome is powerful and well proportioned, with a shallow protruding external surface similar to the dome of Lija church, but with ribs this time and with clusters of coupled pilasters similar to those on the cathedral drum. But the general effect of the dome is less dynamic than those designed by Lorenzo Gafà.

It is the façade which is the crowning glory of this church. As one approaches up the narrow street toward the west front, it is framed in the rigid lines of the houses; then, when one is almost on to the church, the view opens out into the piazza and the façade rises above two flights of moulded steps which sweep forward from the west door like rippling waves. The façade is based on the Cathedral west front, but the planes are more complex and the centre-piece projects more boldly. The scrolled superstructure of the centre-piece is a happier partner to the curved up lines of the two campaniles than the plain pediment of the Cathedral. The pilasters are more tightly coupled. This, with the build up of the steps in the piazza and the similarity of the three doors, gives a tautness to the façade which is sustained until it bursts out in a flaming magnificence above the second restraining band of the entablature.

The last important parish church[301] to be built during the Knights' occupancy of Malta was the church dedicated to St. Publius, the Roman governor converted to Christianity by St. Paul and first bishop of the island,[302] in the suburb of Valletta called Floriana. The foundation stone was laid in 1733 and the church completed and opened to the public in January 1768. The plan is a Latin Cross with deep elliptical transepts and apse. The nave has four bays and an additional half bay to hold the organ gallery and allow room for the western towers. In the original church the aisles must have acted as side chapels, but in 1856 the present aisle chapels were added, barrel vaulted along the line of the nave, thus freeing the aisles for circulation.

The façade was rebuilt in 1771, when the last bay and a half were added, so that as originally planned the church had the usual three-bay nave. The present façade, which consists of a Roman

229

216,218
227

301. Zerafa, *Discorso* p.30, attributes this church to Giuseppe Bonici, the Maltese architect of the Customs House, Valletta, as also does Calleja, *Giuseppe Bonici* p.5.
302. ACTS xxviii,7.

portico flanked by two tall towers, was added in 1882 replacing the old façade and western towers.[303]

The original dome, placed on an octagonal drum pierced by rectangular round-headed windows, did not rise high above the pedestals and vases at the corners of the octagon, but the surmounting lantern was of a slightly taller proportion to those usually found on Malta.

Centrally planned churches in Malta

Although the larger Maltese parish church was invariably designed on the Latin Cross plan, many of the chapels of the langues and the various monastic houses in Valletta (as well as numerous small churches of the later period built in the outlying villages) were designed with central plans based on the square, the circle, the octagon, the oval, and other related shapes. The chapels in Valletta, where money was readily available and fashion more earnestly sought, are rich examples of the architecture of the seventeenth and eighteenth centuries.

Though most of the centrally planned churches date from the end of the seventeenth century, there may have been at least one which was built in the sixteenth century and which still seems to have retained parts of the original plan : this is the church of St.

38 Catherine of the langue of Italy which was designed by Gerolamo Cassar[304] in 1576,[305] abutting the auberge of the langue in Merchants' Street, Valletta.

233 The present church is an octagon with a chancel set in a rectangular box. The semicircular windows on the side façades, which now come in the centre of the side walls inside the church, remind us of Cassar's work;[306] and the heavy squat pilasters at the corners of the façade, now pierced with recessed panels, are typical of him.[307] As the east wall of the church is, and always was, fixed by

287,57 the earlier building of the auberge d'Italie (1574), we must assume

---

303. The 19th century façade was designed by the Maltese architect Nicola Zammit. The church was seriously damaged in April 1942, when the dome and part of the façade were demolished.
304. Paribeni p.99. But there is no mention of this church in the list of buildings designed by Cassar as given in the ARCHIVES 1579–80–81 fol.270. It may have been built after 1581.
305. However, Fleming p.175 states that it was built in 1576. It was enlarged in 1683.
306. Aisle windows of Conventual church, Valletta.
307. Façade of Conventual church of St. John's, Valletta.

that the original church occupied the approximate position of the present one and was thus centrally planned, or extended the full

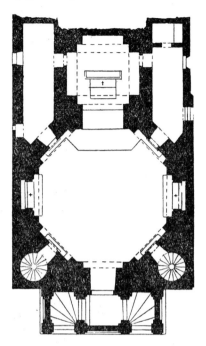

38. *Valletta. St. Catherine of Italy.*

length of the rectangle and was thus a longitudinal plan of stumpy proportions. Without further evidence the latter hypothesis would seem more reasonable, but we cannot exclude the possibility of a centrally planned church existing earlier in Malta than the seventeenth century.[308] And if we assume that possibility we must also assume that it was spanned by a dome.

The present interior is light and pleasant. The panelled pilasters are broken inward across the corners of the octagon, and the recessed chancel makes a convenient arrangement. The dome inside is spacious, with narrow graceful ribs leading up to a central eye which repeats the octagonal shape of the walls, leaving generous panels for carved and gilded decoration.

Caravaggio was called to Malta to decorate this chapel,[309] but it now contains two paintings by other important artists : *The Martyrdom of St. Catherine* by Mattia Preti, which hangs above the high

308. The centrally planned church was a feature of Italian architecture in the 15th and 16th centuries.
309. Paribeni p.90.

altar, and Benedetto Luti's painting of *Our Lady of Sorrows*.[310] The fine porch was added in 1713[311] when the façade was redecorated, and the steps leading to the west door are contained within the porch because the road restricts the area in front of the church. The porch is very similar to that added to the monastery of St. Margherita **234** at Cospicua.[312]

39. *Valletta. Our Lady of Pilar.*

40 Our Lady of Pilar which adjoins the auberge d'Aragon in Valletta is not a true centralized church, probably because of the narrow site. It has a two-bay nave which opens out into an octagonal centralized area, and then the space closes down again as it passes into the deeply recessed square chancel. Behind all this is the vestry, and a corridor which runs to it along the side of the nave and central area and against the back wall of the auberge.

The church was begun about 1670 and considerably improved in

310. Scicluna p.211.
311. Paribeni p.99.
312. Braun, *Works of Art* p.2. The monastery dates from the 17th century, but the porch was added later, and the line of the old pedimented porch is still visible above.

1718.[313] Its interior is richly decorated and the high altar is par- 235
ticularly magnificent. With its radiating apse it is similar in
character to the east end of St. Nicholas parish church at Siggiewi. 206

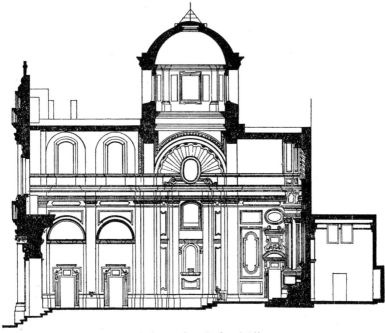

40. Valletta. Our Lady of Pilar.

A plain austere dome, with a high drum, rests on the octagon and
is probably not meant to be seen externally; it cannot be seen from 39
the narrow street in front of the church. The façade is tall and
narrow because of the restricted site, and it has superimposed orders
of about equal height, the upper columns and pilasters being slightly
more slender than the lower ones. The centrepiece projects slightly
and has two segmental arches, the upper one flattened. The full
width of the church is covered with a pediment. Because of the
sloping level of the street the façade had to be raised on a plinth
which accommodates the different levels.

If in 'Tal Pilar' the centralized qualities are doubtful, they are
certainly not in the Sarria chapel at Floriana. Lorenzo Gafà 212,213
designed it and it was built in 1678.[314] It replaced an earlier chapel

313. Braun, *Works of Art* p.5.
314. Braun, *Works of Art* p.5.

dating from 1585. Although this was only his second known work, begun two years after the parish church of St. Nicholas at Siggiewi, it has all the power we associate with his architecture. Because the chapel is circular, no giant scrolls were required to connect the dome to the drum and translate one shape to another. But the form of the dome is strong, with grouped ribs coming down on to grouped pilasters, and the projection of the cornice kept small so as not to break the line of the dome and the vertical walls. Both inside and out, pilasters are raised up on pedestals, but the interior is slightly smaller so that Gafà is able to introduce his favourite attic band above the internal cornice before the springing of the arch, and before the level of the external cornice is reached. In this way the springing starts at the same level inside and out; the inner surface of the dome is a true hemisphere, the outside slightly flattened to give the necessary extra depth at its base.

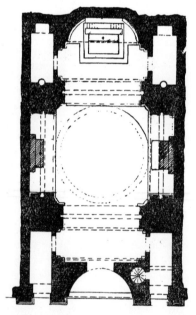

41. *Valletta. St. Roch.*

The plan of St. Roch is an attempt to build a centralized church on a narrow restricted site, of the type which abound in cities like Valletta.[315] The entrance is set in a deep niche to allow people respite before passing from the street into the church. The usual flights of steps and ample plateau of the parish churches or the

315. Plots are made up in this way because of the high value of the frontage onto an important street.

atrium treatment of the small village churches was not possible in busy Merchants' Street. The façade had to be built up to the **236** pavement, and yet room had to be provided to allow people to enter. St. Roch is admirably arranged within these limitations. The concave entrance draws in the congregation which is steadied by the cross emphasis of a rectangular compartment before it enters the central domed area of the church. As the eye passes on, its movement is slowed down by the rectangle containing the high altar and the vision is finally enclosed and turned back onto the altar by the concave apse. It is an ingenious plan. Complete segregation of the central area is achieved by the four barrel vaults which surround it and support the dome. The dome is invisible from the street and it **237** is only possible to see it from the roof tops. For this reason it is made a plain statement. The octagon, pierced with unmoulded segmental-headed windows, supports a low dome, and the transition from the octagon to the circle is disguised by five steps which are set back across the surface of the dome.[316] The façade, though difficult to see fully because of the narrowness of the street, is an equally fine composition made up of a balance of plain surfaces and a subtle play of curves. The concave entrance is contained between two slightly projecting wings of Corinthian pilasters. Each wing has a segmental pediment so that the sky line sweeps over from each side and then up again to the plain raised bell-cot in the centre. The architect of this charming little church is not known.

Smaller country churches with centralized plans

The large parish churches which were required to hold large congregations could best be designed in the form of a Latin Cross;[317] but the small country churches and chapels, used mainly for confession and private devotion, could be planned quite conveniently as centralized buildings, usually square outside, and domed. Malta has numerous examples of this type of church dotted about the countryside, built during the eighteenth century. These are all similar in their general arrangement and differ only in detail.

St. Margaret in Siggiewi, built in 1707,[318] stands out into the **245**

---

316. The dome is similar, but of course much smaller, to that proposed by Bramante for St. Peter's, Rome.
317. The clergy have always favoured this plan shape and opposed the centralized plans for larger churches. This was particularly the case with St. Peter's, Rome.
318. Braun, *Works of Art* p.27.

street and is visible on three sides. It is an attractive little church with a shallow dome on a squat octagonal drum, which gives an octagonal space inside the church. The interior is lit from a graceful buttressed lantern and from a window in one side. The façade has the usual pilasters defining the shape at the corners with small broken entablatures above, the main entablature being carried around the church on a recessed plane. The centrepiece, carrying a stone cross, is linked to the vases by Vignolan scrolls, and the bell-cot is placed on one of the side walls above the window, and not, as is usual, in the centre.

247,244   St. Peter's church in Lija and St. Roch, Mdina, were both built in the same year, 1728,[319] and they have the same characteristics as St. Margaret's, Siggiewi : the same giant order, this time Ionic at Mdina, and the same corner pilasters pronouncing the general shape of the church. St. Peter's church has a circular window, and both have a decorated framework over the door. St. Peter's has a raised plateau in front, its boundary marked with stone posts and steps. When space was available this plateau was always provided. St. Roch is a particularly serene example sparsely applied with gracious decoration.[320]

The most charming examples date from the first three decades of the eighteenth century, and there is a large number which I have not described or illustrated here. Toward the middle of the century the façade tended to become a little too complex for churches of this size, though many are admirable works of architecture. 'Tal 246   l'Abbandunata' at Zebbug, started in 1758, has a rich and impressive example. The treatment of these church façades is effective because the climax is sustained, and the building up is constant to the central feature of the great scrolled lantern and cupola. The same Baroque treatment applied to a palace or other secular building is seldom successful, because the façade is too spread out to sustain and concentrate the interest on the centre. The stone of this church is 'plastic,' moulded in the mason's hand to innumerable planes and surfaces where the light strikes across the surface of the building. Every artifice of curve and contour is employed, but beneath it all we can still discern the rudimentary characteristics of the small Maltese church : the giant corner pilasters, the central windows, and the two small windows which, low down against the

319. Braun, *Works of Art* pp.10 and 14. St. Roch was rebuilt in 1728.
320. It is a pity we do not know the names of the architects of more of these charming little churches.

plinth, flank the door. The area in front of the church is laid out in the most elaborate fashion. The street curves in a serpentine shape along the side and across the front of the church. At one end of the curve, and at the back of the church, a campanile is placed; and in front a raised plateau, walled and with seats against the inside of the wall, comes forward decreasing in width. The front wall of the plateau is slightly concave in shape and a flight of steps sweeps forward in a convex shape across the centre, playing against the concave line of the wall. This is the final stage in the development from the early atrium of Our Lady of Victory at Ta Qali.   127

The last two small churches which I shall describe are the little church of St. Mary of Porto Salvo in Hamrun, built in 1736, and   248,251
St. Bartholomew at Zurrieq. The first consists of a square box about eighteen feet across, with a wide recessed panel on each side supporting a thin arch which in turn supports the drum and the dome. The altar is set in a niche and a side door leads to a long corridor which passes down one side of the church. In spite of its small size the church has a rich façade of many planes. The two tall Corinthian pilasters have slightly lower Doric pilasters flanking them and standing on lower bases. The architect of this church is not known, but the similarity between the raking cornice on the south wall   248
inside the church and the armoury door of the Magisterial palace in   249
Valletta, should be noticed. Both are unusual; both spring from the centre of the corona and curve outward.

St. Bartholomew at Zurrieq, built in 1774, only twenty-four years before the Knights were forced to leave Malta, shows all the characteristics of small church architecture of the second half of the eighteenth century.[321]

Centrally planned churches of the 18th century in Valletta

In 1612 the church of St. James was built in Merchants' Street,   241
Valletta, at the expense of Fra Pietro Gonzales de Mendoza, Grand Chancellor of the Order;[322] in 1710 it was enlarged by the Maltese architect Giovanni Barbara.[323] This enlargement must have been little less than a complete rebuilding. The plan is based on the oval

---

321. Except the original treatment of the main door. It has a sculptural richness and freedom which is rare in Malta and which borders on the licentious.
322. Scicluna p.211.
323. Fleming p.175.

with entrance doors onto two of the city's crossing streets. The altar is recessed in a deep niche opposite the main door and another niche is placed opposite the secondary door. There are eight pairs of coupled pilasters around the oval, with coupled ribs leading to an oval opening in the cupola lit from the lantern. The pilasters are placed with alternate large and narrow intercolumniations to allow room for doors and large niches in the wider spaces. This church is said to have been derived from the best work of Borromini in Rome,[324] but I can see little connection, either in style or in plan arrangement. Though the architectural embellishments are not as

222–226 academic at at Lija parish church, which Barbara designed sixteen years earlier, they are still a long way from the flowing wall surfaces

42 which characterize Borromini's work. The plan of St. James is a straightforward statement : its walls following the line of the oval, not weaving in and out like in the fluid plan of S. Carlo alle Quattro Fontane in Rome.[325]

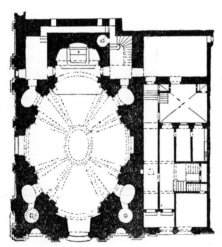

42. *Valletta. St. James.*

Barbara's plan combines the advantages of the centralized plan with the directional line from west to east, retained in accordance with the ideals of the Counter-Reformation Church. Centralization is preserved by the cross axis from the side door to the altar in the opposite niche.[326] Paldini painted the picture of *St. James* which now

241,242 hangs in the church. The screen façade of superimposed pilasters is

324. Bonello, article *Malta* p.45.
325. Scicluna p.211.
326. It is very similar to Vignola's Sant'Anna dei Palafrenieri, Rome. Cf. Fasolo, *Schemi centrali* in ARCHITETTURA E ARTI DECORATIVI 1931.

much richer than that applied to St. Saviour parish church at Lija,
and shows how Barbara's taste changed as he grew older. He was
probably well over forty when he designed this façade for St. James'

43. *Valletta. St. James.*

church, and it has few details in common with the Lija façade. The
pilasters are richly grouped and the doors and windows ornately
carved. The crowning cartouche over the central window is particularly magnificent. He has mixed the vernacular with imported
Roman detail. The curved supports of the lower windows are
traditionally Maltese, the door and window pediments and supports;
and the festoons in the upper frieze are imported. Where at Lija he
was content to leave wall surfaces unadorned, here he has obviously
felt compelled to panel and carve the blank walls on each side of
the central window.

The small Nibbia chapel, now in ruins, was built in 1731.[327] It lies at one end of the Great Hospital in Valletta. A sad loss as it was once a charming little eight-sided building of dignified proportions!

St. Barbara, the church of the langue of Provence in Kingsway, was begun in 1739 to the designs of the Maltese architect Giuseppe Bonici.[328] Its plan is based on the oval shape which is contained in the narrow rectangular site, but the interior is less centralized than St. James. The oval is extended eastward to an enlarged area containing the high altar. This tends to elongate the oval and there is no strong cross axis as in Barbara's church. It is a tall building and has superimposed orders both inside and out. The façade is rigidly tied between planes of upright pilasters and horizontal bands of entablatures and lintels. The skyline is severe, with the straight and triangular shapes of the cornices. Only the centrepiece of the lower order, which breaks out into a broken pediment and into the round-headed niches above, disputes the severity of this academic façade.

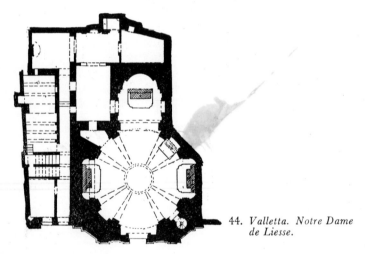

44. *Valletta. Notre Dame de Liesse.*

There is never anything loose or ill-considered in Bonici's architecture; he is a model of control and discipline. His Customs House at Valletta, begun when he was sixty-seven years old, is one of the finest works of the Academic School.

The plan of Notre Dame de Liesse, which was rebuilt in 1740,[329]

331–332

44

327. Zammit, *Valletta* p.46. Original chapel 1619. Rebuilt 1731.
328. Zammit, *Valletta* p.36.
329. Calleja, *Works of Art;* Zammit, *Valletta* p.47. Built on the Marina in 1620 by Fra Giacomo Chenn de Bellay, Bailiff of Armenia. Rebuilt in 1740 at the expense of the langue of France. The plan is similar to S. Maria de' Miracoli, Rome (1662), but with side chapels less deeply sunk.

is similar to St. James by Giovanni Barbara, but it is worked round a circle instead of an oval shape. The rhythm of the intercolumniation is the same, with the wider parts over the three chapels

45. *Valletta. Notre Dame de Liesse.*

(there is no side door because of the site of the church) and the main door. The chancel is more deeply sunk than it is in the earlier plan. The Liesse church has a fine low dome moulded with bands of curved stone and buttressed with shallow heavy ribs which work down the line and become scrolls against the walls of the drum. Whilst by no means identical, the façade which was added to the church[330] of Our Lady of Victory in Valletta in 1752, has much in common with the Liesse church, and may well have been designed by the same architect. Both façades have the following features: the wings of the façades are splayed back, an unusual motif; the centrepiece is raised up as a rectangular block, and joined to the wings with Vignolan links; broken segmental pediments are used over the central door, and repeated above on one of the entablatures;

243

330. The plan of this church is much earlier than the façade.

finally, both churches have a single campanile. The one on the Victory church had to be placed half-way along the side of the nave because of the restricted site, and the flat roof of the campanile gives it a different character. It was probably never completed. The Liesse campanile is placed on one of the splayed wings of the façade and the large amount of masonry between the façade and the circular interior gives it a stable foundation.

The Augustinian church in Valletta, originally the work of Gerolamo Cassar,[331] was rebuilt in 1764[332] in the Baroque style. The new church is set within a square, so that the main body formed a Greek Cross with a square crossing and four double-square bays.[333] The corners between the Greek Cross and the outer wall are thus also square, roofed with small domes and lit by lantern windows. The arms have curved ends similar to the apse; but the apse is set further back, making the east-west arm of the church one bay deeper. It is a tidy, well thought-out plan, confidently handled. The interior has coupled unfluted Corinthian pilasters, and these are applied to half-pilasters so that the entablature, with its double break, has a jagged line of cornice. The attic band, made popular by Lorenzo Gafà, is again used, and above it the vault is a mass of rich decoration and colourful painting. In contrast to this richness, the four corner chapels are restrained and done in a plain dove grey. The clerestory windows are typically eighteenth century, rectangles with semicircular openings attached to the top and the bottom, though these are narrower than the rectangles. The façade, which from its style could have been built any time after the middle of the eighteenth century, is mainly made up of a series of shallow planes which advance and recede, and this sometimes diagonally, across the face of the church. It is a façade of superimposed orders with a centrepiece and wings joined by recessed panels. One western tower has been built and another was obviously intended. The carving and decoration, which are small in scale, are in fact almost apologetic, and confined to door and window heads and a small shy centrepiece at the summit of the façade.[334]

331. ARCHIVES 1581 fol.270.
332. Galea, *Malta* p.12.
333. This was a favourite arrangement of Bramante's, e.g., SS. Celso e Giuliano in Rome and Alessi's S. Maria di Carignano in Genoa.
334. The resemblance should be noted between the dome of this church and that by Barbara on St. Saviour parish church at Lija (1694). Galea, *Malta* p.12 says that this church of the Augustinians in Valletta was rebuilt by Dom. Cachia in 1764.

Summary of the characteristics of Maltese churches

The early church plan developed by the Maltese masons was a plain rectangular box spanned with arched ribs. Its shape was dictated by the method of construction they had developed in an island almost devoid of timber. The flat ceiling on arched ribs was gradually replaced by the barrel vault supported on arched ribs. This type of church was built as late as the end of the seventeenth century and the large Conventual church of the Order in Valletta 153 was designed in this manner. The Knights on their arrival added transepts and choirs to some of these Maltese churches, and these inspired the building of a number of large parish churches laid out in the form of a Latin Cross, but with the same method of roof construction which remained in constant use on the island until Lorenzo Gafà introduced the Roman Baroque cross vaults. This increased 220 the amount of light in the nave and transepts and freed the surface of the vault for use as a great decorative field of painting.

In Malta the centrally planned church seems to date from about the end of the seventeenth century[335] and after 1700 a large number were built, both as churches for the langues and the monastic orders in Valletta, and as small chapels in the villages which crowd the island.

Domes were placed over the crossing, first to the churches to which choir and transepts had been added, and later to the new larger parish churches, so that the dome became a great architectural feature dominating each village. It is possible to look across the island and pick out each village in turn, identifying it by the dome of its parish church. One of the earliest domes on the island was the low saucer dome, placed on a low circular drum, over the new crossing of St. Gregory at Zejtun, built soon after the Knights' 130 arrival in Malta. It had no ribs and no projections, and there were no windows in the drum. The saucer dome, on a high lighted drum, was developed from this prototype. The first example is the old parish church at Lija, built in the sixteenth century. Here for the 133 first time the drum becomes the church's source of light.[336]

---

335. There is the possible exception of St. Catherine of Italy in Valletta, built in 1576.
336. This dome, with its small projecting cornice to the drum, and its plain masonry surface, reminds me of earlier examples in Sicily. Its silhouette is like that of the 12th century dome on the Annunziata dei Catalani in Messina.

We have fully considered the possibility that Gerolamo Cassar may have planned a dome for the Conventual church.

Qormi (1584) is the earliest large parish church with a dome, but from its style of buttresses and ribs this seems to be much later than the church. Tomasso Dingli was the first to make important early contributions to Maltese dome construction, and until the latter part of the seventeenth century his work was the prototype. His domes are spherical inside, resting on a plain octagon with a parapet, so that externally the dome does not rise high above the level of the parapet.[337] The drum is large and pierced with windows, and there is also a top lantern with windows. Decoration is sparse and confined to pilasters at the corners, or alternatively, traditional Maltese mouldings with a simple cornice. At Attard parish church Dingli supports the main drum by two subsidiary saucer domes over the transepts. This form of dome is found on such other churches as Cospicua (1637), besides those designed by Dingli.

The magnificent domes designed for St. Nicholas at Siggiewi, St. Catherine at Zejtun, and the Cathedral at Mdina, are the result of Lorenzo Gafà's training in Rome; and they dominate the architecture of Malta in the last years of the seventeenth century. The dome and drum at Siggiewi are extremely tall, but these proportions are corrected in the later designs where Gafà has sculptured monumental works with all the recession and projection of Baroque design. His ribs are invariably coupled (except on the Sarria chapel in Floriana) and these lead into great rolling scrolls on the entablatures, broken straight across the corners of the octagonal drums and down onto serried rows of coupled pilasters.

In contrast to Gafà's work, the dome which Giovanni Barbara designed for Lija parish church is less ambitious. The dome sinks lower onto the drum, like the earlier domes; the scrolls rise out of the silvery surface of the dome. The Augustinian church at Valletta has a similar one.

Some domes were never intended to be seen externally because of the built-up character of the site. The dome of St. Roch in Valletta is an example of this. The church was altered in 1681 and the dome probably dates from this alteration. The octagonal drum, pierced by eight segmental-headed windows, is built up above the cornice with five steps, and the outer surface of the dome begins from the top step.[338]

---

337. Cupola of S. Annunziata at Marsala is similar.
338. Cf. Bramante's design for St. Peter's in Serlio III, 1551, and there are

In the eighteenth century Domenico Cachia followed the ideas of Lorenzo Gafà when he designed the dome for the church of St. Helen at Birkirkara, but the design is more reserved and less dynamic 229 than the earlier ones, and Cachia has returned to the Maltese tradition of sinking the surface of the dome and omitting Gafa's intervening band between dome and drum.

Centrally planned churches were roofed with domes, though these domes usually followed the Maltese tradition and were not pronounced externally. Lorenzo Gafà's Sarria chapel, as one would 213 expect, is the exception. Oval plans, of course, required oval-shaped domes : St. Barbara, Valletta (1739) has one of these.

There are three types of church façades which were used in Malta and these were all originally derived from Italy. The first is the typical Jesuit façade of two superimposed orders,[339] with the centre-piece raised up to correspond to the extra height of the nave and joined to the wings by Vignolan links.[340] Gerolamo Cassar's Augustinian church (1571) is the first façade of this type in Malta, though 152 the superimposed orders are omitted and only the general outline shown. It then develops in various ways : sometimes with western towers added to the wings as at St. Lawrence, Vittoriosa (1691), or it may be merely applied to a rectangular screen as a facing, a treatment seen in the eighteenth century church of the Magdalene in Valletta. The Gesù in Valletta and the Matrice in Gozo are two typical examples of this type.

The second type consists of a screen façade[341] of superimposed orders, divided into three bays, the centre one crowned with a pediment.[342] This façade is common on the larger churches and is some-

at least six other domes in Book IV, 1537, which have stepped domes. Antonio da Sangallo produced a design, which is similar, for the mausoleum of the Medici family at Montecassino. Cf. Palladio 1570, drawing of the temple of Vesta.

339. Derived from such churches as S. Maria in Vado at Ferrara by Ercole Grandi and Biagio Rossetti, S. Benedetto in Ferrara, and later Antonio da Sangallo's S. Maria in Sassia, and Guidetti's S. Caterina dei Funari (both in Rome).

340. This term is used because, like the term ' Palladian motif,' it explains an architectural motif most commonly associated with that particular architect, though it was used earlier by others.

341. The use of the screen façade is very old. There are many Romanesque examples in Italy, and the 15th cntury façades of S. Maria di Collemaggio at Aquila and S.M. dell'Anima in Roma by Giuliano da Sangallo, bear little relationship to the churches which lie behind. Giovannoni p.196 shows that the Italian church façade was often considered as a separate architectural entity and a separate work of art in itself.

342. This was developed from Michelangelo's designs for S. Lorenzo, in Florence.

times used with western towers, either superimposed onto the wings
or added to the extremities of the wings. St. John's, Valletta (1573), and Qormi parish church (1584) are examples where towers adjoin this type of façade; and Zebbug parish church (1599), the Cathedral at Mdina (1697), and the church of St. Helen at Birkirkara (1727), are examples where the towers are superimposed. Our Lady of the Pilar (c. 1670 improved 1718), the Carmelite church, St. James (1710) and St. Barbara (1739), all in Valletta, are examples of this second type of façade without towers.

The third and last type of church façade is developed from the ancient temple front. The whole façade is embraced under a raking pediment, so that in silhouette it is similar to the ancient Roman temple. It is best suited to a single cell building, as the temple was, and is therefore the logical façade for the early Maltese churches. These are astylar and have a low raking cornice of Grecian proportion. Alberti applied the temple front to a triple nave church at S. Andrea at Mantua and introduced a rhythm of two narrow intercolumniations flanking a wide central one. These corresponded to the narrow aisle chapels and wider nave in the church behind the façade.[343]

The use of the giant order on this type of façade in Malta appears on the late sixteenth century chapel of St. Anthony the Abbot at Verdala, near Rabat, and is used by Tomasso Dingli on his façades at Attard (1613) and the old parish church at Birkirkara (1617). He uses only corner pilasters and there is no indication on the façade of the division of the interior into nave and shallow aisle chapels. Dingli was the main exponent of this type of façade, but later examples include St. Roch at Mdina (1728), 'Tal l'Abbandunata' at Zebbug (1758), and St. Francis in Valletta (1681).

A very popular variation of this type of façade is where a bell-cot is placed at the apex of the pediment. This treatment occurs on the early astylar façades, such as St. Gregory at Zejtun; and it becomes a feature of the small churches of the mid-seventeenth century and eighteenth century. It had the advantage that it could be applied with equal ease to both longitudinally and centrally planned churches. Giant orders with bold entablatures were used, and the pediment was replaced by the bell-cot, which was joined to the

---

343. The all-embracing temple front was used in the 15th century in Italy, but often with superimposed orders below the pediment. Filarete's project for the façade of the Bergamo cathedral in his *Trattato di architettura*; Francesco di Giorgio on the Chiesa del Calcinaio at Cortona (1485); and Rosellino on the façade of Pienza cathedral.

corner pilasters by Vignolan links. The following churches are among the many examples of this type : St. Angelo, Zejtun (1670); Conception church, Zebbug (1677); ' Tal Hlas,' Qormi (1690); St. Catherine, Qormi (seventeenth century); St. Margaret, Siggiewi (1707); and St. Peter, Lija (1728).[344]

146
148,245
247

The use of the giant order for a façade flanked by western towers is a final deviation of this type. This occurs on the parish church of the Annunciation at Balzan (1669–95).

200

The constant use of bell-cots on the smaller churches, and bell towers on the larger churches, is a Maltese characteristic. It is not normally found on Italian[345] churches, but is common in Spain, the Spanish colonies, and Spanish-dominated Sicily.[346] Most of the small Maltese churches have a bell-cot in the centre of the façade, as for example on the chapel of St. Anne in Fort St. Angelo at Vittoriosa (*c.* 1534). The bell-cots are joined to the cornice or parapet, in the later churches, with Vignolan links. Our Lady of Sorrows (1590) at Hamrun, however, has a small campanile at one side of the façade.

131

134

Gerolamo Cassar was the first Maltese architect to use western towers. He used them on the Conventual church of St. John (1573–77), where they project forward on the flanks of the façade. After that, these tall towers are used in various positions. At Qormi (1584) they continue the line of the wings and are set back from the central face of the façade. At Zebbug (1599) the towers cut into the corners of the wings. At Birkirkara one campanile only is attached to the north transept. At Qrendi (1620) two cut into the corners of the transepts and at Siggiewi (1675) they continue the ends of the transept wall westward. At Vittoriosa (1691) they are applied to the wings of the façade and at the church of St. Dominic the façade recedes in a great concave curve between the two towers, in a

155

166

176
183
196
203

344. All these dates are taken from Braun, *Works of Art.*
345. The exceptions are S. Biagio at Montepulciano (1518–28) (only one tower was built), which was perhaps inspired by a drawing for a church with western towers made by Giuliano da Sangallo and illustrated in Loukomski, *Les Sangales* Pl. III; various designs for St. Peter's, Rome; and drawings of churches with western towers in Serlio. Also, S. Anastasio in Rome by Giacomo della Porta and the cathedral at Frascati (1700) by G. Fontana both have western towers, but show Spanish influence.
346. The following are just a few of the Spanish churches which have western towers: the cathedrals of Santiago and Cadiz; the basilica of Marfa; the cathedrals of Merida in Yucatan, Cuzco, Puebla, Mexico City, Lima, Panama, and Ilascala in Mexico. In Sicily and the Kingdom of Naples there are examples at S. Domenico, Palermo (18th century); S. Michele in Caltanisetta (1570–1622); S. Giovanni in Ragusa (after 1693); S. Annunciata at Airola by Vanvitelli; and S. Filippo Nero at Naples (completed early 17th century).

manner similar to S. Agnese in the Piazza Navona at Rome.

Most of the towers are crowned by spires. In the early churches by the Cassars and Tomasso Dingli they are plain and usually octagonal[347] but later, starting with the designs of Lorenzo Gafà and developed by Barbara and Cachia, they are much more ornate and Spanish in flavour.[348] The finest examples are to be found on the **227** church of St. Helen at Birkirkara (1727).

The way in which the western towers are linked to the end walls of the transepts in some of the Maltese churches is, so far as I know, a feature almost unique to Maltese architecture.[349] These screen walls, usually pierced by arched openings, hide the nave buttresses and continue the roof line of the transepts along to the entablature of the façade. This screen arrangement may be seen from above in the photograph of the roof of St. Helen's, Birkirkara. The feature **164** appears first in the Carmelite church at Valletta (1573) by Gerol- **189** amo Cassar. Dingli has used it in a modified form at St. Mary's, Attard (1613). The screen wall is carried to the full height, but the rectangular openings, not normally used for providing light, are here cut down into the thick wall of the vault and (in this case) light the nave. He used the same arrangement at Birkirkara. These screens **191** are used in Naxxar parish church but they are probably later than the main body of the church. They also appear on the parish **215,223** churches of Zejtun (1692), Lija (1694), Luqa (1650), St. Helen's, **228,230,218** Birkirkara (1727), and the Cathedral at Mdina (1697),[350] as well as several other churches on the island.

347. These rather squat pyramidical spires are found in Sicily. Cathedral at Cefalu (15th century and probably contemporary with Ambrogio da Como's central poritico); S. Lucia del Mela; the Santuario di Gibilmanna; and the 16th century Matrice Vecchia at Castelbuono.
348. This feature is also found in Italy but is probably Spanish influence. S. Atanasio, Rome; Frascati cathedral (1700); S. Annunciata at Airola by Vanvitelli.
349. But St. Paul's, London, has it. Could Wren have known the Maltese examples?
350. Dates from Braun, *Works of Art*.

CHAPTER THREE

Palaces, Public Buildings, and Houses

Early palaces in Mdina and Rabat

THROUGHOUT the late mediaeval period and, indeed, up to
1530, when the Knights of St. John landed in Malta, the architecture of the island was closely tied to its larger neighbour Sicily,
which lay to the north separated by a short stretch of water. Sicilian
influence extended in both the political field and the field of fashion;
but although dominated by her larger neighbour, Malta retained
much of her own individuality and her architecture is stamped with
a vigorous character which contrasts with the conservative quality
of Aragonese work in Sicily.[351]

Both islands suffered the same vicissitudes and Malta felt the effect
of piractical raids and political ferment so that the buildings of the
period, those that remain, are modest in scale and unpretentious.
Mdina, once called Notabile and later Città Vecchia when the new
city was built at Valletta, is the old capital lying on high ground in
the centre of the island, protected by an enceinte and comparatively
safe from the Turkish raids which ravished the towns of the sea-
board. It is in Mdina and its suburb, Rabat, that the important
examples of secular architecture of this period are found.

Early palaces and houses were probably single-storey buildings,
but from the beginning of the fifteenth century two-storey houses
were being built and a second storey was often added to the earlier
buildings.[352] Openings on the ground floor were few and compara-   **254·255**
tively small.[353] In plan the house was divided into three rooms. The
centre room, or hall, had four doors : one leading to the street and
one opposite leading to the courtyard at the back. The two other

---

351. Perkins pp.169–170.
352. e.g. the Norman House at Mdina.
353. Galea, *Malta* p.7.

doors in the centre of the cross walls led into the two rooms, one on each side of the hall. This was the basic plan of the Maltese house or palace. From the fifteenth century all houses had a courtyard at the back and those built on two floors had an outside staircase leading up from the courtyard.[354]

The shape and size of the houses was largely due to the constructional methods that were used and to the shortage of timber, most of which had to be shipped over from Sicily. Thick walls and strong cross walls, and often a slightly irregular plan shape, helped to resist earthquake shocks;[355] and the standard dimensions resulted from the need to carry the first floor upon cross arches placed one *kasba* apart.[356]

In some palaces, the Falzan palace is an example, the upper floor consisted of one large room across the front resting on the arches of the three lower rooms, with an open loggia at the back to which the courtyard staircase led. The upper floor had a flat ceiling resting on wooden cross beams which were probably imported.

252   The Norman House in Villa Gainon Street, Mdina, is a good example of this type of plan. The earliest part of the house originally faced in the opposite direction, onto a road which has now disappeared but which originally ran where the staircase now stands. This part dates from the fourteenth century, and its original door with a thin keystone placed off the centre of the pointed arch is a feature of the period. The house was originally upon one storey. When a second storey was added in the fifteenth century, the ground floor was, as usual, used as a store or for stables and kitchens, and the living quarters were moved upstairs. At the back of the house many alterations have been made and the present shape of the courtyard and staircase dates from the end of the sixteenth century.[357] The large four-centered arches, almost flat at the apex, which are often found in the courtyard of these houses, are probably due to Aragonese influence deriving from Sicily.[358]

All the buildings were plain and the term 'Gothic' may be used

354. The courtyard and the outside staircases are features of Spanish houses, especially in the area around Seville, and of houses in southern Italy and Sicily; e.g. Palazzo del Montalto and Palazzo Bellomo in Syracuse.
355. These are prevalent in Mdina. The Cathedral was destroyed by one in 1693 and again damaged quite recently.
356. About seven feet centre to centre, or five feet between the arches.
357. I am indebted to Mr. Olaf Golcher for this information.
358. There are numerous examples in Sicily and all parts of Italy built throughout the 15th century. Palazzo Bellomo, Syracuse; Palazzo Aiutamicristo, Palermo; Palazzo del Principe, Fondi; Palazzo Fabrizio Colonna, Naples; and Cronaca's Palazzo Guddagni, Florence; are only a few examples.

only with great reservation for the pointed arch of the fifteenth century windows. Ward Perkins has shown the interesting change which took place in the design of palace façades, from the fourteenth to the fifteenth century. 'The earlier buildings were often severely simple externally, but the effect was lightened and unified by the skilful use of such devices as shallow recessed surrounds to the windows and of mosaic-patterns of different coloured stone.'[359]

By the fifteenth century bleak barrack-like façades were in fashion and a conscious attempt was made to obtain this effect. The decoration was reserved for the small window surrounds and the triangular corbels which ran below the cornice and the string course of the first floor. On the Falzan palace these are laid out in a double row below the string course and a single row below the cornice and have small circular balls attached below them. The motif is similar to that found on the Palazzo Montalto (1397) at Syracuse.[360]

The auberges in the Birgu (Vittoriosa)

When the Knights settled in the Birgu they enlarged the old palace in Fort St. Angelo to make it a suitable residence for the Grand Master, and built for themselves seven auberges, one for each langue with the exception of the langues of Provence and Auvergne which were accommodated in the same building. There was no attempt to impose the cloistered seclusion of Rhodes, where the Knights had lived in a conventual enclosure called a *collachium,* separated by a high wall from the rest of the city.[361] In the Birgu the auberges were built alongside other buildings, and sometimes separated from each other by a considerable distance. Thus the auberge d'Italie lay at one end of the city, close to the walls of Fort St. Angelo; the auberge de Castile et Leon stood alone in Quarters Front Street; and the auberges of Allemagne and Angleterre, although joined, faced onto separate streets. Only the three buildings of the auberges of Provence (with Auvergne), France, and Aragon

---

359. Perkins pp.167–175. His article gives a very clear summary of the characteristics of the early palaces. I have only referred to them in so far as their plans are the prototypes of the buildings erected by the Knights, and some of their details were still in use in the 16th century after the arrival of the Knights.

360. Two of the early palaces are described and illustrated in Baerlein, *Two Houses in Malta* in COUNTRY LIFE LXXXVII, 22 June 1940, p.606.

361. Although the general area of the Knights' residences was still called the Collacchio area and subject to special laws. See Cardona, *Officio delle case.*

formed a compact block placed side by side in Britannia Street. Having broken away from the *collachium* the Knights never returned to its seclusion, and when the Convent moved to Valletta the practice started at the Birgu was repeated.

The new auberges were built about 1535[362] and their detail is essentially Melitan, barely touched by the Italian mouldings which **131** were soon introduced. But the chapel of St. Anne on Fort St. **259,261** Angelo (*c.* 1534) and the extensions to the Magisterial palace made in 1555,[363] carried out by the Grand Master de la Sengle, show a **263** break from this Melitan style : the 'fat' mouldings in the cornices of the Melitan buildings are replaced by a cavetto supported on corbels.

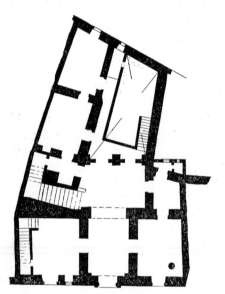

46. *Vittoriosa. Auberge de France.*

The auberge de France has a traditional plan which is similar to the Norman House at Mdina : it has a main block consisting of three rooms facing onto the street, the centre room pierced by four doors, one leading from the street, one leading to the courtyard behind, and two others opening onto the side rooms. Behind the main block there is a covered loggia, with the staircase contained within the walls, leading off from one side; and then directly beyond the loggia is an open courtyard. This house plan occurs time and time again in Malta up to the eighteenth century, but though typi-

362. Perkins p.173.
363. Perkins p.174.

cally Maltese, it is also found elsewhere, especially in Sicily.[364] On the first floor the staircase climbs to another loggia from which the main rooms may be entered. The area occupied by the entrance hall and the right-hand room is thrown into one on the floor above to make a large room which was used as the refectory. All the auberges at the Birgu occupied two floors.

47. *Vittoriosa. Auberge de France.*

The façade of the auberge de France was not completely symmetrical because another room was added to the east end of the first floor of the building;[365] and the balance of the first floor windows, with a narrower space between the two centre windows, is disturbed by the placing of the main door under one of these.

The windows and doors have been placed centrally inside the rooms with the knowledge that the façade could never be read as a detached façade in the narrow street, but only as part of a continuous line of houses.

The large area of wall (especially over the windows), the very plain treatment of the façade,[366] and the simple Melitan cornice moulding, give this, and all the Birgu auberges, a calm restful

364. Though in Sicily the entrance room is often replaced by an open passage leading to loggia and courtyard, e.g. Palazzo Montalto, Syracuse. The central court with rooms built completely around it, and with an external staircase in the court, is a more usual arrangement in southern Italy and Sicily.

365. I feel that the real reason for this lack of symmetry on the façades is that the Knights were still not conversant with the symmetrical architecture of the Renaissance in Italy, and continued the tradition of asymmetrical elevations which they had practised on their auberges in Rhodes.

366. These façades are remarkably like those of the auberges in Rhodes; with the same large bare areas of wall, and the same proportions of the windows, only here in Malta a pseudo-Renaissance decoration has replaced the mediaeval mouldings of Rhodes.

appearance. This auberge is the finest and the largest of the three in Britannia Street. The façade of the auberge d'Aragon completely lacks cohesion, and the windows of the auberge de Provence et Auvergne are too closely packed and irregularly spaced to present a restful appearance; both these façades are without cornice mouldings and they stand one on each side of the auberge de France.

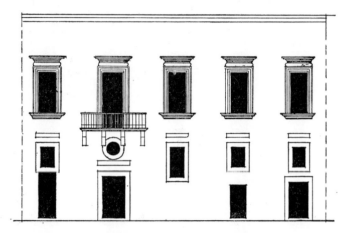

48. *Vittoriosa. Auberge d'Angleterre.*

The auberge d'Angleterre in Mistral Street has a façade of five main windows, with the door and the balcony over the second window from one side. There is a mezzanine floor lighted from the façade, and a characteristic Maltese circular window over the door.[367]

261,263   All these auberges are decorated with Melitan 'fat' mouldings:[368] heavy roll mouldings which are common in Maltese buildings after the arrival of the Knights in 1530 and which continue to be used until about 1620. They occur often in the Birgu, and in some of the early buildings in Valletta as well as in many of the country casals: there are good examples in Mdina, Qormi, Siggiewi, and Zebbug. The mouldings are applied to the three decorative fields of a building: the door, the windows, and, where the building has one, to the cornice. The design is distinctive and uniform except for very small variations in the friezes of doors and windows. Both the

367. It will be remembered that these windows occur over the main doors in many Maltese churches. Later they are used in palaces in Valletta, such as the Dorell, de la Salle, and Rospigliosa pp.159,160.
368. This apt description of the shape of the moulding has been made by Anne Cooke p.29. Whether or not she has invented the title I do not know.

doors and windows are tall and thin in proportion and are surrounded by a triple roll moulding which runs around the sides and
the top. The sill consists of a triple roll moulding, each roll projecting beyond the lower one, capped with a cyma recta curve and
a fillet.[369] Above the door or window there is usually a deep frieze
which is pulvinated, and then the sill moulding is repeated but with
greater projection. Finally a segmental arch, flush with the masonry
wall and undecorated, is constructed over the cornice to relieve the
load. The triple roll (or 'fat') mouldings always increase in depth
as they project, so that the inner, or lower one, is thinner than the
roll on the outside, or top. Variations occur in the frieze. Sometimes it is omitted altogether and a blank wall space left between the

49. *Vittoriosa. Auberge de
Provence & Auvergne.*

head of the door or window and the cornice moulding.[370] On a
window in Old Church Street, Siggiewi, the frieze is decorated with **265**
carved square medallions. The silhouette of the main cornice of the
building is usually similar to the door and window cornice, with a
cyma recta and fillet supported on a triple 'fat' moulding.

The auberge de France in the Birgu has a fine example of this, **263**
and the small sixteenth century house adjoining the church of St. **266**
Catherine of Italy in Valletta has another.

369. Renaissance mouldings in Italy usually only have a fillet over the cyma
reversa curve and not over the cyma recta.
370. This arrangement became popular in Valletta and G. Cassar used it,
but without the Melitan mouldings, on the palace and the auberge
d'Aragon, Fig.283.

The origin of these Melitan mouldings is not clear. They appear after the Knights' arrival in Malta so it is reasonable to assume that they were introduced by the Knights. Both Cooke[371] and Fleming[372] state that they were brought from Rhodes, but I can find no examples on that island.[373] Ward Perkins[374] states that it is hard to find parallel examples elsewhere and suggests that there is little connection with Rhodes, but that the influence may have come from Provence. I have found mouldings, which have certain affinities, on the Castle of Kyrenia in Cyprus, and St. Maria de Melque in northern Spain. In Cyprus the mouldings form the capitals of the columns at the entrance of the castle. At St. Maria de Melque[375] they occur at the springing of an arch. They also surround the buildings at cornice level on the outside, and form a continuous frieze inside, at the level of the capitals of the columns. In neither case are they used in a completely similar manner to those at Malta, and the only resemblance is in the actual fat, bulbous shape of the moulding.

It seems reasonable to assume that the way they were used in Malta was developed on the island itself; and whatever their distant origin they may safely be referred to as 'Melitan Mouldings.'

Early buildings in Valletta

In 1569 Eustachio del Monte began to build himself a house in the centre of the new city of Valletta, acting on the instructions of his uncle, the Grand Master Pietro del Monte. Some writers[376] have suggested that this was the first house to be built in Valletta, but it is certain that at least one house had been begun as early as 1566.[377]

The Council of the Order discussed the provision of a new Magisterial palace for the new city and chose a site on a high point in the southern corner, where the auberge de Castile et Leon was later built.[378]

Eustachio's house, which was built on the site of a main Turkish

371. Cooke p.29.
372. Fleming p.175.
373. I can find no reference to them in Gabriel, *Le Cité de Rhodes 1311–1522* which is the standard work on the architecture of the island.
374. Perkins pp.173–174.
375. Gomez-Moreno, *Inglesias Mozarabes arte español de los Siglos IX a XI*, Madrid 1919, p.24 and Figs. 9 to 11, and Plates II to IV.
376. Simmons p.8.
377. CODEX LAPARELLI, appendix II pp.1–12, gives account of expenses on a house built by Laparelli between 21 October 1566 and 22 March 1567.
378. Scicluna p.199.

battery, was originally 'a simple structure of wood with a dry stone wall to shelter it from the sun,'[379] but this must have been replaced by a permanent stone building very soon after. The Grand Master liked the site of his nephew's house and in 1571 he persuaded the Council of the Order to buy it on the understanding that it should be converted into the Magisterial palace. The general migration from the Birgu to the new city began in that year, and plans were quickly put afoot for the new palace as it was felt that its building would cement the foundation of Valletta and finally overcome the opposition of many of the Knights. Building may have begun in that year,[380] or shortly afterward, to convert the existing house into a much larger building. Grand Master del Monte died in January

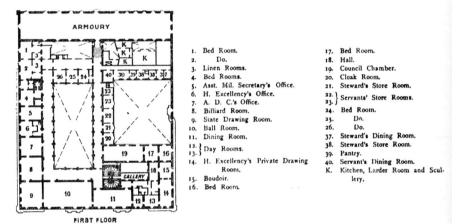

1. Bed Room.	17. Bed Room.
2. Do.	18. Hall.
3. Linen Rooms.	19. Council Chamber.
4. Bed Rooms.	20. Cloak Room.
5. Asst. Mil. Secretary's Office.	21. Steward's Store Room.
6. H. Excellency's Office.	22. Servants' Store Rooms.
7. A. D. C.'s Office.	23.
8. Billiard Room.	24. Bed Room.
9. State Drawing Room.	25. Do.
10. Ball Room.	26. Do.
11. Dining Room.	37. Steward's Dining Room.
12. Day Rooms.	38. Steward's Store Room.
13.	39. Pantry.
14. H. Excellency's Private Drawing	40. Servant's Dining Room.
Room.	K. Kitchen, Larder Room and Scul-
15. Boudoir.	lery.
16. Bed Room.	

50. *Valletta. Magisterial palace, first floor plan.*

1572 and the main work was carried out by his successor La Cassière. Gerolamo Cassar, engineer to the Order, was commissioned to design the new palace and had to incorporate the old building in his new scheme.[381]

The palace is built around two courtyards[382] and the old house of

379. Simmons p.8, and Scicluna p.199.
380. Scicluna p.199, but most writers give the date as 1572, including Bonello, *Old Valletta* p.163.
381. Bonello, *Old Valletta* p.163. 'Eustachio del Monte's house still exists in practically its original condition altered and enlarged by Cassar.'
382. Cassar's plan provided for only one large courtyard. This can be seen in a bird's-eye view of Valletta in A. F. Lucini, *Desegni della guerra assedio et assalti dati dall'armata Turchesa all'Isola di Malta l'anno MDLXV dipinti nella gran sala del palazzo di Malta d'Aleccio et hora intagliata da A. F. Lucini,* Bologna 1631. The palace then had only one gateway. The central block which now divides the courtyard into two was erected under G. M. Perellos (1697–1720).

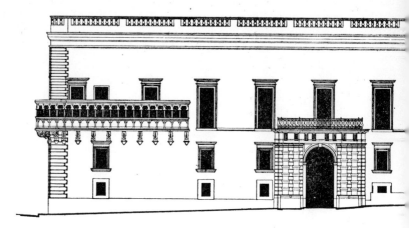

Eustachio del Monte can still be clearly seen in the south-west corner (rooms 12 to 17). Its old part is much more domestic in scale and consists of three rectangular blocks lying alongside each other to help resist thrusts from the arches' ribs which run across them.[383] The left-hand block of the old wing probably had a light well in the centre. The coherence of the rest of the plan is marred by this earlier work being incorporated into it and by later additions. The change of scale is obvious and this impedes the flowing qualities which the plan should possess. But in general it is typical of Cassar's secular work and similar to the plans of some of his auberges in Valletta. The long narrow blocks run the full length of the building, characteristically interlocking at one corner (room 9). This idea of abutting the rectangular blocks at three corners and interlocking at one corner, is strange and difficult to explain. That it was used consciously and not purely dictated by the site or other condition is clear, for Cassar does it so often. The rooms are intercommunicating, and, in addition, corridors surround the courtyards. Corridors are rare in Maltese buildings, but they may have been considered necessary in the palace because of its great size in comparison with the other buildings in Valletta and because of the need to pass from room to room without interrupting council meetings and audiences.

383. The three rectangular blocks can be identified in Fig. 50. One (Nos. 14,15, and 16), two (Nos. 13,18, and 17) and three (No. 12 with the rest of this block mutilated by the later addition of a corridor and room No. 19).

Some of the corridors are very long : the entrance corridor on the first floor is one hundred feet eight inches by seventeen feet eight inches wide.[384]

The main elevation of the palace, which faces on to Kingsway, **279** is disappointing. It shows all the disadvantages inherent in a building which is the work of more than one architect and is built over a period of years. The immense length of the building, about 316 feet, with a façade which has only two floors, would have been difficult to unite into a coherent and unified design without these added complications, and Cassar has made no attempt to get a rhythmical run of windows to assist him. The closer spacing of the windows at one end indicates the smaller rooms of Eustachio's house which lie behind the façade. Three pictures show the growth of the palace façade to its present state.[385] The old house had a tall arched entrance in the middle of its façade bounded by two windows on both the ground and the first floor on each side of the entrance gate. The extension made by Cassar began with the fifth window from the south-west corner and continued to the east. He increased the height of his main rooms on the first floor. The earliest picture shows the façade with the two roof lines.[386] Cassar's portion is considerably higher. The old arched entrance was filled and a window

384. Scicluna p.200.
385. This analysis of the façade is taken from Bonello, *Old Valletta* pp. 163–164.
386. Discovered by G. Preca Mizzi.

inserted on the ground floor and another above. This first floor window is considerably wider than the others (Fig. 51, third from right). The next picture, which dates from the time of Perellos (1697–1720), shows Cassar's roof line carried along the whole length of the façade, but still there is only one entrance gate onto Kingsway.[387] The two parts of the façade are still discernible and the rustication of the old part still runs from top to bottom.

The final print, in the Valletta Museum, which is earlier than 1741, still shows the one single gateway. The wooden balconies have been erected replacing the delicate iron railings of the early balconies. Under the Grand Master Pinto (1741–1773) the two new Baroque gateways were added to the façade.[388] They have coupled Doric columns, heavily rusticated, resting on large solid bases. The strong rustication is typical of the period and similar to many of the fine gateways erected in Malta during the eighteenth century.[389]

Gerolamo Cassar's work on the façade can be seen in the strong bands of rustication which bind the corners of the building. All his secular buildings are treated in this way, but the detailing and the moulding is different in each case. This rustication becomes a sort of hall-mark for his work, and its ponderous character is typical of his Mannerist architecture. The great width of the rustication, the deep cut of the mouldings, and the rhythm of the stones, should be noticed. Those stones on the south-west corner are slightly shorter and broken up in their length. They may be part of the earlier house of Eustachio del Monte altered by Cassar to agree roughly with the other corners of the palace. Gerolamo Cassar's interest in rustication may have been prompted by the assistance of Bartolomeo Genga,[390] or the fashion may have been copied from Laparelli[391] or again by examples he actually saw in Italy. For as Cassar studied in Rome he had the opportunity of seeing this corner treatment on many of the early Baroque palaces,[392] though never was it so powerfully used as it was by him in Malta.

The interior of the palace makes up for the austerity of the façades and the main audience rooms on the first floor are sumptuously apparelled. Whilst the ground floor is vaulted with stone

387. Lucini, *Desegni della guerra*, Bologna 1631.
388. Cooke p.24 wrongly ascribes these gates to Gerolamo Cassar.
389. For example: Fort Manoel gateway (1726) and St. Helen's gate, Cospicua (1736).
390. Genga used rusticated columns on the Palazzo Ducale at Pesaro.
391. CODEX LAPARELLI p.152r. refers to the angle of one of his buildings being *bugnato* (rusticated), with a window beneath an arch.
392. The Palazzo Farnese had rusticated corners and the fashion was taken up by the Palazzi Marescotti, Mattei, Pamfili, and Altieri.

arches, the first floor rooms have lofty wooden ceilings supported upon wooden beams. Because of the great span of the timbers they receive extra support from carved corbels, also of timber, which projects from the walls. The Knights had long experience in this form of construction : they had used it in Rhodes.[393]

The Council Chamber, which measures sixty-nine feet by twenty-five, has a fine set of Gobelin tapestries on the walls which was purchased by the Grand Master Perellos.[394]

The long armoury corridor has a flight of steps at the end and an impressive doorway with a concave entablature and scrolled curved pediments which spring above the keystone and fly outwards, leaving space in the centre for a carved bust.[395] The entrance corridor on the first floor has a carved ceiling painted by Nicolò Nasini da Siena in 1724.[396]

The finest room in the palace is undoubtedly the Hall of St. Michael and St. George, the throne room used by the Grand Masters on solemn occasions. It is a large room measuring eighty-five feet by thirty-seven feet and faces across Kingsway and St. George's Square. The walls are hung with red damask and large mirrors; and the frieze was painted by Matteo Perez d'Alesio.[397]

All the auberges in the new city, and there was one for each of the seven langues[398] in the Order, were designed by Gerolamo Cassar.[399] Each auberge was presided over by the head of the langue and the Knights lived there communally, very like the system of the Oxford and Cambridge colleges, taking meals in the hall, with privileged persons sitting at the high table placed upon a raised platform.[400] The Knights were obliged to dine in the hall at least four times a week.[401]

There is considerable disagreement about the dates when the various auberges were begun and finished; but working from the

---

393. The hall of the Magisterial palace in Rhodes. These wooden corbels also occur in 16th century Spanish ceilings, e.g. Salon de los Concilios in the palace of the Archbishops of Toledo in the Alcala de Herrares. Illustrated in Contreras III p.107.
394. Bedford, *Malta* pp.64–66.
395. Similar to the side altar in St. Mary of Porto Salvo, Hamrun (1763). The same out-turning pediments were used in the Tuileries palace in Paris.
396. Scicluna p.200.
397. Scicluna p.200, gives the dates of this fresco as 1601 to 1622, but Perez d'Alesio died about 1600.
398. The auberge of Angleterre was not built as the langue was forced to disband after the action of Henry VIII.
399. ARCHIVES 1579–80–81, fol.270.
400. Luke p.53.
401. Further information upon life in the auberges see L. Wilkinson, *Auberge de Provence* pp.4–5.

most reliable sources the following order seems reasonable. The auberge d'Aragon, the most simple of the auberges and single-storeyed, was begun in 1571.[402] This building housed the three Grand Priories of Aragon, Catalonia, and Navarre, and was built on the Marsamuscetto side of Valletta. The auberge d'Auvergne of the langue, which consisted of the Grand Priory of Auvergne and the Bailiwick of Lyons, was probably begun in 1574.[403] It was the plainest of the auberges and contained many of the 'fat' Melitan mouldings which we associate with Cassar's early work, and because of this was probably the first auberge completed.[404] The auberge d'Italie was begun in 1574[405] for the important langue of Italy, which comprised seven Grand Priories and five Bailiwicks. This langue had 142 commanderies and was only outnumbered by the combined 248 commanderies of the three French langues. The design of the auberge de Provence is more mature than any of the other auberges and, from the style, the year 1575[406] for its commencement seems reasonable. Considerable alterations were made in 1638. The auberge de France, which once stood in Strada Mezzodi, was destroyed by a bomb in 1942. Very different in style from the other auberges, it was begun in the year 1588[407] and was probably the last designed by Cassar. The auberge de Castile et Leon, though originally designed by Cassar, was remodelled by Cachia in 1744. The seventh auberge designed by Cassar was for the langue of Allemagne and it stood in the Piazza dei Celsi. Little is known about it, for it was demolished to make way for the English church of St. Paul designed by Scamp in 1842.[408]

As the Reformation in England (1534) had almost suppressed the langue of England, no English auberge was built in Valletta's early years. A site was reserved, bounded by Merchants' Street, St. Paul's Street, St. Christopher Street and St. Dominic Street, until it was later appropriated by the Grand Master Nicholàs Cotoner. In the hope of the reintegration of the English langue, Sir James Shelley, brother of the Turcopolier, purchased a plain simple house at the corner of St. Ursula Street and St. Christopher Street, and reserved it for an auberge by notarial deed in 1577.[409] The house is illustrated

402. Scicluna p.212.
403. Scicluna p.210. Built between 1570 and 1574.
404. Cooke p.12 and Pratt p.223.
405. Scicluna p.211, and Pratt p.223.
406. Pratt p.223, but Braun, *Works of Art* p.41 gives the date 1571. Unless the design was altered during erection, 1571 seems too early.
407. Scicluna p.210. However Bonici suggests it was not by Cassar at all.
408. Zammit, *Valletta* p.83.
409. Zammit, *Valletta* p.57.

and commented upon by Bartlett.[410] In 1782 the langue of England was combined with that of Bavaria,[411] and two years later the Bailiff Carner purchased the Palazzo Carnerio, which faces out across Marsamuscetto, for use as the auberge of the combined Anglo-Bavarian langue.

After that short summary of the building of the auberges in Valletta it is necessary now to consider their designs in detail. The auberge d'Aragon, built to the north of the Piazza dei Celsi, is on 283 the Marsamuscetto side of Valletta. This made it reasonably convenient for the Knights whose duty it was to defend the bastion of St. Andrew. The Pilier of the langue was 'Draper' or 'Great Conservator' of the Religion, in charge of supplies for the troops and the hospital.[412]

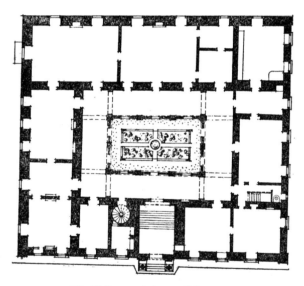

52. *Valletta. Auberge d'Aragon.*

The auberge is a plain one-storey rectangular building. A barrel-vaulted entrance leads into a peristyle surrounding a central court which is approximately twenty-three by forty-three feet. All the rooms which surround the court are intercommunicating and also open through doors onto the peristyle. There is a circular staircase on the left of the entrance leading to the flat roof. The entrance onto the piazza is the only one on the main floor, as the side street,

410. Bartlett p.13.
411. Porter p.304.
412. Zammit, *Valletta* p.39.

Strada Ponente, slopes away rapidly to the north-east allowing one to enter the basement from that street.

The doorway is a typical example of late sixteenth century Maltese work, semicircular headed with the architrave carried right round. The projection of the hood mould and a single large dentil below are characteristic of this type of design, which is used throughout the seventeenth century and occurs contemporaneously in Roman work.

Whilst the plan is clear cut and confident, there is no definite rhythm about the disposition of the rooms; neither is there pronounced symmetry, for the entrance is two feet off the centre line of the courtyard and about four feet from the centre of the main façade.

Though the plan seems similar to those of early Renaissance palaces in Florence and Rome, in actual fact it is a complete reversal. For instead of seeking a complete symmetry on the façade, Cassar has attempted to place the windows and doors centrally in the room, or balanced on the interior wall surface; with the result that, although a regularity has been attempted on the façade with three windows on each side of the door, and the building is tied in with Cassar's usual massive rusticated corners and a continuous cornice, the interfenestration is far from rhythmical. It reads as follows : 4 feet for the rustication on the left, then 10 feet, 10 feet, $9\frac{1}{2}$ feet and 8 feet to the doorway; $5\frac{1}{2}$ feet, 10 feet, 10 feet, 15 feet, and finally another 4 feet to the right-hand rusticated quoins. The façade to Strada Ponente is also unrhythmical with the interfenestration : 4 feet, 12 feet, 20 feet, 12 feet, 12 feet, $15\frac{1}{2}$ feet, $9\frac{1}{2}$ feet, and 5 feet, with 4 feet to the final quoins. Undoubtedly Cassar was influenced by events in Italy, and by this time Palladio had experimented and achieved a complete synthesis of the proportions both externally and internally in the design of his villas at Vicenza.[413] He had published the results of his work the year before Cassar began the auberge d'Aragon[414] and it seems to me that Cassar, dissatisfied by the earlier type of palace plan,[415] was unable to achieve the solution reached by Palladio.

Further proof of Cassar's interest in contemporary ideas in Italian architecture is found in the Mannerist treatment of details of the façade. Below the main cornice there is part of an entablature of

413. Wittkower, *Architectural Principles* pp.51–58.
414. *I quattro libri dell'architettura*, Venice 1570. The Knights acquired a copy of the first edition, but the date of the purchase is not known.
415. e.g. Palazzo Strozzi, Florence, and Palazzo Farnese at Rome.

the Doric order. The frieze is greatly reduced in size and triglyphs are omitted. The architrave is similarly reduced but hanging guttæ have been placed ten feet apart along the length of the architrave, although above them there are no triglyphs. Now this, although characteristic of Cassar's architecture, is most unusual and I know of only two other examples; the cortile of the Palazzo Massimi at Rome, built about 1532 to the designs of Baldassare Peruzzi,[416] and Sanmicheli's Villa della Torre at Valpolicella, Verona (*c.* 1558).

The Doric portico of the main door is later than the main façade, and is not the work of Gerolamo Cassar.[417] Our Lady of the Pilar, the church of the langue of Aragon, was built in 1670, against the back of the auberge and facing onto Strada Ponente, and there is an entrance from the auberge at basement level into the church corridor adjoining the nave and sacristy.

53. *Valletta. Auberge d'Auvergne.*

The auberge d'Auvergne[418] in Kingsway, begun in 1574, was **282** severely damaged by bombs in 1942 and lost its main façade. The Pilier of the langue was Grand Marshal of the Order, Military Commander of all land forces, and over all the Knights with the exception of the Grand Crosses, their Lieutenants, the Chaplains, and the household of the Grand Master. The Knights of Auvergne defended the bulwark of St. Michael, the western outpost of the Valletta defences and the flank of Marsamucetto harbour.[419]

It was of two storeys, with the main storey on the first floor. The ground floor, before its destruction, had shops facing onto Kingsway

416. This was noticed by Anderson, *Architecture of the Renaissance in Italy* p.98. 'The entablature is in this way bereft of its proper frieze, while guttæ are left to lament the absence of their hitherto inseparable triglyph.' Pevsner, *The Mint* p.124, has noticed the Mannerist quality of this Roman palace but has failed to comment upon this particular detail in the courtyard. He gives 1535 as the date of building.
417. Cooke p.14.
418. Zammit, *Valletta* p.38. He says it was built between 1570 and 1574.
419. Zammit, *Valletta* p.39.

with a small mezzanine floor above. Whether this was the original arrangement I do not know, but the practice was by no means unusual at the time, and Palladio in his book points out the economic advantage of letting off the ground floor area on the façade as shops, in palaces which face onto busy thoroughfares.[420]

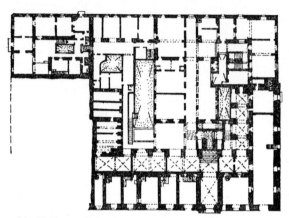

54. *Valletta. Auberge d'Auvergne, ground floor plan.*

Because the door does not come in the centre of the façade, Cassar has resorted to subterfuge.[421] From the eastern corner of the **282** auberge, bounded by rusticated quoins which are more delicate and less restful than usual, the façade runs west along Kingsway with a fairly regular rhythm of three windows each side of a central doorway and central window above. Thus to define this shape, he inserted another rusticated quoin similar to the eastern one, but here he continued the façade westward to include three more windows, and then came to an abrupt end. The cornice is carried along the length of the building and supported on regular strong consoles. Therefore, although the cornice is all-embracing, the façade is split into a major and a minor element and the three western windows 'continue rather lamely to the end of the building.'[422]

The general impression of the façade is austere with windows occupying only a small part of the wall surface. The windows are

420. *I Quattro Libri,* Venice 1570 Bk.II, cap.iii, p.12.
421. V. F. Denaro has suggested that the three left-hand windows were added after 1782 when the langue of Auvergne bought the Casa Caccia from the langue of Italy and incorporated part of this house in their auberge. See: Darmanin Demajo, *Archivio Storico di Malta,* II,2.
422. Cooke p.12 suggests that there were some misgivings about the length that the building should be. I think the arrangement of the façade was necessitated by other conditions in the plans.

tall, with flat projecting cornices similar to those on the palace, and are surrounded with the Melitan triple-roll moulding. It is this feature which has led many writers to suggest that the auberge d'Auvergne was the first completed.[423] The central doorway had double Ionic columns surmounted by the Corinthian coat-of-arms : this had been restored and may have been later than the rest of the façade.[424]

As with most of the buildings in Valletta, the auberge d'Italie in Merchants' Street has undergone many changes since it was designed by Gerolamo Cassar, and it is now difficult to decide which parts belong to the original structure.

The auberge was begun in 1574 for the Italian Knights whose Pilier was Grand Admiral of the Order. According to Zammit it was originally a modest building, but was improved and enlarged by the Grand Master Gregorio Carafa who in 1683 placed his effigy and an inscription over the main door.[425] As no further evidence has come to light regarding the extent of the enlargement, the building must be examined and considered stylistically.

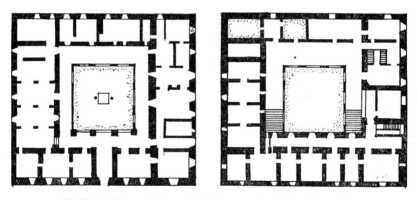

55–56. *Valletta. Auberge d'Italie, ground and first floor plans.*

In plan the auberge occupies a rectangular site bounded by Merchants', Britannia, and Zacharias Streets, with the church of the langue on the fourth side. The church, which is dedicated to St. Catherine, was built in 1576[426] and so must have defined the western boundary of the auberge at that date. Cassar's massive quoins mark the corners of the existing auberge so that it seems likely that it

423. Pratt p.223, and Cooke p.12.
424. Pratt p.223.
425. Zammit, *Valletta* pp.38 and 61.
426. Scicluna p.211. See also Darmanin Demajo, *Archivio*, I,vol.I, p.261–306.

occupied all the site which it occupies today. The auberge is built around a large courtyard which is almost square (fifty-one feet by fifty-four feet) and this agrees with the usual Italian practice. The system of the plan is rotary and is thus similar to Cassar's plan for the auberge d'Aragon and other contemporary plans. The blocks abut in a clockwise direction and overlap at one corner (top left). Again, in a manner similar to that at the auberge d'Aragon, Cassar has tried to place his windows centrally internally and at the same time to get some sort of rhythm on the façade. Because of the number of rooms on the ground floor facing onto Merchants' Street, this has not been achieved, but that the attempt was made is quite clear when we see how he has moved the most western window (Fig. 57, left-hand window) inward and adjusted the two windows in the adjoining room. The main entrance leads into the centre of the courtyard and the rhythm along the façade gives us the following interfenestration between the rusticated quoins: 8, $6\frac{1}{2}$, $6\frac{1}{2}$, 6, 20 (including the main door), 6, 18, and 8 feet. On the mezzanine floor and on the first floor this second (offending) dimension is omitted, the rhythm becomes clearer and the façade symmetrical.

57. *Valletta. Auberge d'Italie.*

Many of the ground floor rooms are spanned with traditional four arches supporting flat ceiling slabs, whilst the entrance and the two rooms to the east have vaulted ceilings. Clearly these rooms were important rooms intended not merely for stables and stores,[427] and in any case there is ample accommodation in the basement for storage.

This leads me to the conclusion that Cassar laid down a plan

427. Cooke p.15.

similar to the one which stands today, bounded by the same four boundaries and having important rooms on the ground floor. Therefore the only enlargements, which are reported to have been made in 1683, must have been made vertically, by adding another storey. The following points tend to support this theory : the staircase of the auberge is insignificant as though it were never intended to lead to important rooms, and yet the present rooms on the top floor are large and commodious. It was either built intentionally unimportant or was squeezed in later. The façade is clearly divided into two, with the ground and mezzanine floors dominating.[428] The band which separates the floors also separates the rusticated quoins. The auberge designed by Cassar may have ended at the cornice level above the mezzanine. Certainly the rusticated doorway seems better proportioned to a building of this size than it does to the present building, even now that its elaborate centrepiece has been added. **291**

The top floor extends along Merchants' Street and a part of Britannia Street, looking down upon the terraces and the courtyard of the rest of the auberge. In order to align the windows with those below and repeat the rhythm of the façade, the relationship of the windows to the rooms has not been considered and there is no internal symmetry. These top rooms are intercommunicating, but they also have a long gallery at the back. To support this the southern peristyle of the courtyard had to be rebuilt with stronger piers, thus its ceiling is some feet higher than the other corridor ceilings and it is vaulted with quadripartite vaults. Finally, the ground floor windows may be sixteenth century with perhaps the console supports added later. The windows on the first floor however are probably later; their slender detailing is seventeenth century, and so also are the slightly projecting balconies below these windows.[429]

The auberge de Provence in Kingsway is of a more advanced **284** design than those hitherto considered and it is difficult to believe that it was designed as early as 1571.[430] Only one writer dates it later, stating that it was begun in 1575.[431] The plan is designed

---

428. Ground floor 22ft. and mezzanine another 13ft. First floor is 24ft.
429. It should be pointed out that these occur on the Palazzo Massimi in Rome, though they are more usual later. All the same, Cassar had used a motif from the Palazzo Massimi on his auberge d'Aragon. The mezzanine windows of the auberge d'Italie resemble the top windows of the Roman palace, but the resemblance is closer to those on S. Caterina dei Funari, Rome (c. 1560).
430. Braun, *Works of Art* p.41, Zammit, *Valletta* pp.37–38.
431. Wilkinson p.7, and Pratt, also states that it was rebuilt in 1638. No evidence is produced to substantiate either of these claims.

around three sides of a courtyard and confined within four streets of the Valletta grid plan. Both the plan and the main façade are more symmetrical than the other auberges, and Cassar, for the first time on a secular building, has adopted a columnal façade of superimposed orders. In this way he has related the façade to the plan, which on the ground floor has nine almost even rectangular rooms along the front; the central one containing the entrance to the auberge is a little wider than the others, and on the façade this distinction is shown by a setting forward of the four centre columns with their entablature. The main entrance hall has a quadripartite vault and leads directly onto the staircase. Unlike the other auberge plans which lead into the courtyards, here the emphasis is on the main suite of rooms above and the staircase leads to them. The siderooms on the ground floor are spanned in the traditional way with arches supporting ceiling slabs.

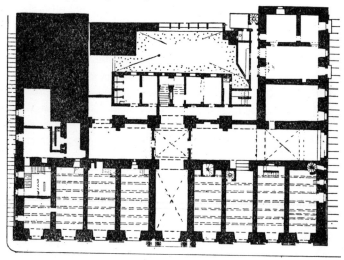

58. *Valletta. Auberge de Provence, ground floor plan.*

The great hall is on the first floor and, large in size, it is one of the noblest rooms in Malta.[432] Richly painted, it has a deep frieze and a wooden beam roof with coffered panels between the beams. Because of the timber ceiling, the building was covered with a timber truss and roofed with a pitched roof. It is therefore one of the few buildings in Malta to possess a pitched roof.[433] The musicians'

432. 90ft. x 46ft. x 45ft. high. Cooke p.12 is wrong in giving the width as 56ft.
433. Part of the Magisterial palace and the Great Hospital have pitched roofs.

gallery was added later, probably after the arrival of the British.[434] Dormitories, storerooms, and stables were in the basement and the horses were led in and out on a ramp from Carvi Street.[435]

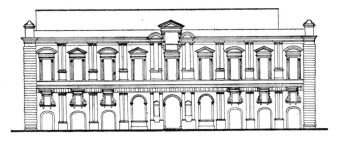

59. *Valletta. Auberge de Provence.*

Cassar has used his ingenuity upon the façade. The great rusticated blocks at the corners, with alternating narrow and wide bands **285** of rounded and squared stones, stand forward like bastions containing the body of the front. But the effect is less austere than is usual with his designs. Perhaps the light character comes from the superimposed columns and the use of the Ionic order, more playful than anything he has used elsewhere. The façade is stamped with Mannerist details, but it is mature and confident and shows no sign of naïvety. It is on a par with Mannerist work in Italy. The alternation of segmental and triangular pediments on the first floor windows,[436] the contrast obtained by using pilasters on the wings and columns for the centrepiece, the further emphasis given to the centrepiece[437] by the fact that four windows are used in each of the **286** wings and therefore do not tend to create minor centres of attraction, and the increased chiaroscuro gained by inserting a large panel just inside the line of the upper pilasters and entablature : these are so competently handled that it is difficult to believe they were designed by Gerolamo Cassar as early as 1571. Most of his work is less subtle than this, yet the design has the Mannerist characteristics which we are used to associate with his name.[438] On the ground

434. Wilkinson p.8.
435. Wilkinson p.7.
436. See Raphael's Palazzo Pandolfini, Florence; the Palazzo Farnese at Rome; and Roman palaces by Bramante.
437. The raised centrepiece is found on many 17th century Venetian villas. For example : Villa Pasole, Pedavena (prov. Belluno); Villa Butta, Belluno; Villa Rudio, Sedico; and Villa Fulcio, Belluno.
438. Pratt says the auberge was rebuilt in 1638. However, it seems impossible to believe that it could have been rebuilt leaving the old quoins of Cassar's earlier building still standing. I think we must assume that the plan is Cassar's, and if we do, it follows that the regular two

floor, above the openings of the shops:[439] the mezzanine windows cut into the architrave (which is itself unusually thin) and the frieze,[440] forcing these mouldings up over the line of the window; and above: the entablature of the superimposed order is left unsupported at the two ends where it abuts the rusticated quoins.

The auberge de France, which stood in Strada Mezzodi on the corner of Strada Forni, was destroyed by bomb in 1942. Because of its position at the crossing of two narrow streets it was difficult to photograph, and there are no adequate remaining photographs.[441]

The auberge was begun in 1588 and is probably about the last building designed by Gerolamo Cassar, who died two years before building operations began.[442] It was built for the large and important langue of France, whose Pilier was the Grand Hospitaller. The langue had an annual revenue of nearly £31,000 and consisted of 113 commanderies in its three grand priories of France, Aquitaine, and Champagne. The Knights of France defended the bulwark of St. James on the land face of the Valletta defences, and the auberge was conveniently placed near these lines.

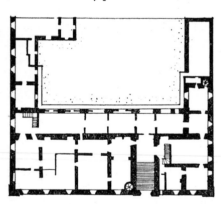

60. *Valletta. Auberge de France.*

storeys with a completely symmetrical façade are also his. As many of the details are Mannerist it seems to point to the conclusion that Cassar did, in fact, design the whole façade, and the contrast with his other auberge façades is just another enigma in his strange variations of style.

439. Cf. auberge d'Auvergne which is in the same street. Without doubt the shops here do seem to be contemporary with the rest of the building.

440. Palladio on the Loggia del Capitano, Vicenza, allows his windows to cut into the entablature but the mouldings of the architrave do not bend up and over the window mouldings. Della Porta on the Palazzo Marescotti in Rome (*c.* 1583) appears to be the first Italian to break the entablature and curve up the architrave mouldings. He does this in the courtyard façade. After that it occurs on the Palazzo Madama and the Palazzo Buonaparte, both 17th century buildings in Rome.

441. Fortunately plans and elevations exist in the offices of the Ministry of Works in Valletta and I have based my information on them.

442. Bonello suggests that Cassar did not design the building but that there was an earlier auberge de France elsewhere in Valletta.

The auberge was primarily a single-storey building, with a large semi-basement for stores, and additional height was obtained for the stores along Old Bakery Street, where the land slopes steeply away to the east. The plan was essentially French. It consists of a long and important block lying parallel with Strada Mezzodi, with an entrance off the centre of the block leading to a long gallery which looks out across the garden at the back. Admittedly, side wings run down each side of the garden, but these are of less importance and the plan is essentially that of a block facing a garden. In this respect it differs from the traditional Maltese plan and also from those auberges, following the fashion of Italy and Spain, which were built with a central courtyard.

61. *Valletta. Auberge de France.*

At first sight the building looked austere and far removed from the balanced façade of the auberge de Provence. The usual characteristics of Cassar's work were there: heavy rusticated corners stopped by a plain frieze and cornice, the large amount of wall surface, plain windows with flat hood moulds and architrave mouldings carried round to frame the openings, and what at first appeared to be a haphazard arrangement of the façade. But upon closer examination this last point was found to be untrue. The windows were not placed on the interior walls for their effect, the internal rooms were irregular and the windows were unrelated to them in plan. The disposition of the windows must then have been determined by the facial effect Cassar wished to obtain. The proof of this is the row of sockets intended to take flag-poles. Though these are small ornaments, the effect would have been very different when the poles were in position and the flags of the Order flying: then the articulation of the façade would have been quite clear. Far from being haphazard, it has been carefully worked out and is a very complex asymmetrical composition. The flag-poles become the main vertical lines of articulation and are placed evenly along the façade from the outside northern rusticated quoin to the main portal.

The windows, being voids, correctly fill the spaces between the flag-poles. Four windows on the north side of the doorway light the small circular staircase which rises to the roof; the four on the other side of the door have no such functional use and are merely included for their effect on the façade. Finally, the short arm of the façade has no flag-pole to break up its bulk and all the mouldings are omitted from the windows so that they hardly appear, and do not distract the eye from the heavy mass of masonry.[443]

The façade onto Old Bakery Street is also an asymmetrical design. The longer block has one strongly rusticated corner and to balance this the doorway is thrown over to the east and the taller plain block is placed at the east end. The effect of this slight rise, clearly not required in the plan for the convenience of the building, is mainly obtained by omitting the cornice moulding : and in this way the mass of this end wing is further increased by the drop of the ground toward the east.

The asymmetrical façades of this auberge are an enigma like so much of Gerolamo Cassar's work. They certainly do not belong to the sixteenth century in style, a century when the architects had endeavoured to impose a certain order and absolute symmetry to their buildings nor do they belong to earlier work where convenience was all that mattered in domestic architecture, and façades were the expression of the requirements which lay behind. This conscious asymmetrical planning belongs at the earliest to the Romantic Revival and more fully to our own times, and yet we cannot doubt the authenticity of this design nor, on the evidence, can we doubt that Cassar's design was fully premeditated. In the details his idiosyncrasies are obvious. On the main portal the coupled columns are gathered onto a single pedestal, but their line is repeated in the line of the panels of the pedestal. The Doric order has both triglyph and dentils. And finally, the window details are typically his.

The Bakery of the Order may have been designed by Gerolamo Cassar. The citation made by Grand Master La Cassière in 1581 refers to Cassar as the architect of the bakeries of the Order, but whether the reference is to this one or to an earlier building is not clear. Zammit states that this bakery was built in 1594,[444] but this

---

443. This is how it reads. We do not know if Cassar intended to add mouldings to these windows, but certainly they were never added and the balance was thereby greatly improved.
444. Zammit, *Valletta* p.42.

would date it eight years after Cassar's death. The building has all the characteristics of an early building and the date 1584 given by another writer seems more reasonable.[445] The building is large and occupies a complete block of the Valletta street plan,[446] being bounded on four sides by Old Bakery Street, St. John's Street, Britannia Street, and Strait Street. The four corners of the building are strengthened by four giant pilasters.

62. *Valletta. Bakery of the Order, first floor plan.*

The plan, being mainly dependent upon structural considerations, is similar to the early house built for Eustachio del Monte and later combined into the enlarged plan of the Magisterial palace, and to the sixteenth century plan of the Orphan Asylum also in Valletta. From one end six long rooms are laid in a row, spanned transversely with stone arches and covered with flat ceiling slabs in the usual way. The rooms are approximately the same width (though they do vary a little) and open courtyards are contained in two of them. By building in this way the thrusts are minimized, each room supporting its adjacent neighbour. Over half-way along the plan the pattern is changed and three rooms are placed in the other direction, the centre one having a courtyard. These rooms are a little wider than the rooms already described. This change of direction stiffens the plan, making it more rigid and more able to resist earthquake shocks.

The sixteenth century Orphan Asylum occupies a large rectangular plot of about 262 feet by 195 feet and, like the Bakery, it follows the early Maltese plan and does not have rooms disposed around a central courtyard in the manner adopted on many of the auberges. The long narrow rooms, though not pleasantly proportioned (for some measure 174 feet by 26 feet), were easy to build as the stone arches could conveniently span them. In utilitarian

445. Cooke p.24.
446. Zammit, *Valletta* p.42. It measures 310ft. by 140ft.

buildings such as these and the Great Hospital pleasant proportions could be sacrificed to convenience. Everything was subservient to the structure. All the walls are thick to resist the strong lateral thrusts, the entrance is small and its axis is blocked by one

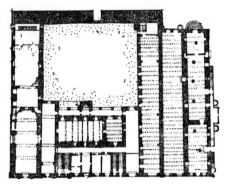

63. *Valletta. Orphan Asylum.*

of these strong walls running across the corridor. The staircases on each side of the entrance are separated by three rooms, and placed where the structure dictates rather than for monumental effect. Windows are placed solely for the purpose of lighting rooms.[447] This produces a certain regularity but otherwise there appears to have been little or no thought put to architectural rhythm.

288 The Great Hospital of the Order was established in the Birgu soon after the Knights arrived in Malta.[448] Bedford[449] writes, 'on the completion of the new city [Valletta] this hospital was transferred to the other side of the harbour, and unfortunately placed on the south-eastern seafront close to the Great Harbour, the inducement to choose this site being that patients might be landed from ships at the mouth of the harbour, and brought in by a covered way below the sea wall into the lower ward of the hospital, without making a tedious and dangerous circuit of the streets. Unfortunately it is thus completely sheltered by the high ground behind it from the healthy north and north-west winds, while it is exposed to the enervating sirocco.' This was in the year 1575.[450]

The Order was justly proud of its Hospital. It had banded together to tend to the needs of the sick and had never forsaken this

447. Compare this with the false windows on the right of the main door in the auberge de France which is about the same date.
448. Bedford, *Malta* p.58 : ' In the chapel however there is an interesting painting dated 1557, with the arms of de l'Isle Adam and the date of foundation, 1533. The Knights arrived in October 1530.
449. Bedford, *Malta* p.58.
450. Bedford, *Regulations* p.ix.

task. The expenditure upon the Hospital was considerable. The silver plate from which the patients ate was valued at £3,449 in 1778 and in the same year the annual expenditure was £7,947, or a daily average of between tenpence and one shilling per patient. This was very high for the time. In addition, a further £614 was spent on the accommodation and maintenance of illegitimate and destitute children.[451]

In view of this it is strange that this was the site chosen for the Hospital, and having been chosen, that more was not made of the architecture of the building. Though the great ward is indeed impressive in its proportions (it measures 185 feet by 34 feet 9 inches by 31 feet high) and is one of the longest rooms in Europe, the general plan does not compare with some of the fine hospitals which had been built in Italy and Spain.

The Hospital, which was built under the Grand Master La Cassière in 1575, was one of the most important buildings erected by the Knights, yet we have no knowledge of the architect. Had it been designed by Gerolamo Cassar it would surely have been mentioned in the citation made by La Cassière.

Partly perhaps because of the site, for the new hospital in Valletta was placed awkwardly across a corner of the street pattern, the layout has none of the architectural clarity and grandeur of such buildings as the hospital of Santa Cruz at Toledo which was designed by Enrique de Egas and built between 1504 and 1514. It has a clear cruciform shape with a chapel at the crossing and long wards where the patients could all see the service in the chapel.[452]

Many sixteenth century buildings, such as Egas' hospital at Santiago de Compostella (1501–11), followed the pattern first used by Filarete in the Milan hospital : of a layout with four courtyards. A plan that is segmental and coherent. Philibert de l'Orme[453] published a project for a hospital on this pattern, so that there is no doubt that this form of hospital was widely known throughout western Europe. The plan which undoubtedly had the most profound influence upon the architect of the Valletta hospital was the hospital of Santo Spirito in Rome which, though of ancient origin, had been reconstructed by Marchionne d'Arezzo upon the instructions of Innocent III, and considerably enlarged under Sixtus IV between 1474 and 1482. The plan consists of a long ward (121m. x 12.40m. x 13m. high) with an octagonal central opening connecting with another

451. Scicluna pp.214–215.
452. Hautecoeur Ia, p.344.
453. Philibert de l'Orme, *Livre d'Architecture,* Paris 1567.

shorter ward to form a T shape. Its siting near the river and the existence of earlier buildings probably dictated, to some extent, the plan of this Roman hospital.

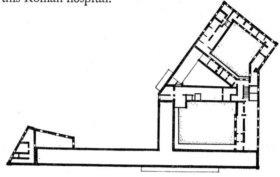

64. *Valletta. Hospital of the Order, first floor plan.*

At Valletta the long ward was on two floors with a basement, and the north-west end of the lower floor opened out into a loggia in the first courtyard. The shorter cross ward was introduced only on the ground and first floors. The windows were comparatively small in order that the wards might be kept cool. Those on the eastern face of the building were combined in single architrave mouldings so that on the elevation they appear tall and narrow, reaching almost from ground level to cornice level. This is a strange and unusual feature of the design. Because of the projecting peristyle this does not occur inside the courtyard, and each window has its own mouldings. Many of the details, such as the main cornice of the building, are rather crude, and the tall panelled pilasters at the corners, with their capitals formed into cornice mouldings, are typical of sixteenth century architecture in Malta and not unlike the work of Gerolamo Cassar.

In the usual Maltese manner the upper floor of the great ward has a timber ceiling supported by wooden corbels.[454] Above it is a pitched roof, one of the few in Malta, trussed with single tie beams. The novel feature of this roof is the way in which rafters are doubled by placing one on top of another to get the required depth of timber. As the wood had to be imported from Sicily, and it would have been much easier to handle and transport the thinner[455]

454. Cf. Hall of St. Michael and St. George in the Magisterial palace and the great hall in the auberge de Provence.
455. The only other explanation could be that they are local timbers, and as none of sufficient girth could be found, thin ones had to be used in this manner.

beams, this form of construction is clearly explained. The roof is covered with buff coloured Sicilian tiles.

Under the Grand Mastership of Perellos in 1662 and again in 1713 large sums were spent in improving the hospital.[456] Some of the money went to provide a library which was formed in 1687,[457] but the major portion of the money undoubtedly paid for the building of a second courtyard placed at an angle of about forty-five **290** degrees to the rest of the hospital so as to align it with Merchants' Street. The new court was higher than the older buildings, and Bedford complains that it blocked out much of the light which should have entered the wards of the hospital.[458]

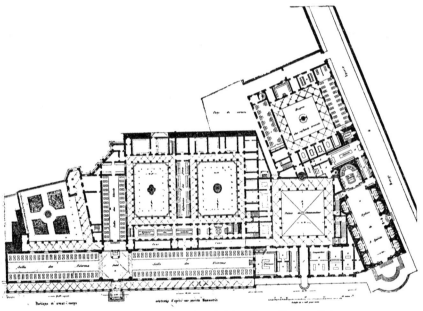

65. *Rome. Hospital of S. Spirito (from Letarouilly).*

At this time Henry Teonge, naval chaplain aboard *H.M.S. Assistance,* visited the island and wrote a description of the hospital in his

456. Bedford, *Malta* p.60.
457. Scicluna p.214.
458. Bedford, *Malta* p.60, and *Report of the Barrack and Hospital Commission, 1863, General Hospital Valletta,* complains that the wards are dark with only fifty square feet of window to 3,000 cubic feet of ward. Wards are dark and dismal, beside being close, and the air is always more or less stagnant. See also Bedford, *Regulations,* and Howards, *Lazarettos of Europe,* 1789, *Malta* p.58.

diary.[459] 'The hospitall is a vast structure, wherein the sick and wounded lye. This so broade that twelve men may with ease walke abreast up the midst of it; and the bedds are on each syde, standing on four yron pillars, with white curtens, and vallands, and covering, extremely neate, and kept cleane and sweete : the sick served all in sylver plate; and it contaynes above 200 bedds below, besyds many spatious roomes in other quadrangles with in; for the chiefe cavaliers and Knights, with pleasant walkes and gardens; and a stately house for the chiefe doctor and other his attendants.'

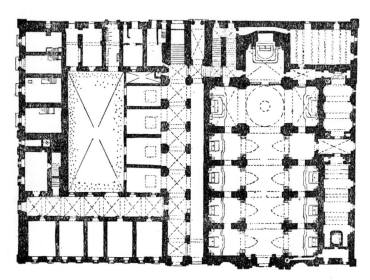

66. *Valletta. University and Gesù church.*

The original College of Studies in Malta, the inception of which was due to a suggestion made by Tomasso Gargallo, was established in 1595 with the aid of a grant of 2,000 scudi made by the King of Spain. A plot of land, 250 feet by 168 feet, which comprised one complete block of the Valletta plan, was bounded by Merchants' Street on the west, Christopher Street on the north, St. Paul Street on the east, and Archbishop's Street on the fourth side. Approximately half of the site, that portion lying to the west, was taken up by the Jesuit church which was built between 1592 and 1600. Its plan followed the Gesù in Rome, with a four-bay nave and seven side chapels; the eighth opening from the nave leading to a door onto Archbishop's Street. There was a dome over the crossing, a deeply-recessed chancel, and two transepts which were no deeper

238-239

459. *Diary of Henry Teonge,* 2 August 1675, p.47.

156

than the side chapels. This is a convenient plan as it fits well into a rectangular space. The church was separated from the remainder of the block by a narrow passage.

The college buildings were first designed with a plan which seemed to rotate in a clockwise direction like those Cassar had evolved for the Magisterial palace, the auberge d'Aragon, and the auberge d'Italie : only here there was no overlapping of the main structure at one corner and the rotation was continuous. The plan revolved around a central courtyard, which was spacious before later additions onto the western cloister wall reduced it in size, and the cloisters ran along the northern and western sides of the court-yard, sheltered from the hot sun and open to the cool mistral breezes. When in 1768 the Jesuits were expelled from Malta, Pope Clement XIV granted permission for their property to be taken over and formed into a university. The University was formally instituted by Grand Master Emanuel Pinto de Fonçeca in 1769.[460]

It would be wrong to assume that the house plans for early build-ings in Valletta fell conveniently into two types : the one type where long rooms are placed side by side,[461] the other planned around a central courtyard.[462] We have already seen deviations due to the preferences of the Knights of the langues of France and Provence, and many of the Valletta buildings show their unwillingness to comply with any complete rule. However, it would be true to say that all the buildings make provision for some kind of internal court or, more usually, for several courts; and that most follow these two types of plans or a combination of the two. Take for example, the pair of old houses which adjoin the church of Our Lady of Victory and back onto the cavalier of St. John. From the Melitan mould-ings on their façades it is clear that they are sixteenth century build-ings and therefore amongst the earliest to be built in Valletta. The doors and windows have flat hood moulds and the triple roll is carried around the windows to form a continuous frame. The cor-nice of the houses is also made up of a triple-roll moulding.

The larger of the two houses has the usual three rooms across the front, spanned by three arches in each, which form three continuous lines parallel with the façade wall. The widest span is thirteen feet. Behind the middle room, or entrance hall, there is a larger room fourteen-and-a-half feet wide, and this seems to have been too wide

460. *Zammit,* Malta p.250.
461. The Bakery, the Orphan Asylum, etc.
462. Magisterial palace, Valletta; auberges of Italy and Aragon; and the University buildings.

for the builder to span it with transverse arches : with the result that
he has had to place a cumbersome and obstructive pier, three feet
three inches square, in the centre of the room and radiate arches

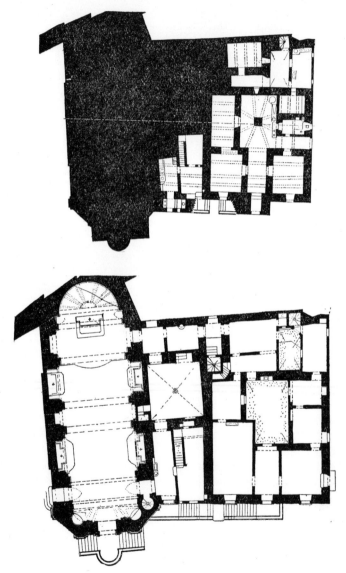

67–68. *Valletta. Our Lady of Victory and two houses, ground and
first floor plans*

from it to the side walls. On the floor above this a space is made into a courtyard, so that the first floor plan is thus designed around this central court.

With the exception of some of Gerolamo Cassar's work most of the early buildings in Valletta are decorated with Melitan mouldings which had been popular in Vittoriosa. One of the best examples is the doorway of the house adjoining the church of St. Catherine of **266** the langue of Italy, which is directly opposite to the last two houses described. Not only are the triple mouldings carried round the door architrave, they are also repeated in the archivolt of the semicircular light above the hood mould, and above on the cornice moulding.

The Dorell palace in Merchants' Street, which has been restored **293** after bomb damage, has one of the best façades of this period. Although this façade is not symmetrical because of the disposition of the rooms behind, symmetry has clearly been considered and the first set of windows are balanced on each side of the door. As the door is lower than the windows, the full height is made up by inserting an oval light over the doorway and framing it with Melitan mouldings. In Maltese architecture[463] this oval window over the door occurs again and again. A few examples are found in Sicily,[464] but in Italy, Sicily, and Spain it was not the normal practice.

There are two important palaces at the lower end of Kingsway which date from the end of the sixteenth century or the early years of the seventeenth. The Pereira palace, which is next to the church **297–298** of St. Catherine, has a plain façade with a plain cornice. This façade is unbalanced with three windows on the right and one on the left of the door, lighting the principal rooms on the *piano nobile*. The decoration is confined to the windows and the door. The focal point of the whole façade is the door and window above. The oval eye over the door is here inserted below the canopy, and above that a recessed arched panel marks the position of the main windows. Later, projecting wooden balconies were added, and these tend to destroy the unity of the façade.

The de la Salle palace, a little further down Kingsway, was built **294–295** about 1600.[465] It was at one time the residence of Ramon Perellos before he was elected Grand Master in 1697.[466] The main reception

---

463. Pereira palace, Valletta. In some cases it is replaced by a circular window, e.g., De La Salle palace, Valletta (*c.* 1600). It is used also on many church façades.
464. e.g. Badia delle Verginelle, Acireale.
465. Cooke p.12 says it was built in 1650, but the details of the palace rather suggest an earlier date.
466. Zammit, *Valletta* p.88.

room on the first floor is particularly noteworthy. It is a room of fine proportions, very spacious and measuring approximately thirty-three feet by twenty-one feet by twenty-one feet high. Pilasters and elaborate cartouches are painted on the walls.

69. *Valletta. Flores College.*

The façade of the palace has large areas of plain wall surface with small window openings. This effect is increased over the upper windows where the hood mouldings have been omitted. The main door has the usual window over it, but this time it is circular and

70. *Valletta. De la Salle palace.*

quite large. The hood is for this reason pushed high above the door and its large consoles are placed close against the mouldings of the circular window, so that the hood seems completely divorced from the door which it should protect. Similarly, the first floor windows

160

have hoods which are completely detached[467] and the windows have no apparent rhythm. At the corner of the building, on St. Nicholas Street and Kingsway, there is a heavy rusticated pier with a chamfered edge, but this rises only to the height of the first floor windows. The Spanish looking balcony, which sweeps around the corner above the pier, may be later; but if these balcony supports were not included in the original design, there seems little reason for the sudden cessation of the corner piers abreast the first floor windows. But the arrangement of the parts of this façade lead us to the conclusion that reason played a small part in the composition.

During the last years of the sixteenth century and the early years of the seventeenth century, many houses were built in the country and in the villages which show the characteristics seen in these Valletta palaces. Whilst the country houses were in character more austere and often semi-fortified, and the village buildings more modest in size and decoration, there is one in particular which should not be neglected.

Qormi is a village particularly noted for its richly-carved doorways and balconies, but the carvings on the façades of the Stagno palace are most original and interesting. It was built in the year 1589.[468] The main façade of the palace faces on to a narrow street and is quite plain, with the exception of carved door and window surrounds : there is no cornice moulding. The triple rolls of the Melitan mouldings are even fatter and more bulbous than usual, but they are strangely combined with delicately carved leaf decoration on the consoles which support the window pediments. These consoles rest upon grotesque heads and tall narrow panelled pilasters which lie against the architrave of the windows. The frieze is richly carved with a flat strap decoration and all the mouldings are unorthodox by any but Maltese standards. One of the doorways, later altered when an arch was inserted into the lintel of the door, has a similarly richly carved frieze decorated with heads placed in rectangular panels. The carving of these friezes is more reminiscent of Spanish colonial work from Peru or Mexico than anything usually associated with Malta. The heads have an untamed appearance strangely disquieting. The palace opens on one side onto a walled garden and one of the first floor windows leads onto a balcony which is continued along the garden wall where a stone staircase

274,276
300–302

---

467. This was the usual practice in the 16th century. Gerolamo Cassar designed windows like this on the Magisterial palace and the auberge d'Aragon.
468. Braun, *Works of Art* p.19.

leads down to the garden itself. The windows are placed on the façade just as they occur, to light the interior, and there is no attempt at symmetry.

The roof is flat, and leading onto the roof there is a circular staircase contained within a small domed structure.

Small palaces and houses in the 17th and 18th centuries

Some of the houses which date from the early years of the seventeenth century continue the design of the Stagno palace at Qormi, but usually with more regular façades. Those built about this time which face onto the long axis of Hospital Square at Zebbug,[469] have large areas of wall surface unrelieved by decoration and no surmounting cornice. The central house has a more or less symmetrical façade with three windows on the first floor. These windows are tall in proportion and have early triple roll with Melitan mouldings, a bulbous moulded sill and a canopy raised clear of the architrave moulding. The ground floor windows and secondary doors are surrounded by a raised architrave, plain and undecorated. This façade foreshadows the seventeenth and eighteenth century, but the origin of the developments must be discussed before the Maltese examples are illustrated; for Maltese secular architecture during these two centuries formed the culmination of a trend of thought which sprang from the ideals of the Renaissance in central Italy and which ripened consistently through three styles of architecture in Rome : the High Renaissance, the Mannerist period, and the Baroque. Although the stimulus was Rome, there is no country in the world where this architectural treatment was more universally adopted than in Malta.

Toward the close of the fifteenth century in Italy, in addition to the principles normally associated with the Renaissance style of architecture, two tendencies are apparent. The first is a process of simplification and a desire on the part of some architects to abandon the superfluous.

Almost at the same time as the ancient Roman orders were being studied, measured, and copied, a reaction set in against the ornateness of these orders. Alberti realised the significance of the architectural orders,[470] the manner in which they defined the shape of the

469. Nos. 15–17 St. Anthony Street and Hospital Square.
470. *The Architecture of Leon Battista Alberti in ten Books,* translation by James Leoni, London 1755 and 1955, Book VI, Cap.2. He describes

building and broke down the overall dimensions into easily assimilated sizes, and he repeated his formula in architectural works. A man of strict upbringing, he applied the orders with Classical correctness, but successors evolved an architecture which retained the significance of the orders, with their basis of post and lintel design 'applied' to give coherence to a façade, but which omitted all the detail and decoration of the Roman prototype. Thus buildings were framed with plain vertical strips representing pilasters and supporting further plain strips which represented the supported entablature. In this way their palace façades had a unity and interrelationship which was immediately apparent, and avoided the straggling appearance so often the fault of the astylar façades.

This process of simplification is clearly evident in the painting of the *Derelitta*[471] by Botticelli.

In architecture the early examples are usually on small buildings and applied somewhat tentatively. Bramantino used this treatment on the interior of the Cappella Trivulzio at San Nazzaro, Milan;[472] but Bramante was the first architect to use it regularly. At S. Maria presso di San Satiro in Milan he used these strip pilasters and entablature both on the elevation facing on to Via Falcone and on the lantern of the sacristy.[473] On the upper storey of the Tempietto in S. Pietro in Montorio he used plain pilasters; panelled and without capital mouldings (this is his most advanced example, if not his most successful), and on the lantern of the dome of St. Peter's, according to the drawing in Serlio,[474] a further simplification of the orders took place. It has been previously established that Bramante was loath to accept the antique capital and preferred to evolve models of his own design; this is a step further along the path of revolt against the adoption of Roman examples.

The second reason for the adoption of this form was not so much a revolt against the use of antique orders, but rather a desperation at the difficulties involved in their use in certain circumstances. Two of the shortcomings in the application of Roman orders to the façades of palaces and tall churches were, firstly, the lack of con-

ornament, by which he means the application of the orders to a building, as 'a kind of additional brightness and improvement to Beauty' where *beauty* is the proportion of the building and the relationship of the parts.
471. In the Galleria Pallavicini, Rome.
472. Illustrated in Venturi, *Quattrocento* II p.763, Fig.696.
473. On the lantern there are very plain capital mouldings and the architecture is also slightly decorated.
474. Serlio III. For a further example see Bramante's design for the façade of S. Maria presso di San Satiro, *c.* 1480, now in the Louvre.

centration which one felt in observing a building made up of tier upon tier of architectural orders; and secondly, the realization that superimposition was limited by the five known orders of classical architecture. This unsatisfactory state of affairs is shown in the projects of Filarete[475] and in such church façades as S. Zaccaria in Venice, San Maurizio in Milan, and S. Paolino at Lucca by Baccio da Montelupo.

Architects often found themselves hampered by practical considerations when designing palaces which required floors of different heights and proportions other than those laid down for the use of the superimposed orders by Vitruvius;[476] and though occasionally it was possible for them to incorporate several floors within the embrace of one order, this was not always convenient. Again, in churches this difficulty could be overcome by applying a screen façade whose proportion need bear no relationship to the body of the church behind. One very clear example of this may be seen on Giuliano da Sangallo's façade of S. Maria dell'Anima, Rome, but at the best it is no more than a makeshift solution.

There were two ways of overcoming this dilemma. Either the architect could employ a form of decoration which had been used in the past, but which was capable of variations of proportion, and here the solution that suggested itself was the caryatid,[477] or he could use a form which had no precedent and was thus not tied to rigid proportions to the extent of those forms established by rule or usage. To do this he must either omit all decoration and merely suggest an order of no established form, or he must form one of his own. Bramante omitted decoration on the upper order of the Tempietto as he wished to keep it subservient to the main Doric peristyle; and Francesco Laurana formed a pilaster of three panels where he required one of unusual width on S. Francesco at Palermo.

Intent upon composing a façade of many planes in depth, Baroque architects found this treatment of plain pilaster and entablature of great use, for it could be applied behind the normal full pilaster and entablature, to act as a shadow and to leave a sunken panel behind. Some delighted in serried rows of columns or pilas-

475. Filarete, *Trattato dell'architettura*.
476. Vitruvius V Chap. vi, para. 6.
477. Caryatids date from their use on the porch of the Erechthium at Athens. Alberti used them to increase the height of Corinthian pilasters in the nave of the Tempio Malatestiano at Rimini. Other examples see: Tombs of Pius V and Sixtus V in the Sistine chapel, and top floor of Palazzo Stanga at Cremona.

ters[478] but others found the constant repetition of carved capital too florid and ornate, and were pleased to use this process of simplification.

Although Baroque in conception, this use of plain pilaster strips to form receding panels was not confined exclusively to the period normally associated with the Baroque. Raphael used them on the upper floor of the façade of the Palazzo Caffarelli Vidoni at Rome, and even earlier they were used inside the house at Mantegna at Mantua[479] by the school of Alberti in 1466. Serlio, that precursor of the Baroque, illustrates examples in Book IV and the so-called Book VII.

Therefore in the Baroque period we find the culmination of this simplification, in major works of architecture, falling into two distinct types, but closely related as I have described. Type one had plain strips representing pilasters and entablatures, replacing the more ornate orders. With the large palaces of this period the need for this became more obvious. Type two also had the plain pilaster and entablature, but with no break or moulding between them, using them either set back behind the order or in serried rows to form receding or advancing panels. There are numerous examples of both types in Rome, which was the centre of the movement and also of the artistic world in the sixteenth and seventeenth centuries.

71. *Rome. Torre dell'Orologio on the Convento dei Filippini.*

The top floor of the Belvedere Nicchione in the Vatican is a good example of the first type, and Borromini's elevation of the Convento dei Filippini (1649), below the Torre dell'Orologio, Rome, best illustrates the second type.

478. One of the finest examples of this is on the façade of SS. Vincenzo ed Anastasio in Roma (1650).
479. Illustrated in Venturi, *Quattrocento* I p.223.

From Rome the influence spread over Europe : examples may be found in France, Spain, Germany, and particularly in late seventeenth and eighteenth century architecture in Sicily.[480]

This trend toward a simplification of architectural details, while retaining the advantages of the architectural orders, affected the style of building in Malta from the end of the sixteenth century and throughout the two succeeding centuries. In fact the tendencies were particularly suited to the Maltese temperament and pocket for, in general, the buildings in Malta are more sober and less ornate than similar buildings in Sicily and southern Italy. The large civic buildings, however, still came under Sicilian-Spanish influence and, where money was available, the orders were employed in a rich Baroque manner.[481] These important buildings are described in the next section.

Probably one of the earliest examples of the substitution of plain strips of masonry for pilaster and entablature is to be found on the aisle screen of Gerolamo Cassar's Carmelite church in Valletta.[482] If there is some doubt concerning the authenticity of this screen, there is also some about the lower floor of the old wing of St. Anton's palace at Attard. This wing, which later became the

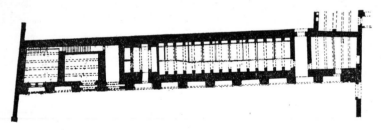

72. *Attard. Palace of St. Anton, stable block plan.*

stables of the enlarged palace, was originally the main body of the palace built by the Grand Master Antoine de Paule soon after his succession in 1625.[483] The plan shows all the characteristics of early

480. Casa di Nutrizione degli *eposte*, Palazzina del Duca di Tremestieri, Palazzo Nava, Palazzo Palmieri, and Palazzo S. Giuliano : all at Catania ; design for the Casa Vaccarini at Portichello and Accademia delle Scienze at Trapani.
481. For a fuller description of the origin of this motif see Quentin Hughes, *Church of St. Catherine 'Tat-Torba' and the Origin of the Simplified Orders of Architecture,* in ARCH I, 1954.
482. The church was built in 1573 but additions and alterations were later made. The façade and much of the interior decorations are later, but there is no evidence to suggest that the aisle screens are also later.
483. Braun, *Works of Art* p.1, states that the stable wing was late 16th century.

Maltese design : the long narrow building, in which the rooms are intercommunicating, is spanned by closely spaced stone arches and buttressed across the front with transverse vaults.[484] This is done in a manner similar to that used by Cassar on the Conventual church at Valletta, but here it is more simple and rudimentary. The simple strip pilaster and entablature is applied to the external wall to transform the succession of transverse vaults to the vertical and horizontal stresses of the building. Doubt arises when we notice that the spacing of the internal beams, usually about five feet centre to centre, bears no relationship to the spacing of the arches and pilaster strips across the façade, which are sixteen-and-a-half feet centre to centre.

It must be remembered, however, that the spacing of the interior arches was governed by the size of the available roofing slabs, but the spacing of the exterior bays depended upon aesthetic considerations and the desire for a regular rhythm along the complete façade. In view of the bay proportions and simplicity of design there seems little reason to doubt that they are contemporary with the rest of the block.

The monastery of the Minor Observants at Floriana founded in the year 1588,[485] was the third building in Malta which had this simplified treatment of pilaster and entablature.

These three examples, dating from the last years of the sixteenth century and all very similar in design, set the fashion which was inspired by work in Rome, and which subsequently affected many secular buildings and at least one church in Malta.[486] Here I shall   **142** confine my description to a few houses which are typical of the development of the style in Malta.

The palace of the Inquisitors at Vittoriosa is the most important   **305-306** early building to exhibit these characteristics. It dates from the end of the sixteenth century, and the small internal courtyard, colonnaded on two sides with pointed arched arcades, is a remnant of the original building. But the palace was extended and improved later to accommodate the Inquisitors and their courts in greater comfort. Several important men, among them two who were later to become Popes, spent some of their time in this palace. Both Fabio Chigi (1599–1667) who became Alexander VII in 1655, and Antonio Pignatelli (1615–89) made Pope Innocent XII in 1676, held

484. These occur only on the east elevation and support a balcony above.
485. Illustrated in Braun, *Works of Art* p.4. The building was destroyed in 1942.
486. The church of St. Catherine at Qrendi has already been described and illustrated.

the rank of Inquisitor at Vittoriosa in their lifetime, as did twenty others who were later made Cardinals.[487]

The dates of the alterations are unknown, but the main façade, an impressive though sombre composition, appears to date from the first half of the seventeenth century.[488] As the layout of Vittoriosa is less rigid and not laid out in a grid pattern like Valletta, the buildings in the city are less symmetrically composed in plan and the palace plan shows the result of this irregularity. It is built around one large courtyard and three small ones, one of which is the early colonnaded court.

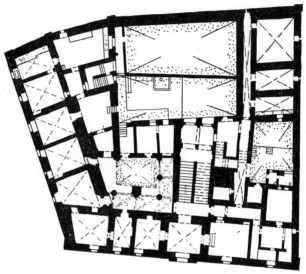

73. *Vittoriosa. Inquisitor's palace.*

In spite of the general irregularity of the plan, the main front has been made completely symmetrical and this only with considerable adjustment. The corner of South Street and Main Gate Street has been projected into the street in order to lengthen the main façade and to terminate it with a right-angle bend (bottom left hand corner of plan in Fig. 73). Transverse vaults span the ground floor rooms and replace the traditional arch and slab construction. The main staircase is also symmetrically placed opposite the main door and in the centre of the main front. The enclosed character of the staircase suggests that it also dates from the first half of the seventeenth century. The main reception rooms on the first floor have flat timber

487. Luke p.85.
488. DICTIONARY OF ARCHITECTURE article *Malta* p.4 gives date of palace as 1684.

ceilings,[489] and are not for the most part intercommunicating, but are approached from lobbies and landings. However, it is the façade which here most interests us. It was designed with two main floors and an attic above the cornice, and is symmetrical with five bays and an entrance in the centre. The ground floor bays are divided by wide piers of rusticated stonework resting on a common base. The rustication is repeated on the architrave of the ground-floor windows, which have accentuated voussoirs and raised keystones curving to a point. This wide window treatment is very similar to one which occurs on the ground floor of the de la Salle palace in Valletta, and which is dated about 1600; but the general arrangement of the façade of the Vittoriosa palace is far more competent than that of the de la Salle palace. In fact, if we believe that it dates from the first half of the seventeenth century, it is certainly one of the most competent palace façades of this period on the island. The rusticated piers give way to smooth slabs on the *piano nobile* and these are divided to represent coupled pilasters.[490] The intervening windows are larger and nobler, crowned with entablature and cornice, and their balconies are tied to the pedestals of the pilaster strips by a string course broken forward over balcony and pedestal.

The attic is subdivided by a string course which joins the plain architrave of the attic windows at the springing of their arches. This subdivision reduces the importance and the apparent height of the

74. *Siggiewi. Summer palace of the Inquisitor.*

attic storey. An impressive sombre façade has been aimed at and achieved largely through the abolition of ornate details, whilst at the same time the overall mass of the building is broken down into related units which are more comprehensible.

The Inquisitor had another residence built in the late seventeenth

489. One is illustrated in Luke facing p.89.
490. This use of the coupled pilaster strip without ornament also occurs in Italy. Cosimo Fanzago uses it on the palazzo Gentile at Barletta (*c.* 1620) and on the dome of S. Maria Egiziaca, Naples (1651); Carlo Fontana uses it on the façades of Sta. Margherita in Trastevere, Rome (1680) and S. Maria ad Nives, Rome; and Sardi on SS. Quaranta Martiri, Rome.

century at Ghirgenti, near Casal, Siggiewi. This palace is made up of three blocks : the centre one of two storeys and the two wings of three; with a chapel to the north connected by a corridor. The façade is plain, but not severe, and the orders are replaced by un-moulded strips which show the division of the floors and mark the corners of the blocks even though these lie in one continuous face. Even the windows are undecorated and merely surrounded by a plain architrave which projects slightly from the face of the wall. The arrangement of the plan with the three blocks and the extended position of the chapel was dictated by the site, for the palace lies on a long ridge of rock. The centre block has three rooms across the east side and a narrow space on the western side containing the staircase, and in plan is typical of many houses built on the islands in the early years of the eighteenth century. It should be

316 compared with the small house which was situated near the Customs House in Valletta and illustrated in the *Cabreo di Vilhena* (1722–36).[491] It has three rooms, with a staircase at the back. The small

315 country house at Ta Bieb il Gzira (1732) has four rooms across the front with a narrower loggia containing the staircase and opening on to the garden at the back. It is essentially the same as

83 at Santa Vennera.[492]

308   The Armeria palace at Zurrieq was also built in the last years of the seventeenth century and was used as an armoury during the Grand Masterships of Pinto, Ximines, and de Rohan, and was eventually sold to Saverio Verario Crispo in 1784. Its façade, stripped of decoration, illustrates the move toward simplicity which took place in these years. This façade is broken down by means of panels separated by plain pilaster strips, the base is painted a darker colour, and the centre of the palace is emphasized by the flight of steps, a balcony on plain corbel supports, and the raised cornice and roof line over the carved figure. A crenellated watch tower was built at the back of the building.

312   The Spinola palace (1688)[493] at St. Julian's Bay is one of the most charming houses of the period, surrounded by a walled garden which on one side slopes down to two small loggias on the edge of the bay; but architecturally it is a compromise throughout. The first floor plan consists of three main units across the front, sub-divided into smaller rooms, with a staircase on the south wall—the side which looks across the garden to the Spinola Road. The great

491. *Cabreo di Vilhena* in the Royal Malta Library, MS. Collection.
492. Both are illustrated in *Cabreo di Vilhena*.
493. Braun, *Works of Art* p.21.

central hall rises to the *piano nobile* and embraces both ground and mezzanine floors. In spite of this simple general layout the plan is not symmetrical : the doors and windows of the great hall and the

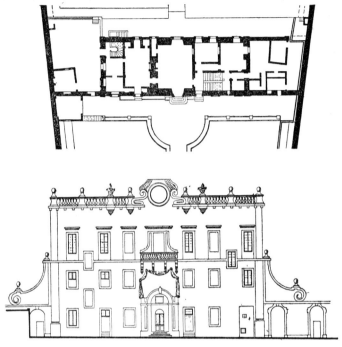

75–76. *St. Julian's Bay. Spinola palace, plan and seafront.*

room above are not placed centrally and the haphazard disposition of all the windows is only partly overcome on the façades by the introduction of dummy window frames. The north façade, which faces the bay, is about 112 feet long, and except for an elaborate centrepiece and the carved balustrade with urns which decorate the skyline, carving is reduced to a minimum. The string courses and the corner pilasters, the main cornice, and the architraves of the doors and windows, are all plain blocks of uncarved stone : even the pseudo-Palladian motif of the central door is merely sketched in flat stone.[494] Although the corner pilasters have bases on the ground floor, both orders omit the capital mouldings for further simplicity. One mezzanine window resentfully punctures the main

494. Palladio produced a similar type of Palladian motif on the garden façade of the Villa Poiana at Poiana Maggiore where no decoration relieves the severity of the expression.

string course and is balanced by a dummy on the opposite side of the door.

The designs which were made with bold pilasters at the corners of the buildings have an interesting origin. In many of the Roman palaces of the sixteenth century rusticated quoins were applied to the corners of the buildings to give apparent strength. These pilasters were tied together by a powerful cornice and quite often a string course at floor levels, which ran the full length of the façade.[495] This was the method adopted by Gerolamo Cassar on many of the Valletta auburges, and it was Cassar who set the fashion in Malta.

Then in certain Mannerist façades, such as the Vigna of Pope Julius in Rome, by Peruzzi,[496] these rusticated quoins and the cornice were replaced by corner pilasters and the full entablature which ran unsupported the length of the building. The apparent instability of this entablature, supported only at its extremities, produced the necessary disquieting effect aimed at by the Mannerist architects. As this feature came into regular use[497] the shock was less pronounced until finally the motif was accepted on the assumption that the solid wall of the building did in fact act as a support to the entablature. In some cases the mouldings of pilasters, capitals, and entablatures, were replaced by plain strips of masonry;[498] and used in these two ways, the motif became very popular in Malta and Sicily. Most of the larger buildings in Malta built during the seventeenth and eighteenth centuries were enclosed within these corner pilasters which, following the proportions of Cassar's quoins, were usually squat and massive.

Some Maltese examples will be discussed in the next section on the larger palaces but, before passing on, I should like to illustrate a typical early eighteenth century example of a small town house from the *Cabreo di Vilhena*. It consists of two floors, with shops on the ground floor and mezzanine accommodation. The main rooms of the house are on the first floor. All three are *en suite* and each has access to a balcony. The street entrance is at the back of the house, and the main staircase is built against the back wall. The façades are plain. On the ground floor a projected plinth course is

495. e.g. Palazzi Farnese, Palma, and Porto di Ripetta.
496. And on his façade on S. Pietro in Montorio, Rome.
497. Serlio IV *Dell'ordine Dorico*: Palazzo Altieri, Palazzo Barberini on the top floor, Palazzo Montecitorio, and Carlo Fontana's project for the Imperial stables at Vienna.
498. Casa Vaccarini, Catania, and the Inquisitor's palace at Ghirenti, are two typical examples.

carried around the doors to form simple architrave mouldings. The main south-east corner of the building is braced with a bold pilaster which runs the full height of the house, broken with a moulding at first-floor level. Windows in the *piano nobile* are more decorated and have moulded canopies. The wooden balconies, supported on carved stone consoles, which are so popular a feature in Malta, were already in evidence at this date (1722–36).

We can see, therefore, that smaller houses have façades which fall into one of three categories: they are completely plain with neither cornice nor carved window frames; or they are pierced by recessed panels which break down their overall size; or they are bound by corner pilasters, often superimposed, and without clear capitals and entablatures.

Many Maltese houses have fine carved stone balconies, the joy **272–276** of Maltese masons. Qormi, and Victoria in Gozo, have some particularly fine examples, but many other villages have a few which are equally good. Early ones date from the beginning of the seventeenth century and are usually solid and supported on bold corbels. The decoration, particularly in Gozo, is incised into a rectangular framework giving some balconies an Arabic flavour. Stylised foliage, disposed in a regular fashion, festoons, and putti or carved heads, form the main features of the carver's skill in earlier examples, but bold balustrades are more common later.[499]

Some balconies are supported upon a cushioned frieze and cornice moulding which is bracketed from the wall in a continuous roll. There is a good example in St. Nicholas Street, Mdina, and others in Zabbar which bear the crescent moon of the Grand Master Pinto (1741–73). This type of balcony usually has a deeply recessed window, with a semicircular or segmental arch.

Although most small windows are severe and plain, some sixteenth century examples are gracefully and delicately carved: refined versions of the Melitan windows are on the Birgu auberges. There is an attractive example on 62 St. Catherine Street, Qormi, where the pediment is still raised clear of the window architrave, and three circular carved plaques occupy the position of the frieze. The sill breaks forward at each side to allow sufficient space for the plant pots which once indicated the number of marriageable daughters confined within the rooms and garden of the house. There are other similar and equally attractive examples of windows of this period in Siggiewi and Zebbug.

499. Though these occur as early as 1620 at 47 Parish Street, Qrendi.

Doorways, too, although influenced from abroad, take on characteristics which become truly Maltese. The most usual modest doorway is the type found on the side of the auberge d'Aragon in Valletta. A roll-shaped frame, often standing on a high plain base,
forms the architrave of the door which is headed by a semicircular
arch with a diameter slightly less than the width of the opening of
the door. The outer moulding of the architrave projects a little
below the springing of the arch and the break contains a single large
gutta.[500] Its final concave shape usually curves in to support the
balcony of the window above. There are variations and some doors
are decorated with strange auricled devices which come from
Spain.[501]

Most large and important palaces have richly decorated doorways
which are illustrated in the next section, but in several villages there
are smaller palaces with ornate doorways modelled on larger examples. 89 de Rohan Street, Zebbug, has a particularly fine one with
Doric columns and entablature running back into the wall, leaving
the cornice moulding, which forms the floor of the balcony, to span
the intercolumniation assisted by a pseudo-entablature which springs
forward over the keystone and is corbelled on a great scroll.

Larger palaces and public buildings of the 17th and 18th centuries

During the last years of the seventeenth century and the first half
of the eighteenth century a number of large and important buildings
was erected in Malta, mainly in Valletta and Mdina. Some were
palaces and some administrative buildings, needed to cope with the
government of an ever-increasing population.

In Valletta, the newly-formed Anglo-Bavarian langue was housed
in a large new auberge which was the gift of the Bailiff Carner in
1696.[502] This langue took over the responsibilities of the old langue
of Angleterre, and its Pilier became Turcopolier, in command of the
Order's cavalry and coastguards. The building was erected on the
Marsamuscetto side of the city and looked out across the Jews'

500. These are common in 18th century Italy and especially in Sicily.
501. The side door of the auberge de Castile et Leon and the main door of
  Notre Dame de Liesse, in Valletta, are modelled on this type. The most
  blatant example is on the first floor windows of the Prime Minister's
  Office in West Street, facing on Queen Adelaide's Square.
502. Scicluna p.212 states that Carner paid £1,408 for a new building in the
  year 1784—this seems to be an error. Pratt p.223 is mistaken in
  supposing that this auberge was designed by G. Cassar. It is much later.

Salley port and the German curtain. It is a monotonous block of
masonry, its main façade punctuated with a regular repetition of
windows which lie six on each side of a slightly projected centre-

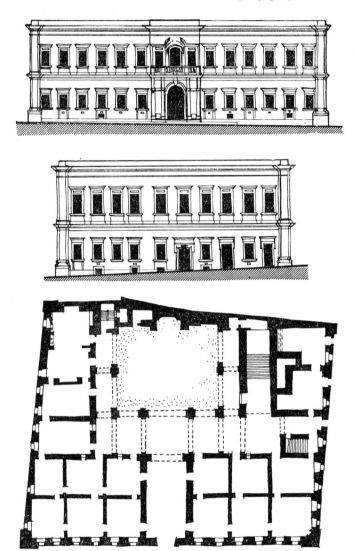

77–79. *Valletta. Auberge de Bavarie, main and side elevations ; plan.*

piece. In order to emphasize the centre further, the main window of
a group of three is semicircular headed and topped with a steeply

broken pediment. The door is typically Maltese,[503] but is blown up in size which makes it appear crude. The windows are delicately detailed, and on the first floor they have pseudo balconies similar to those which were added to the auberge d'Italie. The tall proportions of the windows are further heightened by large projecting panels above them, so that the overriding cornice is high above the lintel for the opening.[504] The designer[505] has made the building seem secure by adding bold pilasters to the corners. Their proportions are massive and their capitals intermingle with cornice and string course.[506]

The building was erected around a court on three sides, with an ample peristyle enlarged along one side. The main façade is symmetrical, and the others are as near symmetry as possible : the entrance hall leads directly to the peristyle and the court. Although the site is slightly irregular, internally the rooms are made rectangular. This shows a keener awareness of proportion and internal shape than was shown by the architect of the earlier Inquisitor's palace at Vittoriosa. There is a wide staircase at one side of the court and the first floor is almost identical with the ground floor. In the courtyard, as on the corners of the façade, there is the same confusion of capital and entablature, and the string course supporting the upstairs balcony seems quite inadequate. The arches of the intercolumniation are wide and depressed to less than a half circle.[507]

319 The Banco Guiratale, or the Municipal palace was built in Merchants' Street, Valletta, about the year 1720.[508] It has a ground floor of noble proportions with a powerfully shaped Doric portal. The entablatures of the columns run back into the wall, leaving the cornice moulding to span the intercolumniation and support the balcony, assisted only by the corbelled keystone. This very same feature was used by Gerolamo Cassar on the porch of the Conven-

---

503. It follows the style of the door on the side of the auberge d'Aragon and many Maltese houses.
504. This gives them a familiar character, similar, at first sight, to the type with detached cornices which had been used by Gerolamo Cassar on the Magisterial palace at Valletta.
505. We do not know the name of the architect.
506. This lack of clear definition in the capital and entablature began with Cassar's architecture but was very common at this time both in Malta and Sicily.
507. There is a similar treatment in the court of the auberge de Castile et Leon.
508. Paribeni p.III describes it as a building of sober lines. Grand Master Zondadari (1720–22), distinguished for his severity and austerity of life, inspired the lines of this building. This is hardly true for, whilst the ground floor has a noble grandeur, neither the first floor windows nor the main cornice and centrepiece can be called sober.

tual church in Valletta and it occurred also on the portico of 156
Zebbug parish church, many years before this palace was designed. 179
It is later used, in a modified form, on the auberge de Castile. 327

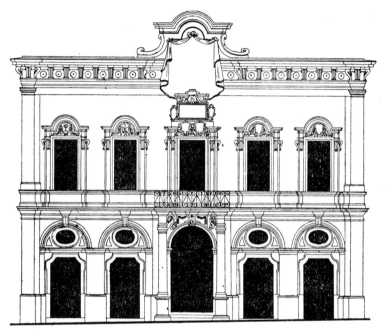

80. Valletta. Municipal palace.

This palace has many points of similarity with the auberge de Castile,
which was built about twenty-four years later : the scrolled centrepiece,
containing carved drapery, is similar; the same carved corbels support the main cornice, though here they are more regularly spaced
with intervening plaques; the first floor windows, their pediments
flat, but with the centrepiece raised to a segmental arch; and the
corner pilasters on the first floor raised up on pedestals, but here
the line of the pedestal is carried across the façade and integrated
with the plain projecting balconies. The ground floor pilasters have
no entablature, but their capital mouldings are also carried across
the façade to form a string course. Beside the main door there are
four other openings on the ground floor for shops; these are spanned
with semicircular-headed arches resting on plain squat pilasters and
the arch is further pierced by an oval eye. In this way the tradi-

tional Maltese oval window is introduced and an added depth is imparted to the Baroque façade.[509]

In 1730 Giovanni Barbara designed the Municipal palace in the old capital,[510] a fine building which has a strong French flavour. The plan is French, with an open courtyard, and the palace is set back around three sides of it. A screen occupies the fourth side and separates the court from the road. The main door, which is one of the finest of the period in Malta, is also suggestive of France, and the banded columns are similar to those used by Philibert de l'Orme on the Tuileries (1515) :[511] the proportions are noble and the carving is much to be admired. Segmental-headed windows, which mark the basement on each side of the main door, are constantly used by eighteenth century architects in France.[512] And the courtyard wings, with open balconies on three floors (two contained within the fluted Doric pilasters), and their very flat-headed arches, could have been inspired by the nave and clerestory treatment of many French churches of the Early Renaissance.[513]

A typical Valletta palace of this period, together with a small adjacent house, is illustrated in the *Cabreo di Vilhena* (1722–36). The palace, which was called Correa House, was built by Fra Antonio Correa de Sousa before 1689,[514] on the corner of Old Bakery Street and Old Theatre Street. It had three storeys, with a mezzanine between the ground and first floors. A part of the ground floor was let off as shops.

The façade was divided into three sections, each defined by heavy squat pilasters, Doric below and Ionic above, the lower order with no proper entablature, but with a string course carried across the building. The small first-floor windows had projected stone balconies, but the main windows on the second floor had slightly projecting stone balconies which were solid and of wide proportion.

509. The same arrangement occurs on the Palazzo Marescotti at Rome (*c.* 1583) by della Porta and the Palazzo Pamfili, Rome; there are several examples in Serlio IV.
510. Scicluna calls it the Magisterial palace.
511. These banded columns were in fact invented by de l'Orme and were called French columns. He considered that, where the shaft was not monolithic, it was more logical to show the breaks in the shaft. The French column was illustrated in *L'Architecture de Philibert de l'Orme*, Paris 1567, Liv.VII, Chap.xiii.
512. They often occur in northern Italy, especially around Milan.
513. In particular, the chapel of the Jesuit College at La Flêche and the church of Saint-Paul-Saint-Louis at Paris, where the large order embraces two storeys and the clerestory is introduced with balustrades and flattened arches.
514. Bought by the Manoel Foundation 18 October 1732. I am indebted to Mr. V. F. Denaro for this information.

Because of the height of the second floor, the main portal was flanked by Doric columns on tall pilasters, and from the broken entablatures great scrolls swung up and out to support a balustraded

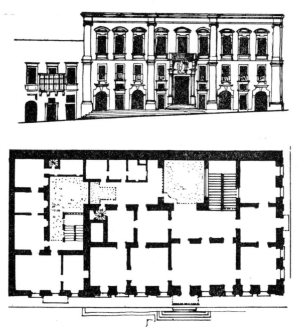

81–82. *Valletta. Correa House.*

balcony in front of the central window. The space below the window was filled with an elaborate cartouche of the arms of the family : thus the door seems similar in conception to the main door of the Municipal palace in Valletta and the narrow lintel of the balcony is supported in its wide span only by the spikey protrusions of the ornate shield. The plan is compressed and consists of four main rooms across the front, two others down the side street and a staircase and small court at the back, the staircase leading onto a covered loggia.

The Leone palace at Santa Vennera, which is sometimes referred to as the Vilhena palace, was built in 1730, and is also illustrated in the *Cabreo.* Here is a country villa spaciously laid out on the Palladian pattern : a more or less symmetrical plan, consisting of a central block with wings projected forwerd. The main block is typically Maltese, with three rooms across the front and narrower rooms behind, one of which contains the staircase. The plan lacks

319

the precision of Palladio's work.[515] At the back a large formal walled garden is laid out on a strong axis.[516]

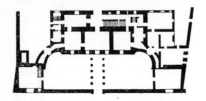

83. *Santa Vennera. Leone palace.*

The Manoel theatre in Valletta, begun in 1731, is one of the oldest in Europe. It was named after the Grand Master, and for its inaugural performance the *Merope* by Francesco Scipione Maffei (1675–1755) was presented on 19 January 1732. The plan of the theatre was modelled on the theatre at Palermo.[517] The auditorium

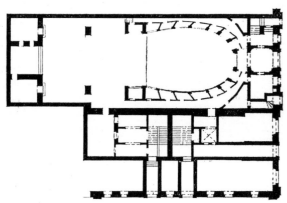

84. *Valletta. Manoel theatre, ground floor plan.*

313 is now egg-shaped, but in the plan in the *Cabreo di Vilhena* it appears as a semicircle with straight sides projecting to the stage.[518]

515. The rooms each side of the entrance are not quite square (17ft. 11in. x 22ft. 1in. upstairs and 17ft. 4in. x 18ft. 11in. downstairs) and the hall has dimensions which are not closely related (26ft. 1in. x 19ft.). For an explanation of Palladio's rhythmical dispositions see Wittkower, *Architectural Principles* pp.63–66.
516. The walled gardens of Malta are particularly noteworthy. Even more than in Italy, the Maltese garden became a collection of open-air rooms, so that one passes from one to another, each clearly defined in shape, each planted in contrasting colours or patterns. Two good examples are: the gardens of St. Anton's palace at Attard and the smaller and more intimate gardens of the 18th century Villa Parisio at Lija.
517. Scicluna p.215.
518. It was repaired in 1844. Alterations to the auditorium may have taken place at this date.

It had three floors of boxes (the top floor consisted of five boxes and open galleries at each side) with two rooms and a staircase placed across the front. The façade was simple and showed three floors with a mezzanine between ground and first. Its windows were kept well into the centre of the façade and bounded by coupled pilasters which embraced the two upper floors, and which rested on a large advertisement panel. There were three doors : the main door, with its meagrely supported balcony, was similar to the one on the Municipal palace in Merchants' Street.

In 1733 Barbara designed the Episcopal Seminary at Mdina.[519] If **322** the source of the nearby Municipal palace was France, no trace of French influence is discernible in the Episcopal Seminary : for this is pure Sicilian, and is thus strongly flavoured by the ideas of the Spanish architects. The ornate porch and sculptured balcony supported upon Atlantes, the recessed centrepiece, the rounded corners which bulge out from the corner pilasters, the ear shapes which are particularly pronounced on the main windows, and the flaming vases set above the crowning cornice : all find their counterpart in Syracuse and Palermo and the Baroque cities of Italy.[520]

The reconstruction and remodelling of the auberge de Castile et Leon in Valletta was the most important architectural operation of **325–326** the eighteenth century in Malta. The auberge was originally designed by Gerolamo Cassar, but it is unlikely that any of the earlier building now remains visible. Some writers have suggested that the massive corner pilasters may be the remnant of Cassar's earlier building, but I see no reason to assume this in view of the fact that stumpy pilasters on two floors were a common feature of Maltese buildings in the eighteenth century. Nor does it seem possible that Cassar's original façade could have been as large as it now is. The reconstruction was carried out by Cachia in 1744, during the Grand Mastership of the Portugese Emanuel Pinto. It is certain that Cachia visited Sicily and southern Italy before undertaking this work, and studied the Convent of S. Nicola (S. Benedetto) at Catania (1693–1735) and the Prefettura at Lecce; the latter building in particular becoming his source of inspiration for

519. Calleja, *Works of Art* p.90.
520. It is strange that Luke p.78, who is so correct when he points out the usual restrained character of Maltese Baroque, should single out this particular building, which is surely one of the exceptions to the rule, and liken it more to the 'restrained domestic Baroque of Salzburg and Vienna than the frenzied extravangances of the architects of the period in Sicily and Calabria,'

the Valletta palace.[521]

Both the façade and the plan are the finest works of architecture in eighteenth century Valletta. The façade is rich, yet not over ornate, and has pleasing proportions. The rhythm of pilaster, recessed panel, and centrepiece projection, is enlivening, and the recessed rustication of the ground floor gives the building a solidity which is needed because of the large wall surface above the main floor windows. The decoration is reserved for the corbelled cornice,

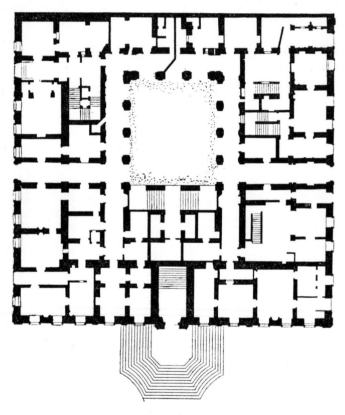

85. Valletta. Auberge de Castile et Leon.

327-328   the windows and, above all, for the very rich central focus which is here most admirably handled, so that the palace shows none of the lack of concentration apparent in many of the sprawling palaces of Baroque Rome. Both in the proportion of the façade and the crispness of the detail Cachia has outshone his master from Lecce.

521. This is pointed out by Briggs, *Baroque Architecture* p.119, and Sitwell, *Southern Baroque Art* p.303,

Its plan is the only example of monumental Baroque planning in domestic architecture on the island. However, most of the dimensions vary from point to point and it is not absolutely regular in its detailed measurements. These variations are almost certain to be due to the result of imposing a new plan on Cassar's earlier auberge. The building is arranged around a central court, with the large main block at one end containing a central entrance hall approached up a flight of steps from the Castile Square, and from the courtyard through the staircase block. The wings are double down the sides and single at the back. The courtyard is more sombre than the exterior of the auberge and has a colonnade built on two storeys around the back and sides. The walls are divided by plain clustered pilasters with arched openings set between them, and with sturdy balustrades on the first floor : the ground-floor arches are flattened.

The Castellania, which is in Merchants' Street, was begun to the 329 designs of the Maltese architect Francesco Zerafa in 1748.[522] It replaced an earlier building and housed the Civil and Criminal Courts. Zerafa died in 1758 and Giusseppe Bonici was called in to complete the building, which he did by 1760.[523] The carving was carried out by a Sicilian, Maestro Gian, and it was he who carved the figures of *Justice* and *Truth* on the centrepiece. The chapel of the Castellania was blessed, on the completion of the building, on 15 November 1760 by the Vice-Prior Constano.

The façade is symmetrical and on two floors. The upper floor (the *piano nobile*), is shown by the large windows and the single large recessed panel on each side of the centrepiece. The ground floor is let off for shops and the keepers have living accommodation in a mezzanine floor above each shop. The individual character of the eight shops is expressed in eight recessed panels on this floor. As with so many Maltese palaces of this period, an attempt has been made to create a concentration on the centre. The corners are defined by bold clustered pilasters, the roof by a strong cornice supported on corbels, and the centrepiece by its triple concave doorway. Its elaborate main window, and raised segmental cornice containing carved paraphernalia, leads the eye into the building. Though much of the detail is crude in comparison with contemporary Roman practice, there is no doubt that the problem has been more successfully solved than it has in such buildings as the Palazzo Madama and the Palazzo Odescalchi.

522. Scicluna p.215. This is now the Public Health Office.
523. Darmanin Demajo, *Archivio Storico di Malta* III, p.207. Rebuilding commenced in 1757.

The crescent moon, insignia of the Grand Master Pinto, is much in evidence on the façade of this palace in Valletta. Pinto was partial to personal recognition and his crest is carved on buildings all over the island. The building is planned around three sides of a small courtyard with the main accommodation on the front. The

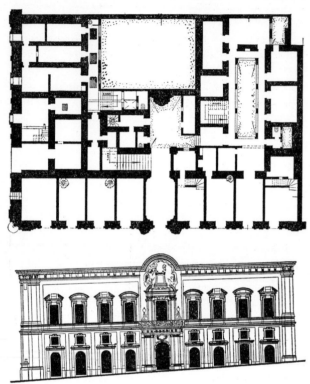

86–87. *Valletta. Castellania.*

ground floor rooms are small, and their walls thick to support the weight of the rooms above. The side wings are broader than those across the front : the left-hand one having two rooms in depth, and the right-hand one is so broad that it required an additional small court to light it. Thus, although the façade is symmetrical, the plan is not; and the entrance lobby leads toward one end of the court and the staircase opens off one side of it. Above, the rooms are intercommunicating and also fed from a loggia which is joined to the staircase.

The Parisio palace, which is higher up Merchants' Street, was built about the same time and has a similar plan consisting of three

blocks built around a courtyard. Its main façade is again symmetrical and the plan is not. The front block is only one room
deep and the side blocks have two rooms in their breadth. The

88. *Valletta. Parisio palace.*

façade is sober and with little emphasis on the centre, save for an
elaborate doorway and a broken segmental-headed window above :
but the front is not long, with only five windows in its length, so
that the expedients adopted in the other palaces need not be resorted

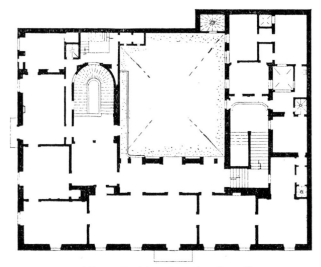

89. *Valletta. Parisio palace, first floor plan.*

to here. The windows have been spaced so that a semblance of
order was obtained on the elevation and more or less regular
spacing occurred inside the main room. One corner has large superimposed pilasters, the lower one being heavily rusticated. It is

185

strange to notice that the joints of the rustication bear no relation-
318 ship to the courses of the masonry. This palace was originally the
property of the Ventimiglia family and was later occupied by
Parisio-Muscati. From the 12th to the 18th June 1798 it was the
residence of Napoleon, and it is now the General Post Office.[524]

From the first quarter of the eighteenth century the tendency of
322 some architects was to react sharply against such decorated façades
310-311 as the Seminary at Mdina and the Archbishop's palace at Valletta.
The movement in Malta was in accordance with the expanding
practice of the Academic School in Italy and the Neo-Classical
School in Spain, and its influence is increasingly apparent in the
last three important buildings I shall describe.

330 The Seminary at Floriana, which was built in 1751, has a very
beautiful delicately carved Baroque door, and richly decorated
ground floor windows (though many are left unfinished, mere slabs
of uncarved stone); the remainder of the building is plain. Windows
are set in plain recessed panels (the centre panel above embracing
three), the first-floor windows are severe, and the main cornice has
no richly carved supports.

By the turn of the half-century funds were considerably reduced
332 and building work cut down. The Valletta Customs House was not
started until 1774.[525] It is the masterpiece of Giuseppe Bonici and a
true building of the Academic School. It was built just outside the
Mina Lascaris on the Marina, facing out across the Grand Harbour
almost at sea level. Bonici was first an engineer, and the solidity of
this building is remarkable. The foundations were sunk into the
waters of the Grand Harbour and the walls, many up to twelve feet
thick, were built up to first-floor level with Coralline limestone to
resist the damaging sea spray. The upper part was built with the
normal Globigerina limestone. The lower floor was vaulted and the
upper rooms had flat ceilings.

The plan is beautifully precise and is symmetrical, with a central
hall cutting through the building, bounded by two shorter rooms.
The remaining space is occupied by a staircase and subsidiary rooms.

The façade consists of superimposed coupled Doric pilasters,
slightly re-entrant at the corners of the building. The lower order is
rusticated with sharp rectangular blocks of masonry. The front

524. The resemblance should be noticed between the top-floor windows and
those on the Selmun palace by Cachia.
525. Zammit, *Valletta* p.72. Planned under G. M. Pinto (1741-73) built
under G. M. Ximines (1773–75) and completed under G. M. de Rohan
(1775–97).

consists of five bays, the centre three breaking forward slightly, the projection being shown by a half pilaster and a double break in the cornice. Three semicircular-headed windows on the first floor contain segmental pedimented windows. The three on the ground floor

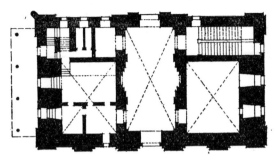

90. *Valletta. Customs House, ground floor plan.*

have their pattern repeated in semicircular-headed door frames. The bases of the pilasters are sturdy and the windows in the wings have triangular pediments to strengthen that wall surface. The main emphasis is on the three centre bays and the base of the corners, where one massive pilaster is used; but playing against this emphasis the façade breaks to and fro like the waves on an agitated sea. The main portal on the north side is a projection set in a recession, well proportioned and sturdy. The rusticated pilasters are strong and join with the alternate stones of the arch ring. The entablature is full, supporting a low balustrade with a plain continuous run. Altogether, the Customs House is a fine building with a strongly Venetian air.

331

It is unfortunate that whilst so many fine buildings were designed by Maltese architects, the last important one to be erected, and thus the last one to be described, should have been non-Maltese. This building was the new library in Valletta completed in 1786[526] and the architect was Stefano Ittar, who came over from Calabria in order to carry out the work.

The Knights had long since established a library where the books of deceased Knights could be deposited,[527] though it was often found difficult to carry out the instruction of the Chapter in this respect. In 1612, Grand Master Wignacourt passed a statute which

526. Braun, *Works of Art* p.41 just gives the date 1786. Scicluna p.112 says it was completed in 1796: surely this is a misprint for 1786. Ittar died in Malta in 1790.
527. Grand Chapter of the Order on 24 May 1555 in the Birgu, under the Grand Mastership of de la Sengle.

forbade the sale of books belonging to deceased Knights. Originally a large hall adjoining the Conventual church in Valletta was used to house the books, but this proved inadequate and they were moved to another part of the church by Fra Pietro Viani. During the eighteenth century the library expanded rapidly for in 1760 Cardinal Giocchino left 5,670 volumes, and in 1763 a further 9,700 books were received from Guerin de Tencin. The need for more space became imperative so in 1776 the Venerable Sixteen decreed the immediate erection of a new building. The expense was deferred by the Bailiff Perez de Sarrio and work was begun by Ittar.[528]

The façade, which adjoins the Magisterial palace and faces onto a small square, is an Academic composition on two floors, its centre marked with a raking cornice and pediment. There is nothing loose in the design : all is orderly and restrained.

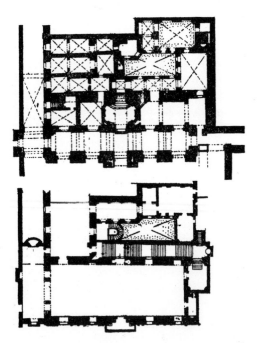

91–92. *Valletta. Library of the Order, ground and upper floor plans.*

The plan follows earlier Maltese practice. The ground floor consists of five long narrow areas, often subdivided, with thick walls

528. Scicluna p.205.

which buttress each other. The first area is an arched colonnade facing the square, and the staircase is in the centre of the second area. On the main floor, the large room of the library lies over these two long areas : this hall measures 138 feet by forty-two feet ten inches and there is another adjoining room, forty-four feet by thirty-one feet. The library was in full use, and already contained some 30,000 volumes, when the French army invaded Malta in 1798.[529]

529. But V. F. Denaro maintains that although the building was completed just before the French invasion, it was not until 1812 that the books were moved to their new premises under the Governorship of Sir Hildebrand Oakes

CHAPTER FOUR

Building Materials and Methods of Construction

Description of the Islands

GRAND MASTER de l'Isle Adam, before accepting the islands, sent Commissioners to examine the countryside and their report gives a fair, if somewhat gloomy, account of Malta in the year 1530. Whilst realizing that the place had tremendous possibilities due to its fine natural harbours, and approving it as the new home for the Religion, they pointed out 'that the island of Malta was merely a rock of soft sandstone, called Tufe, about six or seven leagues long and three or four broad; that the surface of the rock was barely covered with more than three or four feet of earth, which was likewise stony, and very unfit to grow corn and other grain; that it produced abundance of figs, melons, and different fruits; that the principal trade of the island consisted of honey, cotton, and cummin, which the inhabitants exchanged for grain; that, except for a few springs in the middle of the island, there was no running water, nor even wells; that wood was so scarce as to be sold by the pound —which forced them to use either cowdung dried in the sun, or wild thistle, for preparing food.' . . .[530]

However, there was another saving grace, and that was the abundant supply of building stone of the best quality with which they were able to transform a 'residence in Malta (which) appeared extremely disagreeable, indeed, almost unsupportable, particularly in summer'[531] into a 'place which equals in its noble architecture, if it does not excel, any capital in Europe.'[532]

The climate is hot in the summer and, although the mean average rainfall over the last twenty years has been about twenty-one inches,

530. Boisgelin II, p.16. Report of the Commissioners in 1530.
531. Boisgelin II, pp.15–16.
532. Disraeli, *Henrietta Temple,* London 1837.

Malta is generally dry in the summer months. In fact, long periods of protracted drought have been known, and the years 1467 to 1470 are particularly memorable, when not a single drop of rain fell for five years and drinking water had to be imported from Sicily. The abundant good building stone combined with lack of timber which, were it plentiful, would be used sparingly because the hot dry sun tends to draw all the moisture out of the wood, drying it so that it cracks : these have produced a type of building which seems very different from neighbouring Sicily only sixty miles to the north. The houses are rectangular[533] cubes with flat roofs which collect the rain water and lead it to cisterns under the floor of the courtyard. The window openings are small and the face of the house turns inward onto the courtyard, so that the tramontana (which blows cold and icy in the winter) and the humid sirocco (which breathes across the island in spring and autumn) are excluded as much as possible[534] and in summer the interiors kept cool from the glaring sun.

Geology of the Islands

The stones of Malta are laid in five beds : 1 Upper Coralline limestone. 2 Greensand, 3 Blue clay, 4 Globigerina limestone, and 5 Lower Coralline limestone; with the Globigerina limestone bed yielding the most useful building stone. An ideal section through the island reveals two hard layers of Coralline limestone separated by a layer of soft Globigerina limestone.

The Upper Coralline lies along the high ridge of land on the south-west side of Malta; the high strip, that is, which stretches from Kalafrana in the south, through Mdina and Rabat, to meet the three ridges at the north which cut across at right angles to the

533. The exception are the small round houses called *Girna* built of dry wall construction. They are not numerous and seem to have descended from the oval megalithic tombs of Malta and to be akin to the *trulli* of Alberobello in Puglia. Harrison and Hubbard, *Maltese Vernacular* p.77.
534. The winds are important in Malta because of its exposed position, and buildings are often sited to avoid certain winds. The winter tramontana blows 6% of the year and often carries hail; the scirocco for 13% in spring and autumn blows from the south-east, sand-laden from the African desert, it picks up moisture over the sea. The gregale (15%) is a violent, blustery wind which usually blows for period of three days and then ceases as rapidly as it came : it blows from the north-east; and the pleasant cool breezes of the mistral, which are so welcome in summer (29%) blow over the sea from the north-west.

main high mass, and which are also made up of Upper Coralline limestone.

The Globigerina limestone beds occupy the lower land between the ridges and the great central basin of the island, with occasional outcrops of Lower Coralline limestone which become more frequent as we move toward the north-east coast.

As a building stone, the top four beds of the Upper Coralline limestone, which are white and rubbly, are useless except for very rough dry country walls. The stone is very porous, easily breaks up, and weathers into holes very rapidly. The third layer, though the shell casts are smaller, is also useless except for the very roughest of walls. The third layer has a closer structure and is more crystalline, giving it a semi-translucent appearance. Because of the shell casts it has to be carefully selected, but well chosen pieces are used for local buildings in the areas where it outcrops, and the buildings have weathered and endured well. It is quarried at Mellieha, where it has to be carefully selcted as there are fissures containing a soft white powder which makes some of the stone weather badly. It is also quarried at 'Ta Ghalia,' south-east of Mdina, where the stone from the lower beds comes out in large sizes, is hard wearing, and polishes well. It is also quarried in considerable quantity in Gozo where it is referred to as Gozo marble.

The Greensand is useless as a building material for it crumbles in the hand; nor is it suitable for mortar without a great deal of washing. It was used to build the old cemetery at Fort Cambray in Gozo, and 'these walls have weathered away very badly and show the harder fossils in high relief.'[535]

The Globigerina limestone lies in two layers. The upper layer, containing more clayey matter, is a blue or grey colour; the lower one, containing the important building stones, is rose coloured, warm, and soft. Murray[536] has propounded the theory that all the Globigerina rock was a bluish colour when it was raised above the sea bed, but due to oxidization it has slowly changed to a reddish colour. In the passage of time the blue rock will gradually disappear. To support this he describes a wall 200 years old, which has a core of blue rock entirely surrounded by reddish coloured stone, the red zone extending one-and-a-half inches in depth into the wall; the result of oxidization which has occurred since the stones were placed in position in the wall. The oxidization therefore working at a rate of one inch each 133 years.

535. Murray p.465.
536. Murray p.469.

The two coloured layers of Globigerina limestone are divided into nine beds which have been classified by Colson[537] as follows :

1. Top bed. Pale grey rock, well developed in the cliffs above Munsciar. It is soft, weathers badly, and scales off when exposed to the air. It can be used only for rough building.
2. Top nodule seam. Useless for building.
3. A thin layer of soft stone containing nodules of selenite, manganese, etc.
4. A nodule seam with sharks' teeth.
5. A band of greenish nodules partially embedded in the overlying layer.
6. A pale red, yellowish, or bluish rock which weathers badly. Used for rough walls or infilling.
7. A whitish-yellow fine-grained rock with small nodules of chert. It is used largely as a building stone, but is harder to work than 9 because of the cherts. This increases the cost of working it by about a third. The main quarry is at Imghieret. The method of getting the stones out of the quarry is by cutting a four inch trench around the block, then wedging it up from the bottom. The large block is then split into smaller blocks with wedges and dressed to the required size with large, heavy axes.
8. A thin line of nodules, no use for building. This seam is often missing.
9. This seam holds the greatest quantity of the island's building stone. It is pale yellow in colour, mainly composed of very minute fossils. It is soft and easily worked, and hardens somewhat on exposure to the air. It weathers well and in time a light reddish-brown colour. It is easily quarried with wedges and dressed with broad-blade axes. The section through a typical quarry, such as that at Ta Daul, reveals about two feet of surface soil, then six inches to two feet of broken, rotten stone which is called *torba*. The main seam of good stone is between twenty-five and forty feet thick, and below that there is a layer of darker stone, called *saul,* which will not stand exposure to the air. This *saul* is often used for foundations, or in places where it does not come into contact with the air. The Globigerina covers about a third of the surface of Malta.

The Lower Coralline limestone is in many respects similar to the Upper Coralline, but it is generally more crystalline. The harder varieties are known as Malta and Gozo marbles and granites, and

537. Murray p.472.

93. 'Cité de Valete de Malthe' by Pierre Mortier.

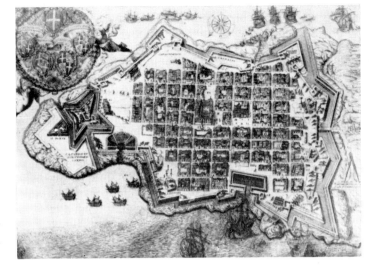

94. Aerial perspective of Valletta and the Three Cities by Carpentier.

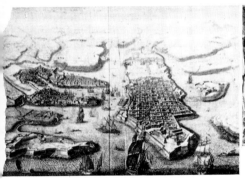

95. Valletta and the Three Cities (18th century Italian engraving).

96. The New City of Valletta (from Bosio).

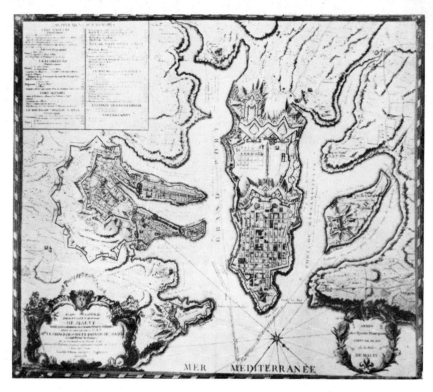

97. Valletta and the Three Cities (engraving of 1757).

98. Fort St. Angelo and Vittoriosa from Valletta.

99. Fort Manoel (from *Cabreo di Vilhena*).

100. Vittoriosa. Sentry-box on Fort St. Angelo.

1. Vittoriosa. Sentry-box on Fort St. Angelo.

102. Cotonera Lines. Zabbar gate, inside (1675).

103–104. Cotonera Lines. 18th century gates between St. Louis and St. James Bastions.

105. Cotonera Lines. Polverista gate and St. Nicholas curtain.

106. Vittoriosa. Main gate to Fort St. Angelo (1690).

107. Floriana. Porte des Bombes (*c.* 1697–1720).

108. Vittoriosa. Advanced gate (1722).

109. Vittoriosa. Couvre Porte (1723).

110. Mdina. Main gate (1724).

111. Vittoriosa. Main gate (1727).

112. Zebbug. De Rohan arch (1677).

113. Valletta. Sentry-box on the junction of
the English and French curtains.

114. Cospicua. St. Helen's gate, outside (1736).   115. Fort Manoel. Gate (1726).

116. Mdina. Lower gate (1724).   117. Zabbar. Hompesch arch (1798).

118. Kalkara. Fort Ricasoli gate (1698).

119. Mellieha. Red Tower (17th century).

120. St. Paul's Bay. Wignacourt Tower (1610).

121. Zejtun. St. Thomas' Tower (1614).

122. Rabat. Verdala palace (1586).

23. Rabat. St. Augustine's church, side door
(1571)

124. Rabat. Verdala palace, door.

125–126. Mellieha.
Selmun palace
(18th century).

127. Mdina. Our Lady of Victory 'Ta Qali.'

128. Zejtun. St. Gregory.

129. Gudia. St. Mary 'Ta Bir Miftuh' (1436).

130. Zejtun. St. Gregory.

131. Vittoriosa. Chapel of St. Anne in Fort St. Angelo.

132. Lija. Old parish church, south door.

133. Lija. Old parish church, dome.

134. Hamrun. Our Lady of Sorrows (*Pietà*) (1590).

135. Rabat. St. Anthony the Abbot in the grounds of Verdala palace.

136. Balzan. St. Roch (1593).

137. Zejtun. 'Tal Ingrau' (1597).

138. Zebbug. St. Roch (1593).

139. Qormi. St. Mary.   140. Qormi. St. Peter.

141. Mdina. A desecrated church (17th century).

142. Qrendi. St. Catherine ' Tat-Torba ' (rebuilt 1626).

143. Qrendi. St. Saviour (1658).

144. Qrendi. St. Catherine ' Tat-Torba,' main door.

145. Zebbug. Immaculate Conception (1677).

146–147. Qormi. 'Tal Hlas' (1690).

148. Qormi. St. Catherine (17th century).

149–150. Vittoriosa. Oratory of the Holy Crucifix (1720).

151–152. Rabat. St. Augustine (1571).

153. Valletta.
Conventual church
of St. John (1573).

154. *ditto.*
The apse.

155. Valletta. Conventual church of St. John, the façade.

156. *ditto*. Detail of main door.

158. *ditto.* Nave buttresses and aisle chapels.

157. Valletta. Conventual church of St. John, detail of blind wall in the oratory.

159. *ditto.* Detail of south sacristy door and window.

160. *ditto.* Sacristy door in Merchants' Street.

161–162. Valletta. Conventual church of St. John, window and door on south side.

163. Valletta. Carmelite church, nave (1573).

164. *ditto*. Tower and nave screens.

165. Florence. Project for façade of S. Lorenzo by Giuliano da Sangallo.

166. Qormi. Parish church of St. George (1584).

167. The façade of a church. (from Serlio V).

168. Qormi. Parish church of St. George, main door.

the colour varies from almost dead white, to red, cream, or a greyish colour. It is divided into two qualities, the first being hard, crystalline, non-porous and between yellowish-brown and white in colour, is easy to work, splitting into smooth straight slabs and weathering well on the building. The second quality is softer and more porous and does not weather quite so well as the first. Both are less porous than the Globigerina stones and are consequently used for foundations (where these are not solid rock) and the lower parts of walls exposed to driving rain, and sea spray which is exceedingly harmful to the Globigerina limestone causing it to disintegrate.

Lower Coralline stone is quarried at Hondak-ir-Rummien, where it varies in colour between dark and light brownish-yellow, and at Ghar-id-Dorf, where it is white or cream-coloured. There are other quarries at Fex Fux, Musta, Madalena, and Malak in Malta, and Sannat in Gozo.

Although there are stone quarries in many parts of the islands, much of the stone used for building houses during the period of the Knights, especially in Valletta, was excavated from the cellars. The crypt of St. John's, Valletta, was the quarry for the church, and most of the lines of fortifications were faced with stone excavated from their ditches.[538] Quantities of stone were dug from the Manderaggio in Valletta where the Knights intended to build a small creek for light craft. And a regulation at one time specified that only Manderaggio stone should be used for building houses in Valletta[539] so that the work on the creek could be finished in the shortest possible time.[540]

Methods of stone construction in Malta

The foundations of Maltese buildings are almost invariably formed by the solid rock, cushioned with a little soil and mortar to get an even surface. The rock in Malta lies close to the surface with rarely more than about a foot of soil to cover it.

The walls of the houses are either single or double. Single walls are one stone thick, that is about eight to twelve inches, and double

538. Flower p.25.
539. Luke pp.50–51 states that it was a regulation of 1562. This could not refer to Valletta's Manderaggio: Valletta dates from 1566.
540. The information is taken from Murray, which contains reports on the building stones by C. H. Colson. For further information see: Boisgelin I; Godwin, *Geology of Maltese Islands*; Spratt; and Hubbard, *Valletta and Three Cities* p.7.

walls are about three feet thick, formed of two single walls of faced ashlar with an infilling of rubble. Three and four storey buildings have double exterior walls increased in width by about six inches for every storey above the ground. The first three or four courses, to about four feet above the ground level, are usually constructed of Lower Coralline limestone, and on those above, the normal Globigerina stone is used.[541]

Where the building is exposed to driving or splashing rain, or likely to absorb much water, either the whole façade, or a band of stonework about ten feet high, is painted with whitewash to form a protective skin. Sea spray rapidly disintegrates Gobigerina limestone, so that houses which face on to the sea often have their façades faced with Coralline limestone. The Customs House in Valletta, which actually stands in the waters of the Grand Harbour, has the lower storey built of Coralline limestone and the upper one of Globigerina limestone. The colour contrast can be seen quite plainly.

Because of the shortage of timber the floors are normally constructed of stone, which has to be supported on stone-arched ribs thrown across from wall to wall and spaced about four feet centre to centre. The ribs are supported by double walls because of their outward thrust. The spandrils of the arches are filled with squared stones up to the level of the keystone, so as to form a horizontal bed for the ceiling slabs. Sometimes the upper courses are cut away to form a better bed, and this takes away the heavy appearance which the full depth of the arch stones would otherwise give to the room. By this method not more than five or six inches of keystone appear under the ceiling.

The same system of arched ribs was used to support the roof of many buildings. Churches were similarly designed, but as their design was developed, the line of the vault was dropped so that it followed the line of the arch: this prevented the interior of the church appearing as a number of narrow cells. With churches, the final development came with the introduction of intersecting vaults and clerestory windows.

The flooring itself consisted of ceiling slabs, three inches thick, laid onto the arched ribs. Two inches of stone chippings were laid onto these and finally three-inch-thick floor stones were laid on top of the chippings. These flags were normally two palmi wide. The finished surface was then scraped and covered with a thin coat of

541. Murray p.468. Globigerina limestone absorbs a quarter of its bulk of water in twenty-four hours, while Upper and Lower Coralline limestone absorbs only 2% or 3%.

warm oil. This hardened the stone, and allowed it to be well polished, as well as forming a surface which kept a beautiful appearance free from stains.

Roof construction was very similar : for all the roofs in Malta (with the exception of about two or three of the early buildings of the Knights, such as the Great Hospital and the auberge de Provence in Valletta) were almost flat. The slabs of stone were laid onto arches in the same manner. The edges of the slabs were bevelled and the triangular-shaped groove, which was left between the edges, was filled with small pebbles which had been soaked in water. The pebbles were set in one part of lime and a similar quantity of *xhahx*.[542] Three or four inches of dry chippings were laid over the slabs to distribute the load and another layer of fine chippings mixed with lime mortar covered these. This top layer had a slight fall to allow the water to run off in the required direction, and in this way it was led from terrace to terrace until it finally fell into a well in the courtyard and was preserved for the use of the household.[543]

The second layer of chippings was well rammed down, and then a mixture of *diffone*,[544] with lime and water, was beaten up to a paste and laid uniformly over the whole surface to a thickness of about three-eighths of an inch. This was thoroughly beaten with wooden rammers, which are semicircular lengths of wood about nine inches long with a four-inch handle. The workmen hit the roof with the flat side of the hammer causing the excess water to run out. As it did so, fine *diffone* dust was sprinkled on to absorb this excess water. When no more water oozed out, women were employed to finish the construction of the roof. The surface of the roof was divided into strips, each two-and-a-half feet : and the women, seated on small stools and barefooted, each took one strip. With trowels, and all working together, they swept the surface of the roof, smoothing it and glazing : all slowly moving across the roof in a regular manner. This process was usually carried out in spring and autumn when the weather is neither too hot nor too cold; and when it was completed a layer of loose straw was placed over the whole roof and sprinkled with water from time to time to keep the roof cool and allow it to harden without cracking. The straw was removed

---

542. Very small chippings mixed into a mortar.
543. Because of the scarcity of water in Malta, regulations have always required householders to collect all the rainwater which fell on their roofs. Thus there are no rainwater pipes on the external façades. Only the water which falls on country churches is wasted and is thrown clear of the walls through long projecting water spouts.
544. *Diffone* is composed of small pieces of broken earthenware pots.

after two or three weeks and the result was a hard roof capable of withstanding the torrential rain and wind of winter and the blistering sun of the long dry summers. This method of construction is still used in exactly the same way today.

The same form of roof was laid over timber ceilings when these were used instead of stone arched ribs. The scantlings were usually made of olive or chestnut imported from Sicily, southern Italy, or the islands belonging to Venice; and these timber ceilings are found on many of the top floors of the auberges and palaces of importance.

Certain farm houses, where rooms were not more than nine feet wide, had their roofs constructed of single slabs of stone which were corbelled out from the walls. The stones were six inches thick and seven-and-a-half feet long. They were covered with three inches of *forba*[545] and on top of that, half-an-inch of *diffone* and lime. The walls were double and filled with rubble stone.

Maltese stone, though fine grained, will crack if not bedded evenly, and in a country where earth tremors occur, steps have to be taken to prevent damage from subsidence.

To counteract this dangerous tendency the pressure on the lintel was reduced by a relieving arch, such as may be seen over the transept door of Attard parish church and over the ground-floor windows of the Magisterial palace in Valletta. When a true relieving arch was not constructed, the stones directly above the lintel were often notched out so that they did not rest on the top corners of the lintel. They are inclined toward the centre and there wedged, leaving a slight gap between the lintel and the courses above.

The tanks in the basements of buildings were usually cut from solid rock, the excavated material being used to build the house or palace. The sides were roughly picked and the surface coated with a quarter-of-an-inch of *pozzolana*.[546] The water was led direct from the roof to the tank and not filtered. After a shower, water in the tanks becomes turbid, but this soon clears, and the water will remain fresh and sweet for years if not exposed to the light.[547]

Globigerina limestone, because of its soft compact character, can be carved with great ease and the Maltese mason has always taken a great delight in his work. The crisp quality of the acanthus capitals on Dingli's parish church at Birkirkara (1617) should be noticed

545. Small stones mixed with argillaceous earth excavated from fissures in the rock, which are generally found to be filled with it.
546. This cement was imported from Italy during the period of the Knights.
547. In Valletta, this stored water supplemented a piped water instituted in 1615 when G. M. Alof de Wignacourt had a long aqueduct constructed from the hills of the city.

for, although the church has fallen into ruin through disuse, the carving is still crisp and sharp as it was when first carved.

On exposure to the air, the stone slowly forms a hard crust so that any carving has to be carried out soon after the stone has been placed in position. If the carving has not been completed in four years, it has to be left uncompleted or the whole stone removed and replaced. Otherwise, once the hard surface is broken the stone becomes very friable and powders away. If this occurs, the damage will spread rapidly to the adjoining stones. In many parts of Malta one can see capitals which have been left as mere solid blocks of stone, uncarved for this very reason. Good stone, on hardening, will last well if this crust is not broken by an iron tool. 229

In spite of the extreme pliability of the material, the Maltese mason has never allowed his art to deteriorate into the licentiousness we find abounding in Lecce, in the heel of Italy, where the masons have taken advantage of a material which is too generous. The classical sobriety of the Maltese has produced an architecture which is always under control and its sight affords relief after the extravagances of Sicily and southern Italy.

I feel that Maltese masonry and Maltese architecture are synonymous, and that Malta is largely impervious to the fashions which sweep like conquering armies across the map of Europe. They fall, a mere incrustation on the solidity of the building beneath, which stands out with a stony accentuation of its corners marking it off as the product of a mason's craft.

It is remarkable that so small an island, under constant subservience to a foreign government, should have produced an architecture which is essentially Maltese in spite of passing fashions; and that a race so small, under constant foreign domination, should have been able to use its native architects almost without exception. Spanish, Italian, and French appear to assist in matters relating to town planning and military defence, but except for Bonamici and Stefano Ittar, no foreign architect erected important buildings in Malta during the period of the Knights.[548]

548. The technical details in the last section are largely based on Major Harry D. Jones *Memoranda,* and on the kind information supplied by Captain Busuttil of the Malta Office of Works.

List of Grand Masters

who governed Malta, with the date of their accession.

Fra Philippe Villiers de l'Isle Adam (French) elected in Rhodes 1521; arrived Malta March 24, 1530.

Fra Pietro del Ponte (Italian) 1534.

Fra Didier de Saint Jaille (French) 1535.

Fra Juan d'Homedes (Spanish) 1536.

Fra Claude de la Sengle (French) 1553.

Fra Jean Parisot de la Vallette (French) 1557.

Fra Pietro del Monte (Italian) 1568.

Fra Jean Levesque de la Cassière (French) 1572.

Fra Hugues de Loubenx Verdale (French) 1582.

Fra Martino de Garzes (Spanish) 1595.

Fra Alof de Wignacourt (French) 1601.

Fra Dom Luys Mendez de Vasconcellos (Spanish) 1622.

Fra Antoine de Paule (French) 1623.

Fra Jean-Paul Lascaris Castellar (French) 1636.

Fra Martino de Redin (Spanish) 1657.

Fra Annet de Clermont de Chattes Gessan (French) 1660.

Fra Rafael Cotoner (Spanish) 1660.

Fra Nicolàs Cotoner (Spanish) 1663.

Fra Gregorio Carafa (Italian) 1680.

Fra Adrien de Wignacourt (French) 1690.

Fra Ramon Perellos y Roccafull (Spanish) 1697.

Fra Marc'Antonio Zondadari (Italian) 1720.

Fra Don Antonio Manoel de Vilhena (Portuguese) 1722.

Fra Don Ramon Despuig (Spanish) 1736.

Fra Don Emanuel Pinto de Fonçeca (Portuguese) 1741.

Fra Don Francisco Ximenes de Texada (Spanish) 1773.

Fra Emmanuel de Rohan-Polduc (French) 1775.

Fra Ferdinand de Hompesch (German) 1779.

Biographies of Architects and Military Engineers

Attard, Giovanni. Maltese architect and engineer employed by the Grand Master Alof de Wignacourt to complete the Wignacourt aqueduct,[549] built between 1610 and 1614 to carry water to the new city of Valletta nine and a half miles away. V. Bontadino de Bontadini of Bologna and Fra Natale Mesuccio of Messina had originally been commissioned to build the aqueduct.[550] Attard was the tutor of the Maltese architect Tomasso Dingli.[551] The Grand Master was annoyed that the foreign engineers he had called in showed insufficient spirit to complete the work, so he commissioned Attard to redesign the aqueduct. Attard's plans were finally carried out by Bontadini.[552] Attard was buried in the parish church at Lija.[553]

Barbara, Giovanni. Maltese architect born about 1670 and died in 1730.[554] He was famous both in Malta and abroad as a military engineer. He was employed upon the Floriana Defences and built the Sa Maison skew arch, sometimes called the *arco Barbara,* a work which is rightly considered by many to be a marvel of construction.[555] His architectural works include : the parish church of St. Saviour at Lija (1694),[556] the church of St. James for the langue of Castile in Valletta (1710)[557] the Magisterial palace at Mdina (*c.* 1732),[558] and the Seminary in the same city (*c.* 1732).[559] He was born in Casal Lija and now lies buried there.[560]

---

549. Zerafa, *Discorso* p.24.
550. Bonello article *Valletta.*
551. Calleja in L'ARTE PERIODICO PATRIO No. 66, Anno III, p.5.
552. Zerafa, *History of Art* p.173.
553. Calleja, *Works of Art* p.102.
554. Tencajoli p.2. Sammut *Profili* p.14 gives the date of his birth as 1660.
555. Galea, *Architecture* p.12.
556. Braun, *Works of Art* p.10, and Zerafa, *Discorso* p.30.
557. Fleming p.175, and Zerafa, *Discorso* p.30.
558. Zerafa, *Discorso* p.30.
559. Zerafa, *Discorso* p.30. If Tencajoli is correct in the date of Barbara's death, then this must be a posthumous work.
560. Zerafa, *Discorso* p.30. He also states that Barbara studied in Rome, and introduced the style of Borromini to Malta. This is hardly true as his work at Lija is much nearer the Academic School in its architectural style.

Bellavanti, Nicolo. Italian military engineer called in by the Grand Master Claude de la Sengle to prepare designs for the defences of the Birgu before the great siege of 1565. He carried out the perimeter defences, 'comprendendovi dentro la penisoletta a ponente di esso, dominante dal Forte S. Michele, e che ebbe da allora il nome che ancora porta, La Senglea.'[561]

Bonamici, Filippo. The biography of Bonamici needs to be clarified as errors have been made by both Maltese writers and the contributors to the ENCICLOPÆDIA ITALIANA.[562] There was a Filippo Bonamici, an Italian architect, born at Lucca in 1705 and who died in 1780. He was the brother of Castruccio Bonamici, the Italian historian. He became secretary for Latin letters to Pope Clement XIV and canon of St. John's, Lateran. He is best known for his literary history *De Claris pontificiarum epistolarum scriptoribus.*[563] Filippo visited Malta and rebuilt the Gesù church in Valletta.[564] According to one authority[565] he also designed the parish church of St. Paul at Rabat, though this work was probably only the addition of a new façade and the redecoration of the interior. He is also mentioned as the architect of the dell'Anima church and St. Nicholas (Souls in Purgatory)[566] in Valletta. To summarise the findings : two architects of Lucca are mentioned in the Italian encyclopædia, Filippo having visited Malta according to Bonello, and Francesco according to Manchini. Both are eighteenth century architects. The churches he/they designed in Malta were built in 1594 (Calleja), *c.* 1600 (Zerafa), 1575 (Valletta Museum), and 1600 (Zammit). The style of these buildings seems to be eighteenth century, and I would suggest that the Maltese writers have given the dates of the original buildings, and have not realised that Bonamici was an eighteenth century architect.

561. Paribeni p.64.
562. Some Maltese writers say he was an early 17th century architect called Francesco Bonamici. Manchini, article *Lucca* in ENCICLOPÆDIA ITALIANA p.559 states that there was a Baroque Francesco Bonamici from Lucca who designed the breakwater and many civil buildings in Malta. Zammit, *Valletta* p.42 calls the architect of the Gesù, Valletta, Francesco Bonamici, so it is possible there were two architects from Lucca, and Francesco visited Malta.
563. However Bonello, article *Malta* p.45 and article *Valletta* p.933, states that Filippo visited Malta and rebuilt the Gesù.
564. Calleja, *Works of Art* p.38 Engineer Bonamici was architect of the Gesù which was built in 1592 during the reign of G. M. Verdale. And Zerafa, *History* p.173, 'About this time (*c.* 1600) the churches of del Gesù and dell'Anima were built by Bonamici.'
565. Valletta Museum file of photographs. It also gives date 1575, but this must refer to the original building.
566. Braun, *Works of Art* p.36, states that it was built in 1762. Calleja, *Works of Art* p.58, states that Bonamici designed this church, see Calleja, *Giuseppe Bonici* pp.5–6.

Bonici, Giuseppe. Maltese architect born in 1707. From an early age he showed an inclination for architecture and at twelve he was continually drawing, with little assistance from his elders. Helped by his father, he entered the studio of Giovanni Barbara, and, under his direction, carried out work on the Floriana Defences.[567] It is not known how long he spent with Barbara, but by the time he had reached the age of twenty-six he had begun to design on his own. This design was for the parish church of St. Publius at Floriana, the last important parish church to be built during the period of the Knights. Its foundation stone was laid by Bishop Paolo Alferan in August 1733. In 1739[568] he began the church of St. Barbara for the langue of Provence in Valletta. When middle-aged he designed the church of Nadur in Gozo and in 1760[569] completed the Castellania in Valletta, which had been begun by Francesco Zerafa in 1748. In addition to these works he designed several houses in Valletta. The Customs House in Valletta is his last and in many ways his finest work. It was begun in 1774.[570] Its foundations rest in the waters of the Grand Harbour,[571] and because of its position the masonry has suffered badly from the sea spray blown against it in the *gregale*. Bonici died in 1779 at the age of seventy-two.

Burlo, Paolo. A Maltese military engineer at the time of the great siege of 1565.[572] He was praised by Bosio[573] for his valour in action, along with Andrea Cassar and Paolo Micciola.

Cachia, Antonio. A Maltese architect who made alterations to the Valletta Library designed by Stefano Ittar in 1785.[574] He also rebuilt St. Mary of Porto Salvo in Merchants' Street, according to one authority, in the year 1804. This church was originally designed by G. Cassar in 1571.[575] The younger Tigne entrusted him with the construction of Fort Tigne.[576]

Cachia, Domenico. Maltese architect born about 1700 and died in 1790.[577] In 1735 he began the parish church of St. Helen at Birkirkara[577,578] which replaced the old parish church designed by

567. Calleja, *Works of Art* p.148. He was a pupil of the engineer Tigne.
568. Zammit, *Valletta* p.37.
569. Fleming, p.175.
570. Zammit, *Valletta* p.72.
571. Zerafa, *Discorso* p.30.
572. Zerafa, *Discorso* p.21.
573. Bosio.
574. Rutter p.89.
575. Zammit, *Valletta* p.33, and Calleja, *Works of Art* p.48.
576. Calleja, *Works of Art* p.48.
577. Sammut, *Profili* p.15. He gives the Christian name as Giuseppe.
578. Rutter p.142.

Vittorio Cassar and Dingli. The new church was completed in 1745. In 1744 he remodelled the auberge de Castile et Leon in Valletta,[577,579] and considerably enlarged it. The original auberge had been designed by Gerolamo Cassar in 1574. In 1764 he rebuilt the Augustinian church in Valletta,[580] the original again having been built by Gerolamo Cassar. He also designed the Selmun palace[577] on Mellieha ridge.

Campi, Scipione. An Italian military engineer, the son of Bartolomeo Campi, was born in Pesaro, and died in Liege in 1579. He found himself in Malta after the great siege of 1565, where he came in company with several other engineers to consult upon the new city of Valletta then being proposed by Laparelli assisted by Gerolamo Cassar. He noted several errors and suggested improvements in Valletta and on the older defences, including work on Fort St. Michael and the bastions of St. Jacob, St. Peter, and St. Paul. He left designs of what was required to be done in the Birgu and Isola.[581] Returning to Italy, he was sent to Flanders by Serbelloni, where he served under Don John of Austria and assisted in the building of Mosa Fort on a hill not far from Namur. He was probably wounded in the attack on Maestricht, for he lay ill at Liege, where he had been brought with the other wounded, and died there in 1579. He left a manuscript *Parere di Scipione Campi sopra la fortificatione della città di Valletta, circa* 1566, which was later incorporated with that by Cassar in Spina's work.[582]

Cassar, Andrea. A Maltese military engineer who served with the Knights during the siege of 1565.[583] He was praised by Bosio[584] for the valour he showed in destroying a Turkish wooden tower.[585]

579. Zammit, *Valletta* p.71.
580. Galea, *Architecture* p.12. Calleja, *Works of Art,* says that the church owed its erection to P.M. Fra Giuseppe Zammit. The belfry is modern.
581. Spina, *Pareri sulla fortificazione della Valletta,* MS. 1594.
582. Promis, pp.728–731.
583. Zerafa, *Discorso* p.21.
584. Bosio.
585. Vertot IV p.66: 'Les Turcs par le moyen de cette machine tuerent d'abord beaucoup demonde; mais un Charpentier Maltois, appellé André Cassar, habile dans son art, ayant examiné la construction de cettex tour, fit ouvrir dans la muraille, et directement vis-a-vis ce chateau de bois, une canoniere, ou il plaça une coulevrine chargée de chaines de fer; et au moment que les Turcs fairoient semonter cette machine, il fit mettre le feu au canon qui la prit par le milieu, et la mit en pieces; en sorte que les soldats qui etoient au plus haut teage, furent precipitéz en bas, ou ecrassez sous ses ruines et ses debris.'

Cassar, Gerolamo. A Maltese architect whose work has been more publicised than that of any other architect in Malta.[586] He was born in 1520 and died in 1586.[587] In architecture and military engineering he was a student of the Maltese engineer Evangelista della Menga and the Italian Francesco Laparelli.[588] 'During his stay in Malta Francesco Laparelli so well trained a young Maltese[589] of perfect character called Gerolamo Cassar in the building of fortifications, that without Laparelli's help he could continue very well and perfect the buildings of the city of Valletta. As soon as news came that the Turks were directing their attention to Cyprus, he wished to show his work for the benefit of the Republic of Venice, so he got permission from the Grand Master and Council to leave Malta for that purpose. . . . Gerolamo continued after that to the great satisfaction of the whole Convent and he deserved to be recommended by the Order, both for himself and for his relations; especially having had two of his sons received among the servants-at-arms, the elder of whom, having taken up his father's profession, made rapid advances in fortification : designing the well-known tower of Sarza on the shore of the island of Gozo. The other, Fra Gabriello, who turned out to be so valorous in arms and was trained in all the military exercises with great care, especially in horse keeping, died as Commandatore of the Venerable Langue of Provence.'[590] His work may be the result of a naïve untrained approach to Renaissance architecture, or strongly influenced by Mannerist tendencies then prevalent in Italy; or again, may be a combination of the two, Cassar having learned his lesson from the Italian architects who had broken away from the rigid, balanced, and logical architecture of Alberti and Bramante. The fact remains that some of Cassar's buildings seem far more Mannerist in their treatment than any contemporary work in Italy. According to the Registrar of the Council of the Order,[591] the Grand Master La Cassière praised Gerolamo Cassar for his work as engineer and architect to the Order and his citation mentions buildings designed

---

586. He is the only Maltese architect mentioned in the DICTIONARY OF ARCHITECTURE.
587. Sammut, *Co-Cathedral.* Ryan pp.141–142.
588. Zerafa, *Discorso* p.21. Promis p.715 gives 1560 incorrectly as date of birth, and both 1590 and 1594 for date of his death (p.717).
589. They were almost the same age. Laparelli was actually one year younger.
590. Malta Library MS.21 pp.260–261, translated from a note taken from Mons Imbroll Cap.xix 1570. *Stuomatum Melitensuum Liber Septimus, collection of notes made in 1755.*
591. ARCHIVES 1579–80–81, fol.270.

by him before the year 1581, which is the date of the citation. He is credited with the following buildings : the seven auberges to the langues,[592] the Magisterial palace (1574) (or 1571),[593] the Conventual church of St. John (1573–78),[594] the parish church of St. Paul, the church of St. Mary of Porto Salvo, the Carmelite church (1573),[595] the church of St. Augustine (1571),[596] of St. Mary of Jesus :[597] all in Valletta; the buildings for the bakery and the mills, as well as several private houses. In addition to these he is attributed with the designs of the following buildings not mentioned in the citation : the church of St. Catherine of the langue of Italy in Valletta (1576),[598] the Augustinian church and monastery in Rabat,[599] St. Paul Shipwrecked, Valletta,[600] the Capuchin monastery in Floriana,[601] Verdala palace (1586).[602] After Laparelli left the island, Cassar was appointed chief military engineer and directed work on the fortfications of Valletta until his death in 1586. The full text of the citation from Archives of the Order MS. 439 *Liber Bullarum* fol.270 verso, reads :

> Frater Joannes Levesque, etc. Iniversis et singulis principus ecclesiasticis, etc., et terrarum constitutis salutem. Notum facimus, et in verbo veritatis attestamur come il magnifico Hieronimo Cassar Maltese nostro e di nostra Religione donate sue confratre et ordinario architettore et ingegniero nostro per molti anni n ha servito nel detto suo officio, videlicet dal anno 1565 insino hoggi et dal tempo di quel crudelissimo et inordito assedio di Turchi et autri barbari, dove non sparagnando punto la persona sua, emo rappresentatose a ogni pericolo per reparare le ruine fatte da Inimici con L'artigliaria, mantendo sempre la gente coperta e sicura dalli quitidiani assalti si terribili et doppo detto assiedo essendo determinato che questa nosura citta Valletta l'havesse da fabricare se retrovo dalla prima linea continuamente insino al giorno present in compagnia d'altri Ingigneri mandati dalla Maesta Cattolica del Re di Hispania procurando con agni affectione de ridurre cosi important fortezza nel termine e perfectione ch'al presente. Similmente ha designato li setti palazzi chiamati

---

592. There is some argument about the date of these auberges. See details in the text under the heading of each auberge.
593. Dates given by Braun, *Works of Art.*
594. Sammut, *Co-Cathedral.*
595. Calleja, *Works of Art* pp.55–56. The façade and the interior marble work are by Signor Bonavia and are both recent additions.
596. Galea, *Architecture.*
597. Calleja, *Works of Art* p.50. Façade was altered later by Mario Blunde in 1688.
598. Fleming p.175.
599. Braun, *Works of Art* p.20.
600. Zerafa, *Discorso* p.24 says this church was designed by Garagona.
601. Calleja, *Works of Art* pp.64–65, 1588. Cassar drew the plans and the work was carried out by a Neapolitan Padre Raffaello Camifferi who came to Malta at the invitation of the Grand Master Verdale. Portico and parts of interior were later. Destroyed 1940.
602. Rutter. Enlarged under Lascaris (1636–57). Refers to garden layout.

albergi delle sette lingue nei quali consiste il corpo di tutta nostra **Religi**-one il nostro Palazzo magistrale et quel che importa ha designato l'ecclesia nostra maggior conventuale di san Giovanni Battista reducendola in perfectione, non cessando dire che da se sono usciti tutti li disegni delle chiese particolari cioe della parrochiale di San Paolo, di Porto Salvo, del Carmino, di Santo Agostino e Santa Maria di Giesu ove al presente s'officia di continuo ha disegnata ancora tutti li edificii tanto di forni e molininquanto di case di nostri Religiosi et altri particulari dove non ha verso tempo con tanta sua lodabil diligenza, aggiongendo che non ha mancato ponere si buona forma la fortezza di San Michele et la Victoriosa citta che furono assediati et maltratti dal inimico in detto assedio con la lororfuriosa artigliaria. Similmente nella città vecchia et nell'isola del Gozzo ha ordenato molti ripari secondo li bisogni che sono occorsi, et al presente tuttiavia continua nel medesimo servito con ogni sua diligenza et leude amato da noi et da tutto il popolo del nostro dominio, onde noi accioche li suoi lodevoli meriti in ogni tempo et loco dove bisogbara appariscano li babbiamo fatto le presente nostre lettere patente et attestationi in cuius rei, etc. Bulla nostra Magistralis in cera nigra, etc. Datum Melitae, etc. Dei XVIII Maii MDLXXXI.

To this list of buildings Calleja, *Works of Art,* p.114. adds St. Gregory, Zejtun, referring, of course, to the alterations and additions made to the east end of the church. I have not seen this attribution in any other book and would be inclined to treat Calleja's statement with some reserve in view of the other errors which occur in his book. A short biography of Gerolamo Cassar appears in *L'Arte periodici Patrio-bimensile* Anno I, No. 2, 7 December 1862, p.4, and Promis, *Biografie di Ingegneri Militari Italiani* pp.715–7, taken mainly from the information in Bosio, *Istoria della Sacra Rel.* III, pp.417,425,611, and 612. Promis states[603] that Cassar left a manuscript entitled *Parere di Mo. Gerolamo sopra la fortificatione della città di Valletta,* written about 1566, when many engineers were engaged in discussing these defensive works. This manuscript, together with the *Parere di Scipione Campi,* were later collected together by a Florentine named Spina, who in 1594 composed a report (still unedited) based on these two manuscripts. I have not been able to trace it.

Cassar, Vittorio. Maltese military engineer and architect and son of Gerolamo Cassar. He became a serving brother in the Order of St. John. He designed several coastal forts including : Fort St. Thomas at Marsascala,[604] Fort St. Lucian in Marsaxlokk Bay,[605]

603. Promis pp.717 and 731.
604. These buildings are ascribed to him in Zerafa, *History of Art.* Braun, *Works of Art,* gives the date as 1614. Parish of Zejtun.
605. Braun, *Works of Art* p.13 gives the date 1711. If so this cannot be V. Cassar's work. But Zerafa p.172 says that Cassar designed this fort. Perhaps Braun's date refers to alterations or rebuilding.

and the fort on the small island of Comino which lies between Malta and Gozo.[606] He also designed the old parish church of the Annunciation at Birkirkara[607] which was completed by Dingli; the parish churches of Senglea (1580), Zebbug (1599)[608] and the old parish church of Pawla[608] (1626). I have suggested that he may have been responsible for part of the façades of St. Augustine, Rabat, and Qormi parish church (1584). He died in Gozo in 1607 and was buried in the church of St. Barbara at Valletta.[608]

Coglituri, Matteo. Maltese prefect of building when the Knights occupied the island. Grand Master de l'Isle Adam employed him to restore Fort St. Angelo and build fortifications in front of the Birgu (Vittoriosa). He also built the Magisterial palace in Fort St. Angelo, the upper church, also in the fort, which was dedicated to St. Anne and is said to contain ancient granite columns from the Temple of June,[609] and the chief church of the Order in the Birgu.

Dingli, Tommaso. A Maltese architect who was born in 1591 and died in 1666. He was born at a time when it was necessary to fortify the island at the greatest speed, and at an early age, in common with other children who showed the slightest inclination toward architecture, he was put to work in an artist's studio. After studying mathematics he was probably taught the elements of building by Matteo Coglituri.[610] He later collaborated with the Maltese engineer on the building of the Wignacourt aqueduct (1610–14).[611] He designed the old Porta Reale in Valletta (now rebuilt), the Bishop's palace at Valletta for Mons. Cagliares,[612] and completed the parish church of Birkirkara, begun by Vittorio Cassar, adding the Renaissance façade in 1617.[613] He also designed the parish churches of Attard (1613), Naxxar (1616), Zabbar (1641),[614] Gargur (1638), and Gudia (1656). One authority states that he designed the parish churches of Zebbug and Luqa (1656).[615]

606. Zerafa, *History of Art* p.172.
607. Braun, *Architecture* p.19.
608. Zerafa, *Discorso* p.23.
609. Zerafa, *History of Art* p.170, clearly refers to the upper church in the fort. There seem to have been two churches built about this time; one in the fort, and the other—the conventual church—dedicated to St. Lawrence and later rebuilt by Lorenzo Gafa.
610. Calleja, *Tommaso Dingli* p.5. In *Works of Art* pp.104–105 he calls the architect ' Matteo Dingli.'
611. See Attard.
612. Calleja, *Tommaso Dingli* p.6, and Zerafa, *History of Art* p.172.
613. Braun, *Architecture* p.19.
614. Braun, *Works of Art* p.1. Calleja, *Works of Art* p.117 : Gudia begun 1636 and completed in 1656.
615. It seems unlikely that Dingli rebuilt Zebbug church between the years 1621 and 1632 as the photograph in the Valletta Museum suggests. Braun, *Works of Art* p.10, gives 1650.

His ability in architecture was praised by Giovanni de' Medici, with whom he became friendly. Giovanni had been sent over by the Grand Duke of Tuscany in 1639 to inspect and report on the fortifications. Dingli pointed out several defects to him.[616] He is often referred to as 'Dingli of Attard.' This in all probability refers to his birthplace, but may refer to his association with the engineer Attard, from whom Dingli received instruction. He died in 1666 at the age of 75.

Ferramolino, Antonio. An Italian military engineer from Bergamo. Very little is known about his early work, but he seems to have gone with Charles V on the successful expedition against Tunis in 1535 and to have served in the campaign in Sicily. He was entrusted with the defences of Messina in collaboration with the Messinan mathematician Francesco Maurolico. Sent for by Admiral Doria, he built the fort of Menze and the bastion below Monte Vergato to defend the port of Ragusa. He stayed there for four months, and on departure he left a model for further work, which included the fortress of SS. Sergio and Bacco, and a bulwark with a ditch and counterscarp which was never built. In 1541 he was sent by the Emperor to the Knights of Malta, and he lived on the island for many years.[617] He advised the Grand Master on the defences of Fort St. Angelo and the Birgu, and it was he who first suggested the building of a powerful fortress on the hill behind St. Elmo, where Valletta now stands; as, he said, this position would command both ports and bar them to an enemy. However, the Grand Master feared the expense and the adverse criticism this scheme would bring about, so he shelved the idea and set about to improve the existing fortifications. Ferramolino was therefore instructed to raise a cavalier[618] on Fort St. Angelo to as high a position as was possible, so that its batteries might cover the mouth of Marsamuscetto harbour. Besides this, he lowered the ditch between the fort and the Birgu so that the sea might flood it. This ditch later gave admirable shelter to the galleys during the

616. Zerafa, *Malta* p.172. This cannot be the Giovanni de' Medici referred to by Promis pp.747–766, for this Florentine military engineer lived from 1565 to 1621, according to Promis, and he makes no mention of a visit to Malta.
617. Promis p.370 states eleven years, but on page 371 he states that Ferramolino returned to Sicily in 1550—after only nine years in Malta. 1550 also seems to have been the year of his death.
618. This cavalier was built in 1541 and called after the Grand Master the Homedes Bastion, according to Scicluna p.219. The latter incorrectly calls this engineer 'Caramolin.' He is also called by this name in Crocker.

assault of the Turks in 1565.[619] He returned to Sicily to build further fortresses, and in 1550 he sailed with the Spanish fleet against the town of Africa (Maladia). He was killed in the assault on that city.[620]

Firenzuola, Vincenzo Maculano da. A Dominican friar and an Italian military engineer in the service of the Pope. In Rome he designed the Forte Urbano. He was sent to Malta to direct work on the lines which were to be built around the Three Cities. He designed the fortifications on the hills of Santa Margherita and della Mandra and the foundation stone was laid by Grand Master Paul Lascaris Castellar on the 30 December 1638. Work was suspended during the construction of the Cotonera lines, but was later resumed under the Grand Mastership of Ramon Perellos y Roccafull (1697–1720). The lines, which were called after Firenzuola, were completed by Grand Master Vilhena in 1736.[621]

Floriana, Pietro Paolo. An Italian military engineer born at Macerata in 1585[622] and died in 1638. He was the son of a military engineer and soldier who had fought at Lepanto and had advised Don John upon the Goletta fortifications : advice which was thrown over in preference to the suggestions of Serbelloni. Pompeii Floriana acquired considerable fame when events showed the error of Don John's judgement, and his renown was further increased when, in 1576, he published a book of the events.[623] The son acquired the father's confidence and knowledge, and embarked upon a brilliant career of enlarging the fortresses of Europe and his own reputation; and often with little respect for the military necessity and the financial situation of his clients; a fault common to his age.[624] He entered the service of the King of Spain for whom he rebuilt the fortifications of St. Germano (1617). In

619. Bosio III p.198.
620. Bosio III p.275. Others have stated that he was killed in a mine gallery when the Turks exploded a countermine. See Promis p.371.
621. Scicluna pp.221-222. This engineer has often been mistaken for Francesco Fiorenzuoli who prepared the pentagonal citadel at Florence in 1534, working with Antonio de Sangallo.
622. Borgatti article *Fortificazione* states 1584.
623. See bibliography Floriana.
624. Gugliemotti, *La Marian pontificia*, Roma 1887, V p.299. 'The 17th century entered with vanity and swelled up everything which was already swollen, and around existing defences the military architects overflowed with their works of enormous expense which were difficult to guard and which had the very worst moral effect. At that time, and belonging to that school, Pier Paolo Floriana of Macerata, the Lieutenant of Don Mario Barberini, came to Civita Vecchia. To him, and not others, many attribute those long emaciated horn works with their high ravelins in front.'

the following year he reported upon methods of storming Algiers and Tunis. In 1620 he was serving on the eastern front and took part in the assault upon Rosenberg and Newhausel.[625] In addition to these works, he also built defences at Civita Vecchia, Innsbruck, Altenburg, and many other towns; and, according to Borgatti, he designed the hexagonal citadel at Tunis.[626] In 1627 he was nominated Castellan of the Castle of S. Angelo in Rome, and Governor of the armies of Umbria. It was then that he visited Rome and compiled his treatise on *Difesa et ofesa delle piazze*.[627] At the close of 1634, Urban VIII received a request from the Grand Master of Malta for the services of an able military architect. Floriana was chosen and arrived on the island in the following year. On the high ground beyond the land defences of Valletta he built a great walled enceinte upon a rectangular plan, with elaborate ditches, lunettes, teneille, and counterguards: the whole complex being dominated by a horn work of great size. His work came in for considerable criticism and he returned to Italy disgusted with the turn of events. Another Italian engineer and a Commission to investigate the dissatisfaction were requested, and Cardinal Vincenzo Maculano da Firenzuola d'Arda was sent to Malta by the Pope. Floriana was to some extent vindicated, and the defences were carried on to completion. Both these defences, and the new suburb which grew up in the shelter of their walls, were named after their designer. On his return to Italy, Floriana again took up his old appointment as Commander of Ferrara, and on the 28th May 1638 he died in that city. In addition to the major work on *Difesa et ofesa delle piazze*, Promis attributes the following writings to Floriana: *Dichiarazione dell'Ufficio del Sergente generale*, a five page manuscript in the Biblioteca dell'Università, Turin; *Carico del Sergente maggiore*; *Libro di vari segreti, cose militari, d'architettura, ingegneria, ecc.*; and in the Biblioteca Riccardiana collection, Florence, *Relazione dell'ingegnere Pietro Paolo Floriana col discorso a lui tenuto col S. Marescial di Thoiras sopra le fortificazioni della città e cittadella di Ferrara, con la pianta di questa*.[628]

625. Maggiorotti, L. A., *L'Opera del genio italiano all'estero architetti e architetture militari*, II, gives an account of his activities in Hungary.
626. Borgatti article *Cittadella*.
627. Published after his death in Macerata. First edition 1630, another edition Venice 1654. Ayala refers to a London edition published in 1727, but Promis denies its existence, and I have not been able to trace it.
628. For further information see Clausetti, *Pietro Paolo Floriana*.

Gafà, Lorenzo.   Maltese architect born in 1630 and died in 1710 :[629] he was a brother of Melchiorre Gafà, the painter and sculptor.[630] He studied architecture in Rome, where his brother was working. The exact dates of his stay in Rome are not known : Bonello believes he was there between 1699 and 1700, when he must have taken part in the work on the Niccione of S. Giovanni in Laterano. He was sent to Rome by the Council of the Order with the models of the great altar which had been commissioned for the Conventual church of St. John, so that he could supervise the erection of the altar in Italian marble. On his return to Malta he set the fashion for Roman Baroque architecture.[631] He seems to have drawn inspiration from Borromini, whose dome on S. Agnese[632] in the Piazza Navona may have been the inspiration for Gafà's domes, with their coupled pilasters and double ribs.[633] His works of architecture include : the Sarria chapel,[634] Floriana (1678); St. Scholastica, Vittoriosa[635] (1679); St. Lawrence, Vittoriosa (1681);[636] the little church of 'Tal Hlas' at Qormi (1690);[637] St. Catherine at Zejtun (1692);[638] a chapel and perhaps the central dome of St. Paul, Rabat (1692);[639] St. Nicholas at Siggiewi (1693);[640] the Cathedral at Mdina (1697)[641] at the age of 67; and the Matrice at Gozo[642] in the same year. I have also suggested that he may have designed the dome of Zabbar parish church, and if so, this must date after Rainaldi's dome of 1654. Calleja credits him with following additional works : the chapel of the Blessed Sacrament in 1680[643] in the church of St. Paul Shipwrecked,

629. Sammut, *Co-Cathedral* p.61.
630. Bonello, article *Valletta* p.45.
631. Tencajoli p.2.
632. The dome was built up to the lantern by 1654, so if this theory is correct Gafà must have visited Rome between 1654 and the building of the dome of Siggiewi parish church soon after 1676. The high band between dome and drum may have been inspired by Michelangelo's design of the dome of St. Peter's, Rome. Melchiorre Gafà was in charge of the decoration of S. Agnese in 1660.
633. These double ribs are often used in the 18th century. They occur on the church domes in Catania built after the earthquake of 1693, and on S. Maria Egiziaca, Naples, by Cosimo Fanzago soon after 1651. They are later issued by Filippo Juvara on the Superga at Turin (1717).
634. Braun, *Works of Art* p.5. It replaced an earlier chapel of 1585.
635. Critien, *Borgo* p.33, illustrated on p.31.
636. Braun, *Works of Art* p.42. Paribeni p.84, 1697, and Critien, *Borgo* says 1679.
637. ANCIENT MONUMENTS COMMITTEE.
638. Braun, *Works of Art* p.46.
639. Rutter p.126. Braun, *Works of Art* p.27, says 1675.
640. Valletta Museum photograph file.
641. Rutter p.121.
642. Zerafa, *Discorso* p.25.
643. Calleja, *Works of Art* p.46.

Valletta; St. Roch, Valletta (1680);[644] St. Peter the Martyr at Zejtun;[645] parish church of St. Mary at Qrendi[646] (1685–1712); and the dome of Qormi parish church.[647] He was also a sculptor,[648] which may explain his ability to model a superb dome.

Garagona. A sixteenth century architect and painter who designed St. Paul Shipwrecked in Valletta.[649]

Genga, Bartolomeo. An Italian architect and military engineer born at Cesena in 1516, the son of Girolamo Genga. He died in Malta in 1559.[650] He studied painting and architecture, first under his father[651] and later in Rome and Florence, which he visited about the age of twenty-one. He served as an engineer to the Pope and Duke Cosimo, who sent him to review the mainland fortresses of Venice. He built the church of S. Pietro at Mondavio,[652] and, in collaboration with F. Trezi, he designed the Villa di Miralfiore at Pesaro for della Rovere (Guidobaldo II).[653] Also at Pesaro, he prepared a plan for improving the port and made proposals which were never carried out.[654] In 1553 he went to Rome and was presented to Giulio III, for whom he prepared some very beautiful designs for fortifying the Bourg. At the end of 1558 the Grand Master requested his services in Malta and sent Cesare Visconti to Pesaro to obtain the permission of the Grand Duke. After a lot of difficulty, Genga was permitted to sail with Visconti on the 20th January 1558, and they landed in Malta on the 11th March after being delayed by bad weather off Sicily. Genga prepared to fortify the Birgu, St. Elmo, and L'Isola Senglea, and required the whole population to be put to work on these new fortifications. He also enlarged the bulwarks and ditches in front of the posts of Provence, Auvergne, France, Aragon, and Castile; and sent the galleys of the Order to Comino, Gozo, and as far as Sicily in search of brushwood and firewood. Finding that both the

644. Calleja, *Works of Art* p.57.
645. Calleja, *Works of Art* p.114.
646. Calleja, *Works of Art* p.120. Braun, *Works of Art* p.19, states church dates from 1620.
647. Calleja, *Works of Art* p.106.
648. Zerafa, *Discorso* p.25.
649. Zerafa, *History* p.173, states that Garagona completed the church of St. Paul Shipwrecked, which had been designed and started by Gerolamo Cassar.
650. Serra p.526. Milizia, *Memorie degli architetti antichi e moderni,* gives his dates 1518 to 1558, and so does Promis p.249.
651. With whom he designed S. Giovanni Battista at Pesaro and transformed the Ducal palace which had been constructed by Alessandro Sforza.
652. Serra, and Gwilt p.49.
653. Fagnoni p.354.
654. Gwilt p.49.

Birgu and the Fort of St. Michael were too low to fortify adequately, and because the Order's coffers seemed well filled, he again broached the subject of a new city on the hill behind St. Elmo (Ferramolino having already suggested this development), and prepared a model. His plan included a larger area than that which was later laid out by Laparelli, and its front extended forward toward the Marsa so that the guns might cover the high ground at Coradino and the water hole on the Marsa, to prevent the enemy making use of them.[655] Nothing was done on the new city because of the need to improve the existing defences immediately. Genga is also reported to have made designs for some churches and the Magisterial palace.[656] He was the most important Italian architect to visit Malta in the sixteenth century and, although his visit was cut short by his death, he may have helped Gerolamo Cassar and influenced his work. Heavy rustication, a feature of his work on the Palazzo Ducale at Pesaro, is also one of the many characteristics of Cassar's architecture. According to Promis, Genga caught a chill[657] and after seventeen days[658] he died in July 1559 at the age of forty-three. The following letter was sent by the Grand Master to the Duke of Urbino on the 30th July 1588.[659] 'Se alla morte quando dal N.S. Iddio ne viene assignoto il fine del vita nostro potessimo trovar qualche rimedio, dubitersi che V. Ecc. come habbia noticia che il poveretto de M. Bartolomeo Genga, rarissimo fra quelli della profession sua, oltre molt' altre virtù ch'in lui erano, sia morto, ne potessi culpare qua non essersi dato il ricapito necessario. Però come no se possi fuggir il mandato di Sua Mag. ta restaro appresso di quella iscurso, con dirgli esserne restato tanto smarrito et dolente che d'un fratello mio, se così fosse sequito, piu non potrai esser, perchè era ingenrosissimo, ben creato, intendente et gentilissimo. Et veramente all'ultimo, persona che aveva tutte le qualità. . . . Et poichè la mala sorte ha voluto ch'esso non habbia possuto principiare il disegno fatto della nova città ho fatto che in Roma saranno pagati alli suoi figli scudi 500 franchi per il suo travaglio di venir qui. . . . Pregola però poi ch'io resto cece nel principiare questa nova habitatione, sia contenta dirmene il parer suo sopra il disegno mandatogli dal detto Genga senza il

655. Bosio III pp.398–455.
656. Promis pp.252–253.
657. Promis p.253.
658. Vasari III p.268. Vernaccia, *Elogi degli uomini illustri d'Urbino* MS. fol.47. (Raccolto da A. Rosa from MSS of Vernaccia) says that he died on the 30th August.
659. Promis p.253.

quale non voglio a costo alcuno da principio.' Genga wrote a *Trattato di fortificazione* during his lifetime but its whereabouts is not now known.[660]

Giuseppe, Fra. A Capuchin monk responsible for the designs of the Capuchin monastery of St. Liberata, built in 1736, which lies outside the Cotonera lines. He also designed another monastery which was built in Gozo.[661]

Grunenberg, Don Carlos de. Military engineer to the King of Spain in Sicily. He arrived in Malta on the 29th January 1681 and on the 15th March reported to the Council on the state of the fortifications—displaying stone models to illustrate his proposals.[662] The work he proposed was undertaken, and in 1687 he paid another visit to the island to inspect the progress. A further report, dated 26 February,[663] was put before the Council for discussion. Grunenberg proposed that fausse-braie should be built on the foreshore at the forts of Ricasoli, St. Elmo, St. Angelo, and St. Michael to give sweeping fire across the water and provide better protection for the ports. He also advocated building four new batteries on St. Angelo. His scheme was approved but the work was deferred until the completion of the Floriana fortifications, because of lack of funds. However, Grunenberg generously offered to build three of the new batteries at his own expense and the task was undertaken.[664]

Ittar, Stefano. An Italian architect, and a descendant of the noble Italian family of Guidone de Hittar, Counts of Balneo, which had moved from Tuscany to Rome because of political and financial difficulties. His early training was in Rome. Later he went to Spain and in 1765 he was travelling in Sicily when he visited his friend, the Prince of Biscari. It was then that he met the architect Francesco Battaglia, whose daughter he married. He settled in Catania[665] and there worked as an architect reconstructing the city which had been stricken by an earthquake in 1693. In 1768 he was working on the Collegiate church at Catania, which was rebuilt

660. Busca Chap.34 refers to a codex by Captain Genga which is thought to refer to Bartolomeo Genga.
661. Zerafa, *Discorso* p.30.
662. ARCHIVES Vol.262 pp.123–124.
663. ARCHIVES Vol.262 pp.285, 289–291.
664. An inscription was placed over the main gate of St. Angelo commemorating the improvements carried out by Grunenberg, and dated 1690. The original inscription is now in the Valletta Museum. This biography is largely extracted from Darmanin pp.46–53.
665. Zammit, *Biblioteca,* says he was a Frenchman who settled in Messina. Galea, *Malta,* repeats this and says it accounts for the French Renaissance style of the Library.

entirely to his designs. He also designed the Porta Ferdinandea (now Garibaldi) which is 'cold and academically elegant in conception.'[666] The dome of S. Nicola and the churches of S. Placido and S. Martino dei Bianchi, in the same city, are by him. He was called to Malta on the express instructions of the Grand Master, and there designed the fine academic building which is now the Library in Valletta. This was the last important building erected by the Knights was begun in 1786.[667]

Lanci d'Urbino, Baldassare. An Italian military engineer born toward the beginning of the sixteenth century at Urbino[668] and died in Florence in the year 1571. He was a student of Girolamo Genga and later spent some time working at Lucca as a military engineer. He served with the French army, which in 1549 garrisoned the town of Montalcino for the Sienese Republic. His works in military architecture include : work undertaken for Marcantonio Colonna at Paliano and Nettuno; the revised fortress of Ancona for Pius IV; work on the fortresses of Ostia, Civita Vecchia, and the defences of Rome;[669] the rectangular citadel with its four great bastions at Siena, called the Fort of S. Giovanni Battista, which he built for Grand Duke Cosimo in 1561;[670] a large part of the fortress of Livorno (1566–67); and finally in 1569 the important fortress of S. Martino in Mugello.[671] Borgatti[672] states that he designed the hexagonal citadel at Grosseto. He designed at least one church, in the form of a Greek Cross;[673] that of S. Maria della Rosa at Chianciano, when he was engaged in work on the design of that city. He was called to Malta to help in the preparations for the defence of the island, and left Naples in March 1562. Bosio states[674] that he was the most excellent engineer of his day. He made a model of the new city on the hill behind St. Elmo (later Valletta), which had been proposed by Ferramolino and Genga, but his plan was more practical than Genga's, for the city proposed

666. Tosi p.381.
667. Rutter p.89.
668. Paribeni p.82 calls him a Florentine. Promis p.311 says he was born about 1510 and contemporary writers refer to him as the son of a sailor and a native of Urbino.
669. Albenga p.484. (Ittar : see also Fichera I pp.49,100,139,141,163–164, 167–169,173–178, and 193, which gives the buildings attributed to Ittar. Fuller information can be found in Anon. *Cenni biografici su Stefano e Sebastiano Ittar,* Palermo 1880).
670. Borgatti article *Cittadella* X p.495.
671. Borgatti article *Cittadella* X p.495.
672. Albenga p.484.
673. This form of church plan was not much used in Malta.
674. Bosio III p.454.

was far smaller. As the front would thus be much shorter Lanci felt that it could be more easily defended. His stay in Malta was for little more than three months, for in August 1562 he wrote to Cosimo on the progress of the Siena fortifications.[675] In 1564 he wrote numerous letters about the new fort Cosimo wished to build at Grosseto and in the following year he was ordered to make a design for the Rocca at Radicofani on the Tuscan frontier. In that year Terra del Sole was laid out in the form of a 'quadrangolare ortogonale' and Lanci was engaged in the work. I do not know if the general layout was his idea : he certainly designed the citadel,[676] and if the town is his design it would be interesting to find some comparison with its layout for Valletta. In military engineering the features ' Ricorrendo ' and ' Torina draga ' are his invention.[677] He designed and made instructions to help in the preparation of perspective drawings which were based on those described by Daniele Barbaro in his *Pratica di prospettiva,* Part IX, chapter 4, p.192.[678] Preserved in the CODEX LAPARELLI at Cortona there is a *Memoriale, ovvero Discorso di Baldassar Lancia da Urbino sopra delle cose da fortifiarsi, e da far la nuova Città di Malta*; it is in the hand of Laparelli.[679]

Laparelli da Cortona, Francesco. An Italian architect and military engineer born at Cortona in 1521, and died of the plague at Candia on 26 October 1570, at the age of forty-nine. Little is known about his youth except that he worked for Duke Cosimo I and Pius IV, preparing the defences of Civita Vecchia and Rome, and that he collaborated with Michelangelo on the building of S. Peter's. The Grand Master sent to Pius IV asking for a military expert to design the defences of Malta, and Laparelli was dispatched, arriving on the island on 28 December 1566. The Knights feared a fresh attack from the Turks in the spring. Some wished to leave the island, and already the most precious things had been packed and stored ready for dispatch. Laparelli had to decide his plan quickly and in three days he made his proposals, which he later carried out with very few modifications. ' If the Turks do not come it would be harmful and reproachful to leave without being driven away ' he wrote in January 1566. His proposals were (a) to repair the old defective fortifications and (b) to build a new city im-

675. Promis p.319 now in the Archivio di Firenze.
676. Albenga p.484.
677. Albenga p.484.
678. *Dizionario Biografico Universale* III, p 506.
679. Promis p.325.

mediately on the heights above Fort St. Elmo so as to protect the harbours from attack. This new city had first been proposed by Ferramolino, military engineer to Charles V, and later by Bartolomeo Genga and Baldassare Lanci. Supported by the Grand Master and the favourable report made by Serbelloni in March 1566, the new proposals were accepted and opposition overcome. As work was going well he applied for leave in the winter of 1568 and returned to Italy. At the end of the year he returned to Malta, but his stay was short. In 1569 he volunteered for service with the papal fleet, wishing to get into close action with the Turks. His ambition was foiled when plague struck the fleet and he fell a victim at Candia, in Crete, where he died in 1570. His work at Valletta was carried on by the Maltese engineer Gerolamo Cassar. Michelangelo said of Laparelli that 'all his life he studied fortifications with more passion than sculpture and painting.' But Laparelli was not only responsible for the fortifications of the new city. He also planned several buildings and obviously considered the architectural and town planning aspects. The CODEX LAPARELLI contains on page I, 'the plan in perspective of a noble house of the sixteenth century on two floors,' and the second appendix, running to twelve pages, refers to the accounts of expenses made between 21 October 1566 and 22 March 1567 in respect of a house Laparelli had begun to build in Valletta. This makes it clear that the layout of the streets was considered from the beginning and that building of houses actually begun before the enceinte of the fortifications was complete.[680]

Menga, Evangelista della. Maltese military engineer and architect practising in the sixteenth century. He was a teacher of Gerolamo Cassar.[681]

Micciola, Paolo. A Maltese military engineer praised by Bosio for his valorous action during the great siege of 1565.[682]

---

680. These biographical notes are based on Occhini; Venuti, *Vita del Capitano F.L. da Cortona,* Livorno 1761; Mancini, *Contributo dei Cortonesi alla cultura italiana,* Florence 1922 (Deputazione Toscana di Storia Patria); Guglielmotti, *Storia delle fortificazione nella Spiaggia romana 1560–1570,* Rome 1886; are all taken from the same source—the CODEX found in Laparelli's house in Cortona. Sorbell, *Inventario di Manoscritti della biblioteca d'Italia XX,* Cortona pp.93–94, Florence, contains a list of the parts of the codex transcribed by Girolamo Mancini. For further information see: *Dizionario Biografico Universale* III p.526, Florence 1844–45; Articles in ENCICLOPÆDIA ITALIANA—*Laparelli* appendix I p.777; *Cittadella* X p.495; *Fortificazione* XV p.741; *Malta* XXII p.45; and *Valletta* XXXIV p.933.
681. Zerafa, *Discorso* p.21.
682. Zerafa, *Discorso* p.21.

Pardo, Pietro. A Spanish military engineer who designed the original Fort St. Elmo. It was erected[683] under the direction of the Fra Leone Strozzi, Prior of Capua, and consisted of a small star-shaped fort with a ravelin facing onto Marsamuscetto and a cavalier on the seafront. It was captured by the Turks and destroyed during the great siege of 1565. On the Monte del Molino, Pardo designed the star-shaped fort of St. Michael (*c*. 1551–52). Guns were mounted on the fort on 8 May 1552. Additions were made under the Grand Mastership of Claude de la Sengle (1553–57), and in 1716 it was further improved. It has now been dismantled[684] but its shape may be seen in numerous old maps and engravings. Pardo also carried out defensive works in front of Fort St. Angelo and the Birgu.[685]

Quinsani di Montalcino, Antonio. An Italian military engineer who was called to Malta by Grand Master La Vallette to assist Lanci and Bartolomeo Genga upon the new city of Valletta.[686]

Saliba, D. Matteo. Maltese architect who designed the parish church of St. Catherine at Zurrieq (1634).[687]

Saliba, Sebastiano. Maltese architect who designed the parish church of St. Mary at Ghaxaq (1655).[688]

Sammut, Francesco. Maltese architect who completed the Carmelite church at Mdina.[689]

Serbelloni, Gabrio. An Italian military engineer born in Milan[690] in 1509[691] and died in Italy in January 1580. He was of a noble family and cousin of Pope Pius IV. In his youth he enlisted in the service of the Knights of Malta. In 1531, shut up in Lecce, he defended the town for seven months against the army of the Duke of Milan. By 1542 he was employed by the Emperor Charles V as a military engineer, and Charles sent him to Hungary in that year to assist his brother Ferdinando. Serbelloni took four Italian com-

---

683. Zammit, *Malta* p.136, states that the old fort was enlarged in 1552. It is probable, however, that a new fort replaced a simple watch tower which stood beside the old chapel of St. Elmo, patron saint of seamen.
684. Scicluna p.222.
685. Paribeni p.63. He collaborates the statements made by Scicluna.
686. Paribeni p.82.
687. Zerafa, *Discorso* p.24. Exterior rebuilt 1758 and bell towers added in 1861.
688. Zerafa, *Discorso* p.30. The date is from Braun, *Works of Art* p.6.
689. Zerafa, *Discorso* p.24.
690. Both Promis p.208 and the *Dizionario Biografico Universale* say that he was born in Milan but article *Italia* in ENC. ITAL.XIX p.882 states that he was from Mantua.
691. Promis p.208, and article *Serbelloni* in ENCICLOPEDIA UNIVERSAL ILUSTRADA EUROPEO-AMERICANA, Bilbao 1927, states born 1508, and *Diz.Bio. Univ.* states that he was born in 1503 of a French family.

panies to the defence of Strigonia against the Turks. In recognition of his valour in the Elba Crossing, he was made Maestro di Campo of the Marchese di Marignano. In 1551 he returned to Italy and was made captain of 300 Infantry by Ferrante Gonzaga, and in the following year became Governor of Saluzzo. For his valour in taking Capraia in 1554 he was made General of the Imperial Artillery, and in the following year he put to flight 4,000 Turks who had landed near Piombino. In 1556 he was working for the Duke of Milan on the fortresses at Cortona and San Sepulcro, and it was at Cortona that he came into contact with Laparelli,[692] an acquaintance he was to renew later in Malta. His cousin was made Pope in 1559 and Serbelloni was made Captain of the Guard and Governor of the Borgo in Rome, as well as Supreme Superintendent of Fortification and General of the Church Militia. As engineer in charge of building and water supply, he restored the Vergini aqueduct at a cost of 30,000 scudi. It was at this time that he was referred to by Vasari[693] in connection with a dispute between Michelangelo and Pirro Ligorio. Serbelloni made street improvements in Rome when he opened up four wide long streets near the Vatican. With the fear of a Turkish attack in 1561, Serbelloni prepared the defences of Ostia, Ancona, Civita Vecchia, and the most easily defensible part of Rome, the Borgo. The foundation stone of the great walls, which were to encircle the Vatican and St. Angelo, was laid by the Pope on the 8th March 1561. It was in that year that the Pope received a request for the services of Serbelloni from the Grand Master of Malta. He was willing, according to Promis,[694] to attire Serbelloni with the Habit of the Religion and confer on him the Commanderies of Ferrara and Montecchio, in order to acquire the services of such an important engineer and soldier; but the Pope wanted more, and insisted on the conferment of the Priory of Hungary, which was approved in Council on the 29th February 1562. There is considerable argument about the date of his arrival in Malta,[695] and the Vatican enciente was not

---

692. Occhini p.10. Serbelloni had known him at Cortona in the war with Siena and later supported Laparelli's appointment as engineer on the defences of Civita Vecchia and the Vatican.

693. Vasari, *Life of Michelangelo* IV p.169. He refers to the engineer as Gabrio Scierbelloni. This may account for the error made by several Maltese writers who call him Scabelloni.

694. Promis p.215. *Diz.Bio.Univ.* states he enlisted in his youth. Was he then a member of the Religion when called upon by the Grand Master?

695. Viperano, *De bello melitensi Historia*, Perugia 1564, fol.29 states he arrived in a galley to the relief of Malta during the siege. Cirni said he was in Rome in 1564, and Roseo I, part III said he was not in Malta in 1565.

completed until 1565, but Bosio's report,[696] that he arrived in March 1566, seems reasonable and he was in a good position to give accurate information. In Malta he was consulted on the plan prepared for the new city of Valletta by Laparelli, and this he approved, writing in its praise to the Pope and the King of Spain. Being of a diplomatic disposition he soon gained the confidence of Grand Master La Vallette, who told him of the bad intentions of the Viceroy of Sicily toward the Order. On the 14th March he left Malta and sailed for Messina in a galley of the Order. There he met Don Garzia, the Viceroy, and was so successful in bringing about a reconciliation between the Viceroy and the Grand Master, that the former promised to send immediate aid in the form of money, men, and materials, for the building of the new city. Serbelloni then, acting on the orders of King Philip, inspected the fortresses of Sicily. In 1567 he joined the Duke of Alba as Supreme General of Artillery and Sappers and saw service in Flanders. He returned to Italy and, joining the fleet which had been fitted out by the Pope at Messina, he sailed and took part in the famous Battle of Lepanto in 1571. It was largely through his valiant efforts that the vacillating allies were rallied and won such a resounding victory. He was the true victor of Lepanto. He later saw service in Sicily and improved the defences of Tunis and the Goletta. It was during the defences of the Goletta with Don John and Admiral Doria, that he was captured by the Turks[697] and taken to Constantinople. After an outcry he was eventually ransomed and released, when he returned to Italy. He saw further service in Flanders with Don John of Austria, but there fell ill and had to return to Italy in 1579. At the beginning of January 1580 he died. He wrote the following works : *Memorie di guerra,* an eighty page codex in folio, now in the library of the Cistercians of Morimondo. It was seen there by Argelat (Vol. II col. 1337), who noted that ' Io Pietro Gabrio Serbelloni, MDLXIII ' was written at the end. *Relazione delle cose di Tunisi,* which is contained in volume III of Giordano Ziletti *Delle lettere di Principi,* Venice. And there are four letters in the Vatican library referring to the fortress of Tunis and written in November and December 1573.[698]

696. Bosio XXXV p.739.
697. He has been blamed for the failure of defences at the Goletta, but Promis pp.225–242, in his description of them, exonerates him, points to the Turkish praise of him, and blames the King of Spain for putting Porto Carrero as Governor of the Goletta when he was inexperienced.
698. Promis p.246. There is a long biography of Serbelloni in Piorato, *Scelta d'uomini illustri d'Italia,* 1659; Promis pp.209–246; Bosio XXXV;

Tigne, Chevalier.[699] A French military engineer to the Order who, in estimation and gratitude for his services was raised to the rank of Knight—a singular honour rarely accorded to an artist or engineer.[700] In 1792 he designed and built the fort called by his name,[701] at the expense of the Grand Master Rohan-Polduc;[702] an advanced bastion whose duty it was to assist the garrison of Fort St. Elmo in protecting the mouth of Marsamuscetto harbour. This was the last important building erected by the Order before its capitulation to the French forces under Napoleon. Earlier than this, he had designed the triple range of casemates within Fort St. Elmo.[703]

Tigne, De. A French military engineer who, along with de Mondion, was invited to Malta in 1715 by the Grand Master Perellos to complete the fort which had been proposed by Grunenberg. This fort was situated on the island in Marsamuscetto harbour, and was later called Fort Manoel. De Tigne returned to France, but in the following year he was back in Malta and submitted another report to the Grand Master estimating the cost of work to be £3,500.[704] His report, as well as dealing with the new fort, suggested alterations to the Cotonera and Margherita lines around the Three Cities.

Valperga, Antonio Maurizio. An Italian military engineer, native of Turin, and a member of a Piedmontese family of some note. He was chief military architect to the house of Savoy and wrote the following books on military defence : *Esercito militare a beneficio del nuovo soldato, nel quale si tratta del modo di squadronare, porre in battaglia ogni sorte di militia,* Naples, 1653. *Indirizzo del nuovo soldato, diviso in due parti,* Naples, 1655, which was written

Floriana gives a description of Serbelloni's work on Tunis and the Goletta; and finally a tribute to him occurs in Cervantes, *Don Quixote* I, Cap.39.

699. Boisgelin II pp.311–312 mentions two Knights in the Priory of Aquitaine, in the langue of France : No. 3 René Jacob de Tigne, and No. 108 Jean Jacob de Tigne, out of a total of 110.
700. de Borch, *Lettres sur la Sicile et sur l'isle de Malthe . . . écrites en 1777,* 2 vols., Turin 1782, states that only two men received the honour, the other being Mattia Preti (Vol.I, p.218). This is not strictly true about Preti, who received the Habit before carrying out his works of art in Malta. Pugia, *Fra Mattia Preti nel terzo suo centenario 1613–1913,* Naples 1913, and my biography of Preti. De Borch wrote his letters in 1777, before Tigne had built Port Tigne, so it is evident that he had already done considerable work in the employment of the Order at that earlier date 1777.
701. Paribeni p.122.
702. Inscription over the main gate.
703. Crocker p.45.
704. Crocker p.42.

when he was a prisoner of war at Castelnuovo in 1653 and dedicated to the King of Sardinia in flowing 'words of such pride as would have made Achilles envious.' *Breve discorso dell'avantaggio e disavantaggio delle due piazze di Piombino et dell'elba, et la nuova fortificazione di essa per resistere ad oggi attacco o insulto nemico, et delle grandi conseguenze che ne attribuisce la Corona et la Francia,* Anno, 1649, an unpublished work in the Paris Library. *La fortificazione reale difesa, divisa in piu dialoghi, data in luce a beneficio comune, e particolarmente della nobile gioventù piemontese, contro la fortificazione a roverso,* written after 1678.[705] In Malta he designed the Baroque gateway of Fort Ricasoli[706] and the Cotonera lines which encircle the Three Cities, built under the Grand Mastership of Rafael Cotoner (1663–80).[707]

Vella, Carlo. A Maltese architect who designed St. Philip which crowns the end of the promontory of Senglea (L'Isola). This church was built in the year 1662.[708]

Zabbar, Orlando. A Maltese naval architect at the time of the assault of 1565.[709] He built a boat which was made up of many separate sections. This was considered very skilful because the boat could be easily dismantled and reassembled.[710]

Zerafa, Francesco. A Maltese architect who died on 21st April 1758.[711] In 1748 he began the Castellania in Valletta which was completed after his death by Bonici in 1760.[712]

---

705. Ayala, *Biografia militare italiana* I, p.65 and II, p.125.
706. Paribeni p.132.
707. Zammit, *Valletta* p.56.
708. Zerafa, *Discorso* p.24.
709. Zerafa, *Discorso* p.21.
710. Zerafa, *History* p.170.
711. Scicluna p.215.
712. Fleming p.175.

Glossary

Auberge. Place where brothers ate together and where the different langues assembled.

Atrium. Here refers to the open raised space in front of Maltese churches. It is usually defined by a wall, but not by a peristyle.

Bailiwick. A Priory of the Order.

Bastion. A fortified work built at the salient angles of polygonal ramparts.

Bell-cot. A turret at the west end of small churches in which the bells were hung. Sometimes called Bell-gable or Bell-turret.

Boschetto. A small wood, thicket.

Bulwark. A rampart usually placed forward to protect an entrance.

Campanile. A belfry or bell-tower.

Casal. A Maltese village or town, as opposed to a city.

Casemates. Vaulted chambers for guns.

Castellan of Emposta. Almost the same as Priory.

Cavalier. An inner defence work raised higher than the other lines of fortification. In Malta, usually a five-sided fort.

Citadel. A fortress dominating a city—Last line of defence.

Collacchio. An area reserved mainly for the residence of the Knights.

Commanderies. Priories, Castellany of Emposta, Bailiwicks, demesnes, houses of members, lands and property of the Order.

Convent. The portion of the Order of St. John resident at headquarters.

Counterguard. A protective work in front of a bastion.

Croce Guelfa. Pattern of a window with two square panels above and two rectangular panels below, divided by mullions in the form of a cross.

Curtain. A wall of fortification. A line defended by bastions.

Demi-bastion. A half bastion protecting a curtain.

Demilune. A detached triangular work built in the moat.

Echauguette. A sentry-box corbelled out from the angle of a rampart.

Enceinte. The enclosure of the fortifications.

Escarpment. Ground cut so that it slopes away from a line of fortifications. The face of a line.

Falsa-braca. As fausse-braie.

'Fat' mouldings. Bulbous-shaped mouldings usually in the form of a triple roll placed around sixteenth century doors and windows, or used for canopies of cornices in Malta.

Fausse-braie. A space left at foot of a rampart next to the moat for defence, protected by a parapet.

Grand Master. Head of the Order.

Hornwork. A work outside the main line of fortifications. It is detached from it and usually has two half bastions ending in acute angles on the front to the attack.

Intercolumniation. Space between two columns or pilasters.

Langues. The eight languages or nations from whom the Knights were recruited.

Melitan mouldings. As ' fat ' mouldings.

Order. The semi-military, semi-religious Order of the Knights of St. John.

Outworks. Any defensive works placed beyond the main line of fortifications and detached.

Piliers. Eight conventual bailiffs who acted as presidents of the various langues. ' Pillars or supporters.'

Platform. A level place for mounting guns in a battery.

Rampart. A line wide enough at the top to allow the passage of troops, and usually battered to deflect shot.

Ravelin. A small detached triangular work with two faces.

Redoubt. A small defence post worked into a bastion trace to give initial strength, or an outpost pushed well forward of the main lines.

Religion. The same as ' convent.'

Scarp. The revetted face of a rampart.

Templars. Members of the Military and Religious Order which was suppressed in 1312.

Tenaille. A detached oblong work with the ends projecting outwards at an obtuse angle.

Torus. A large half-round moulding.

Trace. A ground-plan of a defence system.

Turcopilier. English Pilier, or Prior. Inspector of the guards in Rhodes, but in Malta the office was merely titular. (Schermerhorn, *Malta of the Knights.*)

Bibliography

Abela. Giovanni Francesco, *Della descrizione di Malta, Libri V*, Malta 1647.

Abercrombie, *Maltese Baroque* in THE ARCHITECT AND BUILDING NEWS 13–viii–1943, pp.101–105.

Albenga. Giuseppe, *Lanci* in ENCICLOPÆDIA ITALIANA XX.

Alberti. Leone Battista, *De re aedificatoria*, Rome 1485.

ANCIENT MONUMENTS COMMITTEE, *Report to H. E. Field-Marshal Viscount Gort*, Valletta, 16–iii–1944.

(Anon.), *Cenni biografici su Stefano e Sebastiano Ittar*, Palermo 1880.

Arata. Giulio, *L'architettura Arabo-Normanna e il rinascimento in Sicilia*, Milan 1914.

ARCHITECTURAL PUBLICATIONS SOCIETY, *Dictionary of Architecture*, 8 volumes, London 1887.

ARCHIVIO STORICO DI MALTA, Rome 1929 *et seq.*

ARCHIVIUM MELITENSE, Valletta 1910 *et seq.*

Ashby. T.H., *Roman Malta* in JOURNAL OF ROMAN STUDIES, V 1915, pp.28–80.

Ayala. Mariano d', *Dizionario militare francese italiano*, Naples 1841.

Baerlein. Henry, *Two Houses in Malta* in COUNTRY LIFE, LXXXVII, p.606.

Bartlett. *Gleanings of the overland Route*, London 1864.

Bartolo. A., *Mattia Preti* in ARCHIVIUM MELITENSE II No. 17 1914, pp.167–179.

Baumgart. Fritz, *Breslavia* in ENCICLOPÆDIA ITALIANA VII.

Bedford. W.K.R., *Malta and the Knights Hospitaller*, London, n.d.

Bedford. W.K.R., *Regulations of the old Hospital of the Knights of St. John of Valletta, from a copy at Rome and preserved in the Archives of Malta with a translation and notes by W.K.R.B.*, Edinburgh and London 1882.

Bevan. Bernard, *History of Spanish Architecture*, London 1938.

Blunt. Anthony, *Artistic Theory in Italy 1450–1600*, Oxford 1940.

Boisgelin. Louis de, *Ancient and Modern Malta : Containing a full and accurate Account of the present State of the islands of Malta and Gozo, History of the Knights of St. John of Jerusalem*, 2 volumes, London 1805.

Bonello. Vincenzo, *Una città del silenzio a Malta—la Notabile*, in LA VIE DU MONDE VI No. 6, Milan 1938.

Bonello. Vincenzo, *Valletta* in ENCICLOPÆDIA ITALIANA XXXIV.

Bonello. Vincenzo, *Malta* in ENCICLOPÆDIA ITALIANA XXII.

Borgatti. Mariano, *Cittadella* in ENCICLOPÆDIA ITALIANA X.

Borgatti. Mariano, *Fortificazione* in ENCICLOPÆDIA ITALIANA XV.

Borromeo. St. Charles, *Instructions on Ecclesiastical Buildings, translated and annotated by George J. Wigley*, London 1857.

Bosio. Giacomo, *Istoria della sacra religione militare di S. Giovanni Gerosolimitano*, Rome 1594–1602.

Bowerman. H.G., *The History of the Fort St. Angelo*, Valletta 1947.

Bradley. R.N., *Malta and the Mediterranean Race*, London 1912.

Braun. Hugh, *An Introduction to Maltese Architecture*, Valletta 1944.

Braun. Hugh, (and others), *Works of Art in Malta, Losses and Survivals in the War*, London 1946.

Bres. O., *Malta antica illustrata*, Rome 1816.

Briggs. Martin Shaw, *Baroque Architecture*, London 1913.

Briggs. Martin Shaw, *In the Heel of Italy*, London 1910.

Briggs. Martin Shaw, *Mohammadan Architecture in Egypt and Palestine*, Oxford 1924.

Bryan's *Dictionary of Painters and Engravers*, 5 volumes, London 1930.

Brydone. Patrick, *A Tour through Sicily and Malta, in a Series of Letters to W. Beckford, Esq.*, London 1773.

Busca. Gabriello, *L'architettura militare*, Milan 1619.

Calleja. Giuseppe, *Giuseppe Bonici, architetto ed ingegnere* in L'ARTE PERIODICO PATRIO-BIMENSILE III, No. 65, pp.4–5, Malta 1865.

Calleja. Giuseppe, *Tommaso Dingli, architetto ed ingegnere* in L'ARTE PERIODICO PATRIO-BIMENSILE III, No. 66, pp.5–6, Malta 1865.

Calleja. Giuseppe, *Works of Art in the Churches of Malta and the Governor's Palace, Valletta, translated and edited by Rev. G. N. Godwin*, Malta 1881.

Cardona. S.R. Borg, *The Officio delle Case and the Housing Laws of the earlier Grand Masters 1531–69*, in THE LAW JOURNAL, Malta May 1951.

Cecchini. *Siena* in ENCICLOPÆDIA ITALIANA.

Chinnizzi. B., & A. Frangipane, *Mattia Preti detto Il Cavalier Calabrese*, 1914.

Ciantar. Gio. Antonio, *Malta illustrata. Descrizione di Malta isola del mare siciliano e adriatico con le sue antichità ed altre notizie diverse in quattro libri*, 2 volumes, Malta 1780.

Clausetti. Enrico, *Pietro Paolo Floriani, ingegnere militare 1585–1638*, in PALLADIO III No. 1, 1939.

Cluverius. P.C., *Sicilia antiqua cum minolibus insulis et adjacentibus item. Sardinia et Corsica, etc.* Batavia 1619.

Cooke. Anne J., *The architectural work of the Order of St. John of Jerusalem,* MS., R.I.B.A. Final Thesis, London 1929.

Contreras. Juan de, *Historia del arte hispanico,* Volumes 3 and 4, Barcelona 1940 and 1954.

Critien. A., *Holy Infirmary Sketches,* Malta 1946.

Critien. A., *The Borgo Holy Infirmary, now the St. Scholastica Convent,* Malta 1950.

Crocker. J., *History of the Fortifications of Malta,* General Staff, Malta Command, Malta 1920.

Curione. Celio Secondo, *A New History of the War in Malta (1565),* translated into Italian from the original Latin by Dr. *Emanuele Mizzi, and into English by Granville Pacha,* Rome 1928.

Darmanin. J.F., *The Phœnico-Grœco-Roman Temple and the Origin and Development of Fort St. Angelo,* Malta 1948.

Dizionario Biografico Universale, Florence 1849.

Donaldson. Gordon, *A Handlist of Manuscripts in the British Isles relating to Malta* in Bulletin No. 7 of THE INSTITUTE OF HISTORI-CAL RESEARCH, MALTA, Malta 1950.

Donati. Ugo, *Artisti ticinesi a Roma,* Bellinzona 1942.

ENCICLOPÆDIA ITALIANA, Istituto Giovanni Treccani, Rome 1930–38.

Fagnoni. Raffaello, *Villa* in ENCICLOPÆDIA ITALIANA XXXV.

Fedden. Robin, *Crusader Castles,* London 1950.

Ferres. V.A., *Descrizione storica delle chiese di Malta e Gozo,* Malta 1866.

Ferres. V.A., *Il maggior tempio di S. Giovanni Battista in Malta,* Valletta 1900.

Fichera. Francesco, *G. B. Vaccarini e l'architettura del settecento in Sicilia,* 2 volumes, Rome 1934.

Fleming. John, *Malta—Naval Base of the Baroque* in ARCHITEC-TURAL REVIEW, June 1946.

Floriana. Pietro Paolo, *Difese et ofesa delle piazze di P.P.F., Opera non solo utile e necessaria a capitani e governatori di fortezze, manco di sommo profitto a studiosi dell'historia militari così antichi come moderne,* Second edition, Venice 1654.

Floriana. Pompeii, *Discorso intorno all'isola di Malta e di cio che porrà succedere tentando il Turco dal impresa. Fatto da un creato dell'Illmo. Signor Marrio Sforza Cavalier di San Michele e generale delle fanterie di Toscana dedicato al serenissimo Principe Don Giovanni d'Austria,* Macerta 1576.

Flower. Arthur J., *Notes on Renaissance Architecture in Malta* in R.I.B.A. JOURNAL Third series, Vol. 5 No. 2, 1897.

Fogaccia. Piero, *Cosimo Fanzago,* Bergamo 1942.

Fokker. T.H., *Roman Baroque Art, the History of a Style,* 2 vols., London 1938.

Francovich. Geza de, *Algardi* in ENCICLOPÆDIA ITALIANA II.

Frangipane. A., *Mattia Preti,* Milan 1929.

Gabriel. Albert, *La cité de Rhodes 1310–1522,* 2 vols., Paris 1921.

Galea. J., *Mdina, the Silent City,* Malta 1948.

Galea. R.V., *Architecture in Malta,* Malta 1914.

Gatt. J.E., *A Guide to Gozo, largely compiled from 'Le Gozo antico, moderno, sacro e profano' by Sacerdote Gian Pietro Franco Agius de Suldana, canon of the Cathedral of Gozo, 1746,* Valletta 1937.

Gerola. Giuseppe, *Monumenti veneti di Creta,* Vol. II, *Fortificazioni,* Venice c. 1912.

Geymuller. H.von, *Les Projets Primitifs pour le Basilique de Saint Pierre de Rome,* Paris 1875.

Gillet. *Francia* in ENCICLOPÆDIA ITALIANA XV.

Giovannoni. Gustavo, *Saggi sull'architettura del rinascimento,* Milan 1931.

Gwilt. Joseph, *Notizia architettonica italiana,* London 1818.

Harrison. Austen St. B. & R. Pearse S. Hubbard, *Maltese Vernacular* in ARCHITECTURAL REVIEW CV No. 626, February 1949 pp. 77–80.

Harrison. Austen St. B. & R. Pearse S. Hubbard, *Valletta—A Report to Accompany the Outline Plan for the Region of Valletta and the Three Cities,* Valletta 1945.

Hautecœur. Louis, *Histoire de l'architecture Classique en France,* 6 volumes, Paris 1943–50.

Hellwald. F., *Bibliographie methodique de l'Ordre Souverain de Saint Jean de Jerusalem,* Rome 1885.

Hermanin. Federico, *Roma* in ENCICLOPÆDIA ITALIANA XXIX.

Hittorf. J.I., & L. Zanth, *Architecture moderne de la Sicile, ou recueil des plus beaux monuments religieux et des edifices publics et particuliers les plus remarquables,* Paris 1835.

Hughes. J. Quentin, *The Influence of Italian Mannerism upon Maltese Architecture* in MELITA HISTORICA I No. 2, Malta 1953.

Hughes. J. Quentin, *The Church of St. Catherine 'Tat-Torba' and the Origin of the Simplified Orders of Architecture* in ARCH. I, Malta May 1954.

Istituto Poligrafico dello Stato, *L'Italia a Rodi,* Rome 1946.

Jones. Harry D., *Memoranda and Details of the Mode of Building Houses, etc., in the Island of Malta* in PAPERS ON SUBJECTS CONNECTED WITH THE DUTIES OF THE CORPS OF ROYAL ENGINEERS V, London 1842.

King. Georgiana Goddard, *Mattia Preti* in THE ART BULLETIN XVIII No. 3, September 1936, pp.371–386.

Kubler. George, *Mexican Urbanism in the Sixteenth Century* in THE ART BULLETIN XXIV No. 1942.

Lamperez y Romea. Vicente, *Arquitectura civil Espanola de los Siglos I al XVIII*, 2 volumes, Madrid 1922.

Lavedan. Pierre, *Histoire de l'Architecture urbaine*, 2 volumes, Paris 1926.

Lazzaroni. Michele, & Antoine Munoz, *Filarete, scultore ed architetto del secolo XV*, Rome 1908.

Luke. Sir Harry, *Malta—An Account and an Appreciation*, London 1949.

Male. Emile, *Religious Art from the Twelfth to the Eighteenth Century*, London 1949.

MALTA LETTERARIA (RASSEGNA DI LETTERE, SCIENZE ED ARTI), Valletta 1904 *et seq.*

Mariani. V., *Mattia Preti a Malta*, Rome 1929.

MELITA (PERIODICO MENSILE ITALIANO-INGLESE), Valletta 1921 *et seq.*

Milizia. F., *Memorie degli architetti antichi e moderni*, 2 volumes, third edition Parma 1781.

Minniti. Michele, *Siracusa*, Syracuse 1949.

Moschini. Vittorio, *Luti* in ENCICLOPÆDIA ITALIANA XXIX.

Moschini. Vittorio, *The Work of Benedetto Luti in Malta* in L'ARTE XXVI, pp.99–102.

Murray. John, *The Maltese Islands with special Reference to their Geological Structure* in THE SCOTTISH GEOGRAPHICAL MAGAZINE VI 1890, pp.449–488.

Nebbia. Ugo, *Gafà* in ENCICLOPÆDIA ITALIANA VIII.

Nuttall. Zelia, *Royal Ordinance concerning the Laying Out of New Towns* in HISPANIC-AMERICAN HISTORICAL REVIEW IV 1921, pp. 743–753.

Occhini. P.L., *Un grande italiano del'500, Francesco Laparelli a Malta*, Arezzo 1937.

Ozzola. L., 'Il battesimo di Cristo' di M. Gafà a Malta in DEDALO VII 1926–27, pp.131–135.

Palladio. Andrea, *I quattro libri dell'architettura*, Venice 1570, Facsimile Milan 1945.

Paribeni. Roberto, *Malta* in ITALIA ARTISTICA SERIES Bergamo 1930.

Pascoli. Leone, *Vite de' pittori, scultori, ed architetti perugini,* Rome 1732.

Perkins. J. B. Ward, *Mediaeval and Early Renaissance Architecture in Malta* in ANTIQUARIES JOURNAL XXII, 1942.

Porroni. A., *Trattato universale militare moderno,* Venice 1676.

Porter. Whitworth, *The Knights of Malta, or the Order of St. John of Jerusalem,* London 1887.

Pozzo. B. dal, *Historia della sacra religione militare di S. Giovanni Gerosolimitano, detta di Malta,* Verona 1703.

Pratt. Jean, *Mediterranean Stronghold* in THE BUILDER 28.ii.1941 pp.221–223, and 7.iii.1941 pp.243–245.

Pratt. Jean, *Fortifications of Malta* in THE ARCHITECTURAL REVIEW LXXXVI 1939, pp.37–38.

Promis. Carlo, *Biografie di ingegneri militari italiani dal secolo XIV alla metà del XVIII* in MISCELLANEA DI STORIA ITALIANA XIV, Turin 1874.

Rees. William, *A History of the Order of St. John of Jerusalem in Wales and on the Welsh Border,* Cardiff 1947.

Rey. G., *Étude sur les monuments de l'architecture militaire des Croises en Syrie et dans l'île de Chypre,* Paris 1871.

Rossi. E., *Aggiunta alla Bibliographie Methodique,* Rome 1924.

Rossi. E., *Storia della marina dell'Ordine di S. Giovanni di Gerusalemme, di Rodi e di Malta,* Rome 1926.

Rutter. Joseph Gatt, *Illustrated Guide to Malta and Gozo,* ninth edition Oxford n.d.

Ryan. Frederick W., *Malta,* London 1910.

Sammut. Edward, *Profili di artisti maltesi,* Malta 1937.

Sammut. Edward, *The Co-Cathedral of St. John, formerly the Conventual Church of the Order of Malta, and its Art Treasures,* Malta 1950.

Sandys. George, *A Relation of a Journey begun An.Dom.1610. Foure Bookes. Containing a Description of the Turkish Empire, of Egypt, of the Holy Land, of the Remote Parts of Italy, and the Islands Adjoining,* London 1615.

Scamozzi. Vincenzo, *L'idea dell'architettura universale, X libri,* Venice 1615.

Schubert. Otto, *Geschichte des Barock in Spanien,* Esslingen 1908.

Scicluna. [Sir] Hannibal, *The Buildings and Fortifications of Malta* in MALTA AND GIBRALTAR ILLUSTRATED (General Editor : A. MacMillan) London 1915.

Serlio. Sebastiano, *Il primo (— settimo) libro d'architettura di S.S., Bolognese,* Vicenza 1618.

Serra. Luigi, *Genga* in ENCICLOPÆDIA ITALIANA XVI.

Simmons. Lintorn Arabin, *Description of the Governor's Palaces on Malta; of Valletta, St. Antonio and Verdala and a Catalogue of the Pictures,* Malta 1887.

Sitwell. Sacheverell, *Southern Baroque Art,* London 1924.

Sitwell. Sacheverall, *Spanish Baroque Art,* London 1931.

Spratt. T.H., *The Geology of the Maltese Islands,* Malta 1845.

Strickland. Lord, *Malta and the Phœnicians,* Malta 1950.

Strzygowski. Joseph, *Origin of Christian Church Art, translated from the German by O. M. Dalton and H. J. Braunholtz,* Oxford 1923.

Strzygowski. Joseph, *Early Church Art in Northern Europe with special reference to Timber Construction and Decoration,* London 1928.

Tencajoli. O.F., *Artisti maltesi a Roma dal secolo XVI ad oggi,* Malta n.d.

Teonge. Henry, *Diary of Henry Teonge, Chaplain on board His Majesty's ships 'Assistance,' 'Bristol,' and 'Royal Oak,' Anno 1675 to 1679. Now first Published from the Original MS. Edited by C. H. Knight,* London 1825.

Tosi. Luigi Maria, *Battaglia, Carmelo e Francesco* in ENCICLOPÆDIA ITALIANA VI.

Touring Club Italiano, ATTRAVERSO L'ITALIA VII :*Campania,* Milan 1936.

Touring Club Italiano, ATTRAVERSO L'ITALIA IV : *Sicilia,* Milan 1936.

Townsend. Rev. G.F., *English Guide to the Cathedral Churches of Valletta and Città Vecchia.*

Tregellas. Walter H., *Historical Sketch of the Defences of Malta* in JOURNAL OF THE ROYAL ENGINEERS' INSTITUTE paper VIII, Vol. III, No. 10, 1879, pp.185–211.

Uhde. Constantin, *Baudenkmaeler in Spanien und Portugal VI,* Berlin 1892.

Vasari. Giorgio, *The Lives of the Painters, Sculptors and Architects,* Everyman edition, 4 volumes, London 1946.

Vassalio. G.A., *Biografia, Carlo Gimach* in L'ARTE PERIODICO PATRIO-BIMENSILE III No. 68, Malta 1865, pp.4–6.

Vertot. R., *Histoire des Chevaliers Hospitaliers de St. Jean de Jerusalem,* 4 volumes, Paris 1726.

Wilkinson. R.J.L., *The Auberge de Provence and the Malta Union Club,* Malta 1948.

Wittkower. Rudolf, *The Biblioteca Laurenziana, Florence* in ART BULLETIN 16, 1934.

Wittkower. Rudolf, *Architectural Principles in the Age of Humanism,* London 1949 and 1952.

Zammit. N., *La pubblica biblioteca (Stefano Ittar)* in L'ARTE PERIODICO PATRIO-BIMENSILE III, No. 60, Malta 1865, pp.5–6.

Zammit T., *Malta, the Islands and their History,* Malta 1929.

Zammit. T., *Valletta—An Historical Sketch,* Malta 1929.

Zerafa. Stefano, *Discorso sulla storia artistica di Malta,* Valletta 1850.

Zerafa. Stefano, *A History of Art in Malta, being an abridged Translation of the Inaugural Address delivered by S.Z. at the University of Malta in October 1850,* Malta 1850.

Index

237

241

Printed by Suttons, Paignton